DATE DUE			
MAY 03			
MAY 02 1990			
JAN 21 199?			
FEB 10 199?			

McNeil, Horace J

Poems for a machine age

POEMS
for a Machine Age

POEMS

for a Machine Age

Selected and Edited by

HORACE J. McNEIL
Brooklyn Technical High School
Brooklyn, N. Y.

with the editorial collaboration of

CLARENCE STRATTON
Directing Supervisor of English
Senior and Junior High Schools
Cleveland, Ohio

McGRAW-HILL BOOK COMPANY, Inc.
NEW YORK AND LONDON

PRINTED IN THE UNITED STATES OF AMERICA

THE MAPLE PRESS COMPANY, YORK, PA.

FOREWORD

IF BY magic all machinery suddenly went out of existence, the world would be an unfamiliar place indeed, for there is almost no phase of modern life in which it does not play an important part. Not only is it used in the production of our food and clothing and in the construction of our dwellings, but it has turned what were once dreams into everyday occurrences. We make night as bright as day. We travel swiftly on land and water, and fly across continents and oceans. We talk to people who are miles away. We go to the theater, where our entertainment is reproduced from a strip of celluloid, or stay at home and dial a program from the air. We amplify sounds to any desired loudness. We transmit pictures and scenes by radio waves. We even make ourselves comfortable indoors with machine-conditioned air.

That this is a machine age does not mean that it is an unpoetical age. Actually machinery and poetry have much in common. A machine, like a poem, is the product of some-one's imagination. Both affect our feelings or emotions. Who is not stirred by the sight of a powerful locomotive, a mighty ship, or a graceful airplane? Rupert Brooke speaks of "the keen unpassioned beauty of a great machine" in the poem "The Great Lover." Again, like a poem, a running machine usually has a steady throb, known as rhythm, satisfying to the ear; and as a smoothly operating machine is music to a skilled mechanic, a well-written poem is music to an understanding reader.

Of course all modern poems are not about wheels and power. Man has other interests besides machines. He likes the outdoors as is evident from parks, playgrounds, camps, and gardens. He seeks adventure as shown by the many people who travel and explore. He also enjoys stories, not only about modern times, but about older times as well. Whatever his interests, he is almost sure to find them expressed in the poetry of his time.

As a matter of fact, many poems written long ago are modern in thought, for the underlying ideas which are expressed in poetry do not change with time. Adventure is no less exciting because it comes by way of the pack animal instead of the airplane; love is no less real because it exists in a thatched cottage instead of an apartment; and humor is no less entertaining because it comes from the court jester instead of the radio.

The poems in this collection, then, are not all about modern civilization nor of recent writing, but were chosen because they have a meaning for the modern reader in the light of his own experience. So far as they fulfill this requirement they are truly poems for a machine age.

HORACE J. MCNEIL.

CONTENTS

THE CITY

THE WAYS OF MAN

LOOKING AT LIFE

THINGS THAT COUNT

UNUSUAL THOUGHTS

WORD PICTURES

PEOPLE

LOVE

THE OUTDOORS

THE SPIRIT OF ADVENTURE

THE SEA

LOVE OF COUNTRY

WAR

STORIES

ANIMAL LIFE

HUMOR

MODERN CIVILIZATION

A tool is but the extension of man's hand, and a machine is but a complex tool. And he that invents a machine augments the power of a man and the well-being of mankind.

—HENRY WARD BEECHER

MACHINES

DANIEL WHITEHEAD HICKY

I hear them grinding, grinding, through the night,
The gaunt machines with arteries of fire,
Muscled with iron, boweled with smoldering light;
I watch them pulsing, swinging, climbing higher,
Derrick on derrick, wheel on rhythmic wheel,
Swift band on whirring band, lever on lever,
Shouting their songs in raucous notes of steel,
Blinding a village with light, damming a river.
I hear them grinding, grinding, hour on hour,
Cleaving the night in twain, shattering the dark
With all the rasping torrents of their power,
Groaning and belching spark on crimson spark.
I cannot hear my voice above their cry
Shaking the earth and thundering to the sky.

Slowly the dawn comes up. No motors stir
The brightening hilltops as the sunrise flows
In yellow tides where daybreak's lavender
Clings to a waiting valley. No derrick throws
The sun into the heavens and no pulley
Unfolds the wildflowers thirsting for the day;
No wheel unravels ferns deep in a gulley;
No engine starts the brook upon its way.
The butterflies drift idly, wing to wing,
Knowing no measured rhythm they must follow;
No turbine drives the white clouds as they swing
Across the cool blue meadows of the swallow.
With all the feathered silence of a swan
They whir and beat—the engines of the dawn.

A SONG OF POWER

BERTON BRALEY

This is the song of the waters churning,
  Waters harnessed to serve our need;
This is the song of the turbines turning—
  Smoothly turning, athrill with speed;
The song of the dynamos deeply purring,
  Driven by water or spun by steam;
Song of a myriad motors whirring
  With wizardry stranger than any dream.

This is the song of the "juice" which surges
  Over the web of the far-flung lines,
The might of the silent force that urges
  The lathe in the shop, the cage in the mines;
The force that lightens the task of labor
  That harries the dark from the face of earth,
That brings us closer—neighbor to neighbor—
  And spans, in a second, the planet's girth.

This is a song of the Men who master
  Motor, dynamo, fuse, and switch,
Who lift our life to a pace that's faster,
  Who move the world—by a finger twitch.
Men in office and laboratory,
  Men who work with the thunderbolts,
Who outmatch even Aladdin's story
  With a magic lamp—of a million volts!

This is a song of modern wonder,
  Of visions lagging behind the fact
Of glamour over the earth—and under;
  Of torrents fettered and mountains cracked;
Of cities bathed in a glow resplendent,
  Of light and power that serve the farm,
Of nature conquered and Man ascendant
  With Thought the wand that has wrought the charm.

This is the song of the singing wires
  That throb responsive to serve our will,
The song of a Genie that never tires
  But toils for greater enchantments still;
A Song of Now—and the days before us
  With vaster marvels for us to scan
A song whose jubilant lifting chorus
  Rings with the hopes and the dreams of Man!

THE SECRET OF THE MACHINES

RUDYARD KIPLING

We were taken from the ore bed and the mine,
  We were melted in the furnace and the pit—
We were cast and wrought and hammered to design,
  We were cut and filed and tooled and gauged to fit.
Some water, coal, and oil is all we ask,
  And a thousandth of an inch to give us play:
And now, if you will set us to our task,
  We will serve you four and twenty hours a day!

We can pull and haul and push and lift and drive,
  We can print and plow and weave and heat and light,
We can run and jump and swim and fly and dive,
  We can see and hear and count and read and write!

Would you call a friend from half across the world?
  If you'll let us have his name and town and state,
You shall see and hear your crackling question hurled
  Across the arch of heaven while you wait.
Has he answered? Does he need you at his side?
  You can start this very evening if you choose,
And take the Western Ocean in the stride
  Of seventy thousand horses and some screws!

The boat express is waiting your command!
  You will find the *Mauretania* at the quay,
Till her captain turns the lever 'neath his hand,
  And the monstrous nine-decked city goes to sea.

Do you wish to make the mountains bare their head
  And lay their new-cut forests at your feet?
Do you want to turn a river in its bed,
  Or plant a barren wilderness with wheat?
Shall we pipe aloft and bring you water down
  From the never-failing cisterns of the snows,
To work the mills and tramways in your town,
  And irrigate your orchards as it flows?

It is easy! Give us dynamite and drills!
  Watch the iron-shouldered rocks lie down and quake,
As the thirsty desert level floods and fills,
  And the valley we have dammed becomes a lake.

But remember, please, the Law by which we live,
  We are not built to comprehend a lie,
We can neither love nor pity nor forgive.
  If you make a slip in handling us you die!
We are greater than the Peoples or the Kings—
  Be humble, as you crawl beneath our rods!—
Our touch can alter all created things,
  We are everything on earth—except The Gods!

Though our smoke may hide the heavens from your eyes,
  It will vanish and the stars will shine again,
Because, for all our power and weight and size,
  We are nothing more than children of your brain!

ALADDIN THROWS AWAY HIS LAMP

Elias Lieberman

A zooming overhead . . . and steel-framed birds
Swoop by, intent on missions far away;
Within my room a cabinet yields words,
Sings, plays and entertains me night or day.
To signal bells a sentiment arrives
From distant friends, I pluck a wire and talk;
A motor energizes wheels, contrives
A magic car for those who will not walk.
I turn a faucet . . . cooling waters spout
And gladden throats that may be parched for thirst;
I press a button . . . brilliant light pours out
Through globes of glass . . . the darkness flees, accursed.
I need no lamp in which a jinn may dwell;
My commonplace outdoes his miracle.

STEEL

HENRI DEWITT SAYLOR

I have lived and worked in Pennsylvania,
In the coal and iron districts.

I have seen miles of steel mills
With ugly bleak buildings,
Many of them glass-roofed
And so begrimed that they cheat
Their original purpose.
I have seen ingots and bars of cherry-red steel
Glide smoothly by,
Countless stacks emitting black smoke,
Cinders, slag, flue dust everywhere.

Then I have seen the laborers,
Wan-faced, sweated and tired, dust-saturated,
Leave the mill for their homes.

I never see a skyscraper
Without counting the terrible cost in wan faces.

From

SMOKE AND STEEL

CARL SANDBURG

Smoke of the fields in spring is one,
Smoke of the leaves in autumn another.
Smoke of a steel-mill roof or a battleship funnel,
They all go up in a line with the smokestack,
Or they twist . . . in the slow twist . . . of the wind.

If the north wind comes they run to the south.
If the west wind comes they run to the east.
By this sign
all smokes
know each other.
Smoke of the fields in spring and leaves in autumn,
Smoke of the finished steel, chilled and blue,
By the oath of work they swear: "I know you."

Hunted and hissed from the center
Deep down long ago when God made us over,
Deep down are the cinders we came from—
You and I and our heads of smoke.

. . . .

Some of the smokes God dropped on the job
Cross on the sky and count our years
And sing in the secrets of our numbers;
Sing their dawns and sing their evenings,
Sing an old log-fire song:
You may put the damper up,
You may put the damper down,
The smoke goes up the chimney just the same.

Smoke of a city sunset skyline,
Smoke of a country dust horizon—
They cross on the sky and count our years.

. . . .

A bar of steel—it is only
Smoke at the heart of it, smoke and the blood of a man.
A runner of fire ran in it, ran out, ran somewhere else,
And left—smoke and the blood of a man
And the finished steel, chilled and blue.

So fire runs in, runs out, runs somewhere else again,
And the bar of steel is a gun, a wheel, a nail, a shovel,
A rudder under the sea, a steering gear in the sky;
And always dark in the heart and through it,
Smoke and the blood of a man.
Pittsburgh, Youngstown, Gary—they make their steel with men.

In the blood of men and the ink of chimneys
The smoke nights write their oaths:
Smoke into steel and blood into steel;
Homestead, Braddock, Birmingham, they make their steel with men.
Smoke and blood is the mix of steel.
The birdmen drone
in the blue; it is steel
a motor sings and zooms.

. . . .

Steel barbwire around The Works.
Steel guns in the holsters of the guards at the gates of The Works.

Steel ore boats bring the loads clawed from the earth by steel, lifted and lugged by arms of steel, sung on its way by the clanking clamshells.
The runners now, the handlers now, are steel; they dig and clutch and haul; they hoist their automatic knuckles from job to job; they are steel making steel.
Fire and dust and air fight in the furnaces; the pour is timed, the billets wriggle; the clinkers are dumped:
Liners on the sea, skyscrapers on the land; diving steel in the sea, climbing steel in the sky.

PRAYERS OF STEEL

CARL SANDBURG

Lay me on an anvil, O God.
Beat me and hammer me into a crowbar.
Let me pry loose old walls.
Let me lift and loosen old foundations.

Lay me on an anvil, O God.
Beat me and hammer me into a steel spike.
Drive me into the girders that hold a skyscraper together
Take red-hot rivets and fasten me into the central girders
Let me be the great nail holding a skyscraper through blue nights into white stars.

EXPRESS TRAINS

MacKnight Black

Shaped long and arrowy
For tearing the gusty side of space,
Locomotives leap trembling across the still land.
Like rivers of certainty
That flow past our eyes and speak to our blood,
Locomotives and trains
Swell out of the dawn and dwindle and vanish in twilight.
At noon they are fierce as lean gushes of lava,
At night they are eager and lonely as stars.
If anyone look to the earth for his hope,
Or stare toward the rim of the world for peace to his heart,
Let him be answered now by the steel flight of trains,
Let him be comforted
Beside the paths of their cleanness.

THE IRON HORSE

Israel Newman

He stands big-shouldered and august,
This genius of wanderlust.

His mane now blue, now gray, now white,
And streaked and freckled with fire at night.

His glance, a mile-long broom, avails
To sweep the darkness off the rails.

Behind him, knocking at his heels,
A row of cars, a town on wheels

Or—what adopts a slower rate—
That mile of thunder that is freight.

He has his trysts with buttes and mines,
With streams and shacks among the pines.

Far hills, half substance and half air,
Reset themselves to meet him there.

And he is coming to his own
In cities chiseled out of stone.

What horse has borne as great a pack
Of civilization on his back?

ACROSS ILLINOIS

JOHN STOLTZE

The feel of the friendly prairies, the softening shadows of night
That covers the flattened landscape to the distant gleam of a light.

The even swing of the trainload over the singing rails
Between the flowing fences that border the straight steel trails.

The light of a locomotive adown the level track,
A straight white line of brightness cutting the blanket of black.

The roar of the whistling steam, a flickering lighted train;
Once more the soft black silence and the hum of the rails again.

And through it all the darkness, keener than sense or sight,
The feel of the friendly prairies, the shadow of Western night.

CHANT OF THE BOX CARS

Harry Kemp

Consigned for lading, marked for repairs,
We hustle about the world's affairs.
Like the roadbeds, having our ups and downs,
We rock through meadows, we clank through towns.
In a thousand, thousand obscure parades
We gride down valleys, we climb long grades,
Through fields that smell of the fresh-turned sod,
Through the tasseled corn and the goldenrod.
The cattle lift their heads as we pass;
The sheep gaze up from their close-cropped grass.
Shunted, side-tracked, laden again,
Fulfilling the service required of men,
Under cloudy or blue-spread skies
We go with our loads of merchandise;
While the roadbed roars and the whistles call
And the signaling lanterns rise and fall!

PARLOR CAR

Dorothy Brown Thompson

What comfort! through conditioned air
  A radio that blares and squeaks;
Beyond the glass (if one should care)
  The thunderous silence of the peaks.

NEW DYNAMO

GERALD RAFTERY

Locked in the stillness of this mighty wheel
Is force too great to chain with shining steel.

Here is a boulder poised upon a height,
A mammoth balanced reservoir of might.

Here is the force behind a straining wall
That dams a lake where drowning rains yet fall.

Here is a strength like storm and flood and fire—
That man has taught to walk upon a wire.

INDUCED CURRENT

HERBERT MAYO

Around the magnet, Faraday
Is sure that Volta's lightnings play;
  But *how* to draw them from the wire?
He took a lesson from the heart:
'Tis when we meet, 'tis when we part,
  Breaks forth the electric fire.

GREAT TOWERS OF STEEL

Eleanor Foote Soderbeck

Great towers of steel which stride
Across the countryside,
You have no charm of line,
No beauty like the pine
Companioning your way;
His branches toss and sway
When blowzy north winds call,
While you stand firm and tall;
Aloof, you span the stream,
Ignoring ferns which dream
Among the blue-eyed grass;
The playful breezes pass
And touch your singing wires,
Arousing hidden fires
Within me, for I feel
The wonder of your steel;
I marvel at the power
Transmitted through your tower
From northern rivers, where
The eagle soars in air,
To light far homes and free
The wheels of industry.
Strong monuments to men
Who dreamed bold dreams, and then
Made visible their dreams,
You stand for more, it seems,
Than pines, or ferns, or streams.

FIRST FLIGHT

ROBERT P. TRISTRAM COFFIN

The airplane taxied to the station's gate,
A huge and lumbering bird with frozen wings
And all its life in wheels that spun on air.
The organ music died inside. It lay
A dead machine. The passengers climbed in,
And sat down in the belly of the bird.

It was the first air travel for one man.
Tristram Winship buckled the strange belt
Upon him. He felt solemn as the day,
Long ago in childhood, when he sat
The first time in a church and felt the roof
So high above him he must lay his hand
Upon his father's hand and close his eyes.
Something solemn, something like holiness,
Lay before him now. He was to know
The earth a strange, new way, from high above,
In a metal angel built by man.
This angel with an explosion for a heart
And cool, oiled gears for sinews would unroll
The parchment of new heaven and new earth.
Fiercer than the eagle in the dream
That Dante dreamt, this creature built of facts
Would take the airy way and show him more
Than Dante knew. The past was past. Mankind
Had taken over God and dreamed no more.
This slim, steel angel proved it. Here was truth
Compacted of the vitals of the hills.

Fire, motion, sequence, rhythm, law,
Power brought from earth's four ends and bound,
Fire, water, air, and earth arranged
Into a reasoned angel lovelier
Than those Ezekiel saw in awe and wonder,
With four wings moving full of burning eyes,
Who stood on wheels in mystery and flame.

It was good to be inside this angel,
For lately this new world which Tristram knew
Had seemed the less secure; the great machines
Stood idle, and men were going hungry
Beside warehouses piled too high with food.
Something like a doubt in wheels and gears
Had come upon the nations of the earth.
But here was reassurance. This swift thing
That made a continent a narrow strait,
No wider than a single night and day,
Was proof that this new earth was firm and good.
The race had come a longer, wiser way
Since Tristram ran barefooted as a boy
Than Egypt, Greece, and Rome set end on end
And all the centuries of climbing since.
Words came over seas and through the walls
Of houses, every man sat snug inside
A whispering gallery opening on the world.
Heat came in along cool wires to cook
His meat, and winter sent its ice to cool
His drink. White rivers spread out webs of day
Across four thousand miles of night-struck land.
A man-made lamp gave purer light than the sun.
The carriage had a hundred horses now,

And bore them on the very wheels they moved.
Winnipeg and Florida and Spain
Met Norway and Brazil at breakfast time
Upon the table. Every man had hands
In strange and godlike powers night and day.
His pictures moved and spoke, his voice ran out
Halfway round the world. He could command
More slaves than Pharaoh dreamt of, quick as light
And powerful as lightning on the hills.
His house could put a Caesar's house to shame.
His mind moved on new planes, new harmonies
Vibrated on a harp of keener nerves.
Men moved below the sea and through the clouds.
Here was the seal of New Jerusalem
In this creature with a life which man
Had built up out of rods and gears and tubes.
And Tristram now sat in its belly strapped,
Strapped in a ventricle of the human brain,
Ready to ascend and see his world
Unroll like a vision, marvelous and new.

The pilot took his seat. Life like a wind
Came rushing out of nowhere and laid hold
Of this day's angel. All three two-spoked wheels
Became three wheels of many spokes and sang,
And, singing, vanished utterly and left
Serene blue sky where they had been, and song.
The angel trembled, stirred, and bumped along
On wheels beneath it old as the pyramids.
The wind became a hurricane, the ground
Leaped back a blur, the angel took the air
On wheels and wings younger than Tristram was

And most young men inhabiting the earth.
The creature leaned up sharply, the wide world
Tipped sharply down, and ran off on both sides.
The wings spread to the sun an hour high,
Red as a window of the Apocalypse.
The angel headed west, the earth spun east,
White Washington slide under and from sight,
And all was ready for the vision to unroll.

The airplane leveled out, its triple heart
Beat like a law of cosmos in the brain.
High and aloof, it lost the sense of speed,
It stood serene and let the earth go past
Beneath it on its natural, eastward way.
The movement of the land was grave and slow,
Towns, forests, the Potomac winding on,
The patchwork of square fields in brown and green,
Slid under in a rhythmic dignity.
Tristram Winship had expected speed,
This quiet was the quiet of a psalm.
The great clouds stood unhurried on each hand,
The land was calm and golden in the sun
As in the landscapes painted years ago.
Tristram had not felt so still as this
Since he had sat with evening as a boy
Beside a trout stream, with a muted breath.
Serenity lay under on the world,
Peace lay below this angel fed on fire.

It was strange. Two thousand feet in under
Tristram's father as a thin young man in blue
Had walked this very country through the rains

And suns of two years red with agony,
His shoes stuffed full of straw to ease his feet.
Antietam lay below, where Tristram's father
Had tasted bitter powder, and seen men
Die in windrows by him, and had felt
The cold surprise of lead and lain in blood
From high sun to high stars. What would he say,
If he could see his son now high above
The place where he had walked the Civil War?
What would he and his comrades say, if they
Could come up from the grave and see their sons
Ride higher than the eagles overhead?
Surely, they would declare this world was great!
This angel which bore up the sons had made
Their fathers seed of Abraham and Noah;
It had raised the sons up to the things
Their fathers left upon the knees of God.
The children had gone forth from grass and tents,
Built up cities to the clouds and left
Their fathers with the far, forgotten past,
Left them with the ancient dark of earth.
The children were the seed of light and air,
The children of their loins were strangers to them!

And under Tristram's plane the land unrolled
Its pattern of small towns and woods and fields.
The houses did not hurry. They stood white
And independent on their rugs of green,
They pointed up like tents against the weather;
They closed in something precious and alone.
So many people still lived in small houses!
So many small towns still in Maryland,

With spires for their pivots and small gardens
Linking people's lives in chains of green!
Men were so near earth still! There were the graveyeards,
Touching houses and the busy streets.
A man on earth would never guess they were
So beautiful as would one flying over,
They looked like petaled flowers from the air.
And death and life were such enduring neighbors
They looked good side by side to one who flew.
It was like seeing sun and shower go
Over a wide, wide land in harmony.
The towns, though, were but little islands,
The rest was ocean and the waves of leaves.
Trees were still chief citizens of earth,
They hemmed the new and metaled highways in,
They laced the edges of the smallest fields.
The farms were lovelier than Tristram dreamed,
Each a little universe entire.
They had their backs in sun and feet in water,
Their hearts were barns, and all their veins of roads
Came home to barns. The history of man
Was in the scrollwork of the paths he made
From house to well, from orchard to the brook.
From his high station Tristram saw that things
Which meant most to a man were very old,
A tree before a door, earth turned in furrows,
A pathway by a brook, a flower bed,
The sounds of bees and cowbells, clean, new grass,
An acre he had planted, sunlit panes,
A small piece of the world which he had made
To blossom and to breed his children on,
Animals to tend and see the worship

In their big eyes when he brought in their grain,
Doves above a dovecot, a deep sense
That his two hands had had their fingers in
Something vast and holy as the growth
Of seeds to plants, of boughs across a window,
The patterns of the sunshine and the rain.
A man might have great voices in his house
From half the world and miracles of machines
To make him comfortable and safe and warm;
Man was a lover of the wild earth still,
And apples in his fingers gave him joy
And sunset in his eyes. His body moved
In the dance of seasons, night and day,
The holy chorals of the sun and moon.
Blossoms were more than fragrance and delight,
There was a fierce communion, man to earth,
Flower to man, and a stern tenderness,
Tremendous as the moon's grip on the sea,
Reached from the opened daisies to his heart.
The same law spread his hand and swallows' wings,
The same commandment lay inside his bones
As in the roots and fibers of the trees.
Ancient and awful were the heritages
Of his eyes and the eyes of morning-glories;
His brain and the bright brain of the thunder
Had nerves fast rooted in the earth and sea.
A man might fly above the hills or hide
Away from green in cities of made stones,
The ancient loyalties still found him out,
They came on him through air and through blue steel,
They held him in their everlasting arms.
With all his new-found swiftness and strange toys,

The mother held him close and turned him round
As she turned in her march about the sun.
Man's speech was still a mystery, and his feet
Moved with the unpredictable and strange
Loveliness, like God, upon the mountains.
His path was wonder, and his heart a dream,
His ways past finding out, like faith and love.
He was grace and terror like the lynx,
He was grace and gentleness with the lamb,
The loving-kindness in the golden eyes
Of sunflowers, the cruelty of storms,
Mercy in the ripened wheat. His ways
Were beautiful and strange as birth and death.

In the low, deep sunlight Tristram saw
Four little horses and a man behind
Turning hairlike furrows far below,
And they were one and beautiful past words.
They went like evening climbing up the world,
They moved, but all their motion was like peace.
And now along the winding paths across
A hundred fields the cows were coming home,
So slow, so grave, so exquisite, like notes
In music, and men, too, were walking there,
All turning home between long-shadowed trees,
Obedient forever to the law
Of coming night. The men and cows together,
Like children of one mother and like brothers.
Old fealties were moving in the dusk,
The sunset lay across all living kind.
Tristram had never felt so near the earth,
The goodness of it came up through his eyes.
Save for its heartbeat, his great bird was still.

And now the solemn eastward march of earth
Was bringing on the mountains into view,
Blue ridges of the Shenandoah, the long
Parallels of beauty north and south.
The day lay on the western sides of them,
The night was heaped behind their eastern walls.
Tristram saw blue night at work below,
Coming out of forests and of hills,
The ancient, holy twilight was at hand.
The sun was big upon the world's red rim,
The clouds went up like towers at each side,
The motion of the world drew Tristram's heart
Along with it towards the night behind.
The sun was half from sight, though Tristram's bird
With heart magnificent at steady beat
Was headed straight towards it at full speed.
The sun was but a flake of molten fire
Upon the farthest range. The sun was gone.
Only great wings of light in backward flight
Came up behind the world as all grew dark.

The mountains merged, subsided. Little lights
Twinkled into being here and there.
Houses were lit, and towns prepared for night.
The sunset wings were folded down and down.
Along straight lines, faint little fireflies
Crawled home with people in them bound for rest.
Lights blossomed thicker, reached out into rows,
Little man-made blossoms bearing day;
Lights grew to thousands, grew to myriads,
Grew into glory like the Milky Way.
Pittsburgh spread her gardens of man-fire,
A million-candle city, there she lay!

Tristram's heart distended as he leaned
To the wonder opening below
His bird's vast wing. Here was a thing,
A new thing lovely as the ancient hills,
A man could well be proud of, made today!
Tristram held his breath and gripped his seat
Above a universe of patterned flame.
The plane tipped, Tristram glanced above, the stars
Were out in millions on bright millions there.
He had never been so close to them as now,
So bright before, Tristram had never seen them,
Flame upon flame, and sun upon great sun,
Hung in the void of space, with laws between them,
Carrying the substance on which they fed.
Sun upon sun, without seen hands to feed them,
Lit for the aeons, and a symmetry
Which men, ages ago, had known as God.
The lights below were dust motes in a beam
Of light that came across ten thousand years.
The angel Tristram rode in was a May fly
Moving about the feet of sons of God,
Whose heads were in the eternal morning,
Whose lips were full of ancient praise of God.
Vast powers reaching downward from the stars
Held the earth and airplane in their hands.
The heartbeat of the engine died away
Into a heartbeat mightier than the sea;
All things were grown together in one form,
The vigor in the sleeping trees below,
The secret life sealed in primeval rocks,
The small lamps fed on lightning down below.
Dark arrows in the ether overhead,

Winged messengers between the distant suns,
Whispered their way, and bound all things in one.
The airplane was a minnow in a sea
Without a shore, where great leviathans
Left in their wakes the haze of stars unborn,
And love and law bound all things great and small.

The plane leaned over gracefully and reached
Two sudden arms of light towards the ground,
Moved in a lovely circle, headed down.
The world came up, and burst into bright day.
Speed came hurtling back to life. The plane
Rushed on and settled, felt the ground, ran on,
Trembled, slowed, and turned. The wheels returned
Into form with furious flying spokes
Upon the front of it. The wheels ran down.
The heartbeat fluttered once. The plane stood still.
The world grew still. A door was thrown ajar,
And Tristram stepped out on the ancient earth.

COCKPIT IN THE CLOUDS

Dick Dorrance

Two thousand feet beneath our wheels
The city sprawls across the land
Like heaps of children's blocks outflung,
In tantrums, by a giant hand.
To cast a silver spire soars
And seeks to pierce our lower wing.
Above its grasp we drift along,
A tiny, droning, shiny thing.

The noon crowds pack the narrow streets.
The el trains move so slow, so slow.
Amidst their traffic, chaos, life,
The city's busy millions go.
Up here, aloof, we watch them crawl.
In crystal air we seem to poise
Behind our motor's throaty roar—
Down there, we're just another noise.

From

CENTRAL

JOHN CURTIS UNDERWOOD

Though men may build their bridges high and plant their piers below the sea,
And drive their trains across the sky; a higher task is left to me.
I bridge the void 'twixt soul and soul; I bring the longing lovers near.
I draw you to your spirit's goal. I serve the ends of fraud and fear.

The older Fates sat in the sun. The cords they spun were short and slight.
I set my stitches one by one, where life electric fetters night,
Till it outstrips the planet's speed, and out of darkness leaps to day;
And men in Maine shall hear and heed a voice from San Francisco Bay.

MANDARIN ON THE AIR

CHRISTOPHER MORLEY

I

In a pellucid calm of summer sunset
The Old Mandarin sat idling in his bamboo grove.
Putting up his chin, like a cat,
To be stroked by silence
He thought of all the hullabaloo
Passing unapprehended through the air around him.

He was astonished to consider:
In his autonomous ears and nostrils
In the private basin of his brain
Orchestras jostled unheard,
Commercials teemed in his belly;
Orators inspissated the bag of his lungs,
Syllables thridded his lumbars,
His entrails were embryo with palaver,
Electric with spores of speech.

Oh circumambient air
Wherein we live and are,
They should choose with care
Words that go so far.

II

When I first went on the air, many years ago
(Reflected the Old Monologue)
Radio was still primitive.
When a thunderstorm came along

Broadcasting was suspended
Until the kilocycles abated
And the amplitudes quit howling.
In those days they said I used words too long and heavy
For the stripling ether.

But now the air has grown up
And can carry almost anything.
Think of the political and economic brainstorms
That have rumbled through space:
Yet as I look outdoors
It seems still pure, transparent, unblemished—
Even unresentful.

THE SURGEON

W. J. Funk

Now he begins: his fingers feel
The tiny burning bit of steel:
They move, obedient to a star
Unseen by us: his sure hands are
So swift that the swift hands of death
Are held: there is one slender breath
Between the two, so delicate
No calipers can measure it
Save those he holds—*I think there is*
No act so near to God as his.

ON HEARING JAZZ

ALICE PHELPS-RIDER

Something wakes and stirs within me,
Something hidden and barbaric,
Wildly pulsing, oddly beating.
Dimly outlined to my vision
Is a cave, and at its entrance
Glows a fire, while around it
Figures, strangely like, yet unlike
People as we know and see them,
Toss and strain and bend and shiver
As the cold wind strikes their bodies
That have strongly knotted muscles,
And coarse shaggy hair that's matted.
Strange emotions light those dull eyes,
Feelings that are like to ours
As their cave, so stark and cheerless,
Is akin to modern dwellings.
I can hear their tom-toms rattle
In that misty morn of living;
I can sense barbaric rhythms,
I can feel the throb of dancing
In that quaint and eerie twilight
Ere the world had lost its weirdness;
Ere the growth of new-found knowledge
Made us stronger, made us weaker;
Made life brighter, made it darker;
Made souls gladder, made them sorrow
More than in the olden era;
More than in the crimson dawning

When the world was young and fiery,
Strong in body, weak in wisdom.
Was my spirit once encircled
By a body, in those far days?
Was my being near the fire,
Did I swing the bones and rattles?
Was I brawny, lithe and sinewy,
Young in mind and soul and culture,
But with seeds of growth within me?
Did I worship sun and fire,
Dread the winter as a devil
Who would smite and kill and cripple?
Did I listen to the throbbing
And the wild uncanny pulsing
Of those rhythms in the firelight?
When I hear our jazz, I wonder.

APARTMENT HOUSE

GERALD RAFTERY

A filing-cabinet of human lives
Where people swarm like bees in tunneled hives,
Each to his own cell in the towered comb,
Identical and cramped—we call it home.

SONNET ON TURNING A RADIO DIAL

ANDERSON M. SCRUGGS

They are the foes of silence and of time,
These voices from the fringes of the earth,
Thronging the streams of air with stave and rhyme,
Charging the clouds with ribaldry and mirth.
Out of the futile dark the sounds arise,
Whistling their way from cities, strange and far,
Cleaving tumultuous pathways down the skies
Long held inviolate for moon and star.
O little valiant voices of the dust,
Lifting your dreams like torches in the night—
Sing on against that hour when time shall thrust
A lean forefinger to put out your light,
And all the centuried silence of the loam
Like some great tidal wave comes thundering home.

LILACS FOR REMEMBRANCE

Irene Shirley Moran

Endure
The farm? Oh, no.
He left, and now he hears
All day the deafening grind of mill
Machines.

His wife
Can take her ease
In these few rooms . . . the boys
Don't have so far to go to school,
He says.

And yet
On Sunday drives
He passes lilac clumps. . . .
No backward looks, lest they recall
Too much.

HOUSE DEMOLISHED

CHARLES MALAM

The iron dragon nuzzles paving crust
With an insatiable hunger in its maw
For broken granite and for plaster dust.
The black earth trembles where it sets its paw.
The leafless earth gives up a hollow sound,
Wall folding over wall with heavy groan,
Ledge upon ledge bowing to the ground,
And the proud timber, and the quarried stone.
Here was the hall where mysteries came walking,
Faces and strangers' voices from the night.
And here they dined, and here were children talking,
And here were lovers dreaming, where the light
Pours through the rafters and the falling floors
And space returns again to out-of-doors.

FILLING STATION

E. Merrill Root

Giant flagons in a row—flashing in the sun—
Stand beside the silken road where steel coursers run;
Flagons made of crimsoned iron and of crystal glass,
Waiting till some thirsty car pause before he pass.

Wine as green as windy seas—wine a gentian blue—
Wine like crimson clouds that are the sunset's avenue—
Wine for thirsty runners wherein the lightnings wink:
So I stop my courser and drive him up to drink.

Casual man in overalls, you know not what you do,
Pouring wine of lightnings out, magic thunder-brew,
Golden mile-a-minute flame from your giant's cup!
Morning's young: the long road waits: comrade, fill her up.

MACHINES—OR MEN

ELIZABETH NEWPORT HEPBURN

If one were soundproof, like a well-built house,
And proof against the weather—winter winds
And dull reluctant stagnant summer heat—
If one were built for service, like a car,
With shock absorbers for rough traveling!

And if men's souls were radio equipped
So that we thought the thoughts and dreamed the dreams
Of souls attuned to ours . . . imagine it,
The satisfaction of a perfect set
So we could listen in, or turn a screw
Insuring soundless perfect placid peace!

But we are ill-constructed for this age.
We need inventors who could speed us up
And see that we're equipped with everything
To safeguard us against our lesser selves:
Electric torches to illume dark moods,
And radium to kill our secret cares,
To burn out fear and selfishness and greed,
Dread cancers of the spirit . . . killing too
That grim and vicious germ, intolerance.

Thus men would be serene and wise, like gods:
No suffering in such an ordered world,
Since we could all inoculate our young
So they need never know love's bittersweet,
Ambition's cruel spur, or passion's prayer,
The acid bite of failure, of despair.

. . . .

And yet I wonder . . . can machinery
Share in the spring, live through an April day,
Or dream, imprisoned, of love's mystery,
Or hope, in winter, for the kiss of May?

POWER

GRACE NOLL CROWELL

Accompanied by clamor and by noise
  Men turn their fretting engines toward the sun;
They lay their little rails and start their toys
  That shunt and shriek and whistle as they run.

But God flung all his new worlds into space
  To make their ceaseless journeys day and night,
Without a sound or tremor as they race
  Upon their countless centuries of flight.

While we, the passengers of earth, arrive
  To take the journey without scrip or purse,
Unmindful of the power and might that drive
  The soundless pistons of the universe.

TEXAS

AMY LOWELL

I went a-riding, a-riding,
Over a great long plain.
And the great plain went a-sliding, a-sliding
Away from my bridle rein.

Fields of cotton, and fields of wheat,
Thunder-blue gentians by a wire fence,
Standing cypress, red and tense,
Holding its flower rigid like a gun,
Dressed for parade by the running wheat,
By the little bouncing cotton. Terribly sweet
The cardinals sing in the live-oak trees,
And the long plain breeze,
The prairie breeze,
Blows across from swell to swell
With a ginger smell.
Just ahead, where the road curves round,
A long-eared rabbit makes a bound
Into a wheat field, into a cotton field,
His track glitters after him and goes still again
Over to the left of my bridle rein.

But over to the right is a glare—glare—glare—
Of sharp glass windows.
A narrow square of brick jerks thickly up above the cotton plants,
A raucous mercantile thing flaring the sun from thirty-six windows,

Brazenly declaring itself to the lovely fields.
Tramcars run like worms about the feet of this thing,
The coffins of cotton bales feed it,
The threshed wheat is its golden blood.
But here it has no feet,
It has only the steep ironic grin of its thirty-six windows,
Only its basilisk eyes counting the fields,
Doing sums of how many buildings to a city, all day and all
night.

Once they went a-riding, a-riding,
Ovcr the great long plain.
Cowboys singing to their dogie steers,
Cowboys perched on forty-dollar saddles,
Riding to the north, six months to get there,
Six months to reach Wyoming.
"Hold up, paint horse, herd the little dogies,
Over the lone prairie."
Bones of dead steers,
Bones of cowboys,
Under the wheat, maybe.

The skyscraper sings another way,
A tune of steel, of wheels, of gold.
And the ginger breeze blows, blows all day
Tanged with flowers and mold.
And the Texas sky whirls down, whirls down,
Taking long looks at the fussy town.
An old sky and a long plain
Beyond, beyond, my bridle rein.

OBSERVATION

Samuel Hoffenstein

Little by little we subtract
Faith and Fallacy from Fact,
The Illusory from the True,
And starve upon the Residue.

What is the sense in tears or laughter?
The Root of things is what we're after:
But fallen trees will spill their fruit
And worms and darkness keep the root.

Fallen days will spill their sun,
But paper heavens must be won,
And so, while we geometrize,
A bird out-twits us, twice as wise.

Mere matter is not all of marrow;
The harvest leaps not from the harrow,
And a push button will not light
Joy by day, or stars by night.

ODE TO MACHINES

LOUIS GINSBERG

Machines in haughty and presumptuous pride
Are mankind magnified.
Extensions of himself, they merely can
Mirror the heart of man.
They will enslave him, never yielding peace
But goading him to greed and pelf,
Until at last he will arise and cease
Being the prisoner of himself;
Till after suffering of the years,
Man will behold the city as it is:
Skyscrapers, soaring arrogant to view,
Raised by groans of workers under new
And greedier Pharaoh's lids,
Are age-old pyramids:
Till suddenly man will arise and cry
With new-found breath
That once for all, he will refuse to die
Before his death.
But gazing into life for all it means,
He'll snap away the code that smothers;
He'll hail the manifold machines
As brothers:
Turbine and dynamo—dower
Us with a happier hour;
Loom—weave quickly, give
New patterns by which to live;
Plowshare—break up the old
Avarice of gold;

Blast furnace—now refine
An age's new design;
Excavating machine—
Dig deep and strong and clean
Foundations for freedom to rise
Eavesdropping on the skies;
Girder and stanchion and stay—
Build high a better day;
At last, at last,
Riveter—come,
Make firm and fast
Millennium!

THE CITY

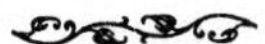

God made the country, and man made the town.

—WILLIAM COWPER

THE EXCAVATION

MAX ENDICOFF

Clusters of electric bulbs
Like giant chrysanthemums
Paint the black cavern
With streaks and blots
Of faded yellow.
In grotesque mimicry
The monstrous shadows
Ape each movement of toiling men.
The stale, pungent odor of unpacked earth
Tickles the nostrils.
Through the wood-plank roof
The dull-booming rumble
Of scampering traffic
Trickles in—
But is swallowed up
By the harsh purr of the drill
As it bites frenziedly
Into the dogged rock.

And overhead, unseen,
A mountain of stone is kept upright
By a slender steel beam
And a theory.

SUBWAY BUILDERS

LAWRENCE LEE

We heard them like besiegers down the street.
  Dark foot by foot they fought the stolid rock,
Until the houses shook beneath our feet
  And windowpanes were rattled with the shock
Of muffled batteries of dynamite:
  All day they fought the hard earth, bone to bone.
And like machine guns through the noisy night
  We heard their sharp drills biting in the stone;
Then great trucks thundered off when they were filled.
  One morning, as men battled underground,
The beaten earth struck back; and some were killed,
  When rock fell on them with an angry sound.
Yet others struggled with the sullen loam;
  And love and hunger and the fear of death
Were dim things in a half-forgotten home
  As they struck earthward with each deep-lunged breath.
They sought the finish like a lunging knife,
  And felt the great joy that all fighters feel;
For they had tunneled through the muck of life
  To lay the stern, straight cleanliness of steel.

I SCARCELY GRIEVE, O NATURE!

HENRY TIMROD

I scarcely grieve, O Nature! at the lot
That pent my life within a city's bounds,
And shut me from thy sweetest sights and sounds.
Perhaps I had not learned, if some lone cot
Had nursed a dreamy childhood, what the mart
Taught me amid its turmoil; so my youth
Had missed many a stern but wholesome truth.
Here, too, O Nature! in this haunt of Art,
Thy power is on me, and I own thy thrall.
There is no unimpressive spot on earth!
The beauty of the stars is over all,
And Day and Darkness visit every hearth.
Clouds do not scorn us: yonder factory's smoke
Looked like a golden mist when morning broke.

WATERFALLS OF STONE

LOUIS GINSBERG

Buildings are fountains jetting stone,
That spurting up with marble crest,
Are frozen and enchained in air,
Poised in perpetual rest

Yet water seeks its level out;
So when these fountains are unbound,
The cataracts of melting stone
Will sink into the ground.

AS TO BEING ALONE

JAMES OPPENHEIM

Why did you hate to be by yourself,
And why were you sick of your own company?

Such is the question, and this is the answer:

I feared sublimity:
I was a little afraid of God:
Silence and space terrified me, bringing the thought of what an irritable clod I was and how soon death would gulp me down. . . .

This fear has raised cities:
The cowards flock together by the millions lest they should be left alone for a half hour. . . .

With church, theater and school,
With office, mill and motor,
With a thousand cunning devices, and clever calls to each other,
They escape from themselves to the crowd. . . .

Oh, I have loved it all:
Snug rooms, the talk, the pleasant feast, the pictures:
The warm bath of humanity in which I relaxed and soaked myself:
And, never, I hope, shall I be without it—at times. . . .
But now myself calls me. . . .
The skies demand me, though it is but ten in the morning:
The earth has an appointment with me, not to be broken. . . .

I must accustom myself to the gaunt face of the Sublime.

. . .

I must see what I really am, and what I am for,
And what this city is for, and the earth and the stars in their
hurry. . . .

To turn out typewriters,
To invent a new breakfast food,
To devise a dance that was never danced until now,
To urge a new sanitation, and a swifter automobile—
Have the life-surging heavens no business but this?

CITY TREES

ANDERSON M. SCRUGGS

There is a poverty that trees may show
From dearth of wholesome sunlight, winds, and rains—
Old trees that press gaunt hands against the panes
Of tenements, like tombstones, row on row.
They are the trees around whose starved roots flow
Only the sweepings of the streets, the drains
Of black, tarred roofs—and smoky yellow stains
Of light are all the sunshine that they know.
How they must yearn—those brick-imprisoned trees—
For mellow slopes of hill where crystal-clear
The rain comes ringing down, where every breeze
Is redolent with mossy earth and flowers;
How like old men by penury made drear,
Silent, they bear the burden of the hours.

SUNSET: ST. LOUIS

Sara Teasdale

Hushed in the smoky haze of summer sunset,
When I came home again from far-off places,
How many times I saw my Western city
  Dream by the river.

Then for an hour the water wore a mantle
Of tawny gold and mauve and misted turquoise
Under the tall and darkened arches bearing
  Gray, high-flung bridges.

Against the sunset, water towers and steeples
Flickered with fire up the slope to westward,
And old warehouses poured their purple shadows
  Across the levee.

High over them the black train swept with thunder,
Cleaving the city, leaving far beneath it
Wharf boats moored beside the old side-wheelers
  Resting in twilight.

COMPOSED UPON WESTMINISTER BRIDGE, SEPTEMBER 3, 1802

William Wordsworth

Earth has not anything to show more fair.
Dull would he be of soul who could pass by
A sight so touching in its majesty.
This city now doth like a garment wear
The beauty of the morning; silent, bare,
Ships, towers, domes, theaters, and temples lie
Open unto the fields and to the sky,
All bright and glittering in the smokeless air.
Never did sun more beautifully steep
In his first splendor valley, rock, or hill;
Ne'er saw I, never felt, a calm so deep!
The river glideth at his own sweet will.
Dear God! the very houses seem asleep,
And all that mighty heart is lying still!

MANHATTAN

MARGARET ELWARD LAWLESS

Manhattan! All your symmetry of steel,
Your golden domes, your bayoneted spires,
Press hard against my heart until I feel
A pagan hand must tend your altar fires;
You drive the birds in exile from your skies;
God from your churches; man in shame to crawl
In awful wonder that the sun dare rise
On such magnificence, a star dare fall,
And yet, my eyes rest on the splintered sheen
Of gray-green waters at your stony edge;
The gallant grass comes back to Bowling Green;
A cowslip blooms upon an East Side ledge;
And when I venture home, my ears will meet
Milano's matchless songs in Bleecker Street!

CITY BIRD

THEDA KENYON

There's a thrush that sings in a shadowy wood,
  And a gull that cries to the sea,
And one dares horizons, and one dares heights;
  But a surer gallantry
Belongs to the little brown bird that nests
  In the crotch of a city tree.

The gull may challenge a northwest gale
  Straight-winged, with a laughing call;
And the thrush fill the frightening wood with notes
  As blithe as a waterfall;
But the bird that nests above city streets
  Sings the bravest song of all.

For the city's leaves are a dusty brown,
  And its dawn is a smoke-thick gray,
And all the fragance that April brings
  Seems very far away;
But the little brown bird in the city street
  Still sings of a dew-fresh day!

SKYSCRAPER

CARL SANDBURG

By day the skyscraper looms in the smoke and sun and has a soul.
Prairie and valley, streets of the city, pour people into it and they mingle among its twenty floors and are poured out again back to the streets, prairies and valleys.
It is the men and women, boys and girls so poured in and out all day that give the building a soul of dreams and thoughts and memories.
(Dumped in the sea or fixed in a desert, who would care for the building or speak its name or ask a policeman the way to it?)

Elevators slide on their cables and tubes catch letters and parcels and iron pipes carry gas and water in and sewage out.
Wires climb with secrets, carry light and carry words, and tell terrors and profits and loves—curses of men grappling plans of business and questions of women in plots of love.

Hour by hour the caissons reach down to the rock of the earth and hold the building to a turning planet.
Hour by hour the girders play as ribs and reach out and hold together the stone walls and floors.
Hour by hour the hand of the mason and the stuff of the mortar clinch the pieces and parts to the shape an architect voted.
Hour by hour the sun and the rain, the air and the rust, and the press of time running into centuries, play on the building inside and out and use it.

Men who sunk the pilings and mixed the mortar are laid in graves where the wind whistles a wild song without words
And so are men who strung the wires and fixed the pipes and tubes and those who saw it rise floor by floor.
Souls of them are all here, even the hod carrier begging at back doors hundreds of miles away and the bricklayer who went to state's prison for shooting another man while drunk.
(One man fell from a girder and broke his neck at the end of a straight plunge—he is here—his soul has gone into the stones of the building.)

On the office doors from tier to tier—hundreds of names and each name standing for a face written across with a dead child, a passionate lover, a driving ambition for a million dollar business or a lobster's ease of life.

Behind the signs on the doors they work and the walls tell nothing from room to room.
Ten-dollar-a-week stenographers take letters from corporation officers, lawyers, efficiency engineers, and tons of letters go bundled from the building to all ends of the earth.
Smiles and tears of each office girl go into the soul of the building just the same as the mastermen who rule the building.

Hands of clocks turn to noon hours and each floor empties its men and women who go away and eat and come back to work.
Toward the end of the afternoon all work slackens and all jobs go slower as the people feel day closing on them.

One by one the floors are emptied. . . . The uniformed elevator men are gone. Pails clang. . . . Scrubbers work, talking in foreign tongues. Broom and water and mop clean from the floors human dust and spit, and machine grime of the day.
Spelled in electric fire on the roof are words telling miles of houses and people where to buy a thing for money. The sign speaks till midnight.

Darkness on the hallways. Voices echo. Silence holds. . . . Watchmen walk slow from floor to floor and try the doors. Revolvers bulge from their hip pockets. . . . Steel safes stand in corners. Money is stacked in them.
A young watchman leans at a window and sees the lights of barges butting their way across a harbor, nets of red and white lanterns in a railroad yard, and a span of glooms splashed with lines of white and blurs of crosses and clusters over the sleeping city.
By night the skyscraper looms in the smoke and the stars and has a soul.

ELLIS PARK

HELEN HOYT

Little park that I pass through,
I carry off a piece of you
Every morning hurrying down
To my workday in the town;
Carry you for country there
To make the city ways more fair.

I take your trees,
And your breeze,
Your greenness,
Your cleanness,
Some of your shade, some of your sky,
Some of your calm as I go by;
Your flowers to trim
The pavements grim;
Your space for room in the jostled street
And grass for carpet to my feet.
Your fountains take and sweet birdcalls
To sing me from my office walls.
All that I can see
I carry off with me.
But you never miss my theft,
So much treasure you have left.
As I find you, fresh at morning,
So I find you, home returning—
Nothing lacking from your grace.
All your riches wait in place
For me to borrow
On the morrow.

Do you hear this praise of you,
Little park that I pass through?

THE LIGHTS OF NEW YORK

SARA TEASDALE

The lightning spun your garment for the night
Of silver filaments with fire shot through,
A broidery of lamps that lit for you
The steadfast splendor of enduring light.
The moon drifts dimly in the heaven's height,
Watching with wonder how the earth she knew
That lay so long wrapped deep in dark and dew,
Should wear upon her breast a star so white.
The festivals of Babylon were dark
With flaring flambeaux that the wind blew down;
The Saturnalia were a wild boy's lark
With rain-quenched torches dripping through the town—
But you have found a god and filched from him
A fire that neither wind nor rain can dim.

CITY NATURE

ESTHER PINCH

I like nature strained through a town,
  Pigeons on the pavements, grass in a park,
Lacquer nights when the rain falls down,
  On golden hieroglyphics, shimmering in the dark.

Flaming sunsets spread beyond the tangles,
  Of smokestacks, clothesline, concrete roof,
Crowds in a snowstorm, rivers wearing spangles,
  And a slim new moon, disdainfully aloof.

CITY BIRDS

Winter Night—Times Square

SPUD JOHNSON

The winds gathered deep in the winter night
And flew down seven canyons to the square,
Making a monstrous whirlpool in their flight—
A maelstrom of the ghostly-lighted air.
Electric signs were blurred and dimmed with dust,
Taxicabs and pedestrians were blown
Together across the asphalt street. A gust
Of icy wind that mounted with a moan,
Shifted, wheeled, and magically swirled
Newspapers in the air like birds
Lost in the night: messengers that twirled
And scattered empty and unimportant words.
These are the wild fowl of the city, but here clings
None of its beauty, written upon their wings.

THIS IS THE CITY CHILDREN MADE

FRANK ERNEST HILL

This is the city children made,
Busy with childhood, being afraid
Of worlds grown up and bare of noise,
Games, and preposterous gay toys.

They built it of blocks—fantastic stone—
Hollowed and windowed, every one,
With stairs piled higher than hills, and cars
Lifting like rockets toward the stars.

And toys with the glitter of wheels they made
That leapt and tooted in proud parade;
And streets they smoothed where wheels could pass—
Avenues shining like roads of glass.

Under the streets more streets were scooped,
Down in the hill roots branched and looped,
Deep under rivers dove from sight—
Trains played in them day and night.

Toys were everywhere . . . toys and toys . . .
Some played at work, some made sweet noise,
Others could add or write or talk,
Some told you when to stop or walk,

Others were magic lanterns showing
What fifty ends of the earth were doing,
And some were stars, turned on at night,
Keeping the streets and the houses bright.

Here in the city the children stay,
Busy with childhood, busy with play—
With games of digging and games of gold,
Of heaping houses in high square mold,

Sweeping their streets and tall stone blocks,
Scattering rubbish, buying frocks,
Dashing forever and up and down
All day in the noise of the great toy town!

This is the city children made,
Busy with childhood, being afraid
Of worlds grown up and bare of noise,
Games, and preposterous gay toys.

CITY TREES

EDNA ST. VINCENT MILLAY

The trees along this city street,
  Save for the traffic and the trains,
Would make a sound as thin and sweet
  As trees in country lanes.

And people standing in their shade
  Out of a shower, undoubtedly
Would hear such music as is made
  Upon a country tree.

O little leaves that are so dumb
  Against the shrieking city air,
I watch you when the wind has come—
  I know what sound is there.

TO THE GREATEST CITY IN THE WORLD

Rolfe Humphries

No permanent possession of the sky
Nor everlasting lease upon the air
Is given any town. *Prepare, prepare*
To see your towers falling! By and by,
Vertical city, delicate and high,
Even your cliffs must crack, topple, and share
The common doom that blunter buildings bear,
Tumble and crumble, disappear and die.
And some day solemn folk, who never knew
Except from ancient hearsay, all your wonder
Of splendid elevating steel and stones
Will come with shovels, rummaging for you,
With dredges pull the river mud from under
Your rusting huddled fragmentary bones.

TOWN CHILD

BARBARA YOUNG

There's a hill somewhere, and a tree and birds;
But I have only the lovely words.

There are roads and rivers to every sea;
But they're only beautiful words to me.

The clouds and sky are over all,
But the towers of town are dark and tall.

So I say them over, the lovely words:
Hill and hollow, and tree and birds.

And they make a song that is sweet to me:
Road and river, and sand and sea.

And I hear soft music, just as plain,
When I whisper, *Meadow and mist and rain.*

And the towers of town grow bright and small,
When I say, *The sky is over all.*

Oh, a flock of words like snow-white sheep
Is a lovely thing for a child to keep!

AUTUMN, FORSAKE THESE HILLS

FRANK ERNEST HILL

Autumn, forsake these hills and dwell with towns.
Change will not take you there. The year will go
Insensibly from summer into snow;
No tower will turn from green to golds and browns.
But here the slopes and hollows burn with death;
Scarlet of leaves, scarlet of butterflies
Flame to their ash. . . . Last flowers shut their eyes.
Bronze bees go stricken in the frosty breath
Of blue-bright noon. Under the black wild grapes
White wine of brooks through leaf-drowned shadow ebbs.
Spiders hang frozen in gray spider webs.
What here was young and bright and swift escapes
In ruin that can never flame at all
Where life is changeless pavement, noise, and wall!

THE WAYS OF MAN

We long for purple distances
Seen only from afar.
We think we want the nearness
Of a million-pointed star.
And reason is unreason
While we are what we are.

—KATHLEEN MILLAY

HE CLIMBS A HILL AND TURNS HIS FACE

LIONEL WIGGAM

He climbs a hill and turns his face
Impudently into space.
He builds a tower that he may climb
Higher still, and measure time.
He fixes Vega, contemplates
Orion, shrewdly calculates
The moon; assembling what he saw
He arrogantly makes a law.
But never can he build a tower
From which to see what passions are.
He cannot fix and name the course
His own heart takes, though he explores
The whole amazing length of heaven.
He is forever baffled; even
Though he knows how worlds evolve,
Himself he cannot solve.

BROTHERS

Elias Lieberman

Noon in the park. . . . A tropic sun
  Dazzles with light and chokes with heat.
Sleepers about you. . . . Notice one
  Stretching his length on a wooden seat.
His face is blotched and puffy and seared;
  Sweat drips from the clammy skin;
Flies romp on a stubble of beard—
  A bundle of dirt with a soul therein.

Noon at the club. . . . A welcome shade
  Dulls the light and cools the heat.
Gentleman seated. . . . Lemonade
  Dashed with cognac and something sweet.
Arms dangling limply down,
  Feet tapping the polished floor. . . .
Yawning and stretching. . . . No one in town. . . .
  Not a soul. . . . What a beastly bore!

ENVY

EDGAR DANIEL KRAMER

I have a brother
  Who has not seen
The white foam flying
  Where tall ships lean;
For he is plowing
  The fields at home,
While I am faring
  The trackless foam.
But while he labors
  Where grass and tree
Are trembling beauty,
  He envies me.

I have a brother
  Whose footsteps turn,
When dusk is falling
  And candles burn,
To where a lassie
  And laddie wait
To hear him open
  The garden gate.
And while I wander
  Far ways and dim,
Though dreams are calling,
  I envy him.

THE SLAVE

James Oppenheim

They set the slave free, striking off his chains. . . .
Then he was as much of a slave as ever.

He was still chained to servility,
He was still manacled to indolence and sloth,
He was still bound by fear and superstition,
By ignorance, suspicion, and savagery. . . .
His slavery was not in the chains,
But in himself. . . .

They can only set free men free. . . .
And there is no need of that:
Free men set themselves free.

INEXPERIENCE

JUNE BREINING

Oh, I will go with carefree laugh—
A lilting song,
And you will smile a sad, wise smile,
Knowing I'm wrong.

Then I'll come back with drooping head,
Hurt and burned,
And you will smile a sad, wise smile,
Knowing I've learned.

THE WORLD IS TOO MUCH WITH US

WILLIAM WORDSWORTH

The world is too much with us; late and soon,
Getting and spending, we lay waste our powers.
Little we see in nature that is ours;
We have given our hearts away, a sordid boon!
This Sea that bares her bosom to the moon,
The winds that will be howling at all hours
And are upgathered now like sleeping flowers,
For this, for everything, we are out of tune;
It moves us not.—Great God! I'd rather be
A pagan suckled in a creed outworn,
So might I, standing on this pleasant lea,
Have glimpses that would make me less forlorn;
Have sight of Proteus rising from the sea,
Or hear old Triton blow his wreathèd horn.

WHEN I HEARD THE LEARNED ASTRONOMER

WALT WHITMAN

When I heard the learned astronomer,
When the proofs, the figures, were ranged in columns before me,
When I was shown the charts and diagrams, to add, divide, and measure them,
When I sitting heard the astronomer where he lectured with much applause in the lecture room,
How soon unaccountable I became tired and sick,
Till rising and gliding out I wandered off by myself,
In the mystical moist night air, and from time to time,
Looked up in perfect silence at the stars.

From

SENLIN: A BIOGRAPHY

CONRAD AIKEN

It is morning, Senlin says, and in the morning
When the light drips through the shutters like the dew,
I arise, I face the sunrise,
And do the things my fathers learned to do.
Stars in the purple dusk above the roof tops
Pale in a saffron mist and seem to die,
And I myself on a swiftly tilting planet
Stand before a glass and tie my tie.

Vine leaves tap my window,
Dewdrops sing to the garden stones,
The robin chirps in the chinaberry tree
Repeating three clear tones.

It is morning. I stand by the mirror
And tie my tie once more.
While waves far off in a pale rose twilight
Crash on a white sand shore.
I stand by a mirror and comb my hair:
How small and white my face!—
The green earth tilts through a sphere of air
And bathes in a flame of space.

There are houses hanging above the stars
And stars hung under a sea . . .
And a sun far off in a shell of silence
Dapples my walls for me. . . .

It is morning, Senlin says, and in the morning
Should I not pause in the light to remember God?
Upright and firm I stand on a star unstable,
He is immense and lonely as a cloud.
I will dedicate this moment before my mirror
To Him alone, for Him I will comb my hair.
Accept these humble offerings, Cloud of Silence!
I will think of You as I descend the stair.

Vine leaves tap my window,
The snail track shines on the stones;
Dewdrops flash from the chinaberry tree
Repeating two clear tones.

It is morning, I awake from a bed of silence,
Shining I rise from the starless waters of sleep.
The walls are about me still as in the evening,
I am the same, and the same name still I keep.

The earth revolves with me, yet makes no motion,
The stars pale silently in a coral sky.
In a whistling void I stand before my mirror,
Unconcerned, and tie my tie.

There are horses neighing on far-off hills
Tossing their long white manes,
And mountains flash in the rose-white dusk,
Their shoulders black with rains. . . .
It is morning. I stand by the mirror
And surprise my soul once more;
The blue air rushes above my ceiling,
There are suns beneath my floor. . . .

. . . It is morning, Senlin says, I ascend from darkness
And depart on the winds of space for I know not where,
My watch is wound, a key is in my pocket,
And the sky is darkened as I descend the stair.
There are shadows across the windows, clouds in heaven,
And a God among the stars; and I will go
Thinking of Him as I might think of daybreak
And humming a tune I know. . . .

Vine leaves tap at the window,
Dewdrops sing to the garden stones,
The robin chirps in the chinaberry tree
Repeating three clear tones.

OPPORTUNITY

Edward Rowland Sill

This I beheld, or dreamed it in a dream:
There spread a cloud of dust along a plain;
And underneath the cloud, or in it, raged
A furious battle, and men yelled, and swords
Shocked upon swords and shields. A prince's banner
Wavered, then staggered backward, hemmed by foes.
A craven hung along the battle's edge,
And thought, "Had I a sword of keener steel—
That blue blade that the king's son bears—but this
Blunt thing—!" he snapped and flung it from his hand,
And lowering crept away and left the field.
Then came the king's son, wounded, sore bestead,
And weaponless, and saw the broken sword,
Hilt-buried in the dry and trodden sand,
And ran and snatched it, and with battle shout
Lifted afresh he hewed his enemy down,
And saved a great cause that heroic day.

THE LITTLE GODS

Abigail Cresson

Oh, you may sing your gypsy songs
Of winding trails and free,
Of days of roving and of love—
But sing them not to me!

For I—I love my little house,
So let the strange roads call;
I'll huddle by my cozy fire
And hear them not at all.

My chairs, my twisted candlesticks,
My great, soft feather bed—
Think I'd change them for the camp,
And no roof overhead?

I'll eat my food from china plates,
With silver fork and knife,
And not with twigs from dirty tin
As must a gypsy's wife.

Ah, do not whistle from the lane—
I'll never heed your call—
I'll hear the ticking of my clock,
The embers as they fall.

PASTORALE

MILDRED WESTON

Only cows can loll at ease,
Canopied by apple trees,
Ruminative, dreaming over
Yesterday's sweet clover.

Man cannot forget for long
He sold Eden for a song.
Of what comfort is it now
To be wiser than a cow?

Lucky beast, whose worries fail
To outwit a switching tail.
Thoughts are more perverse than flies.
Only cows find Paradise.

THE WAYFARER

STEPHEN CRANE

The wayfarer,
Perceiving the pathway to truth,
Was struck with astonishment.
It was thickly grown with weeds.
"Ha," he said,
"I see that none has passed here
In a long time."
Later he saw that each weed
Was a singular knife.
"Well," he mumbled at last,
"Doubtless there are other roads."

CONTRARY JOE

L. A. G. STRONG

Through every sort of trouble Joe
  Hanged tough and stubborn on.
Nine times they said he'd have to go,
  And twice that he was gone.

Good sense was what he'd never learn,
  But obstinate would bide:
For when things took a better turn
  The mazehead up and died.

IDEALISTS

Alfred Kreymborg

Brother Tree:
Why do you reach and reach?
do you dream some day to touch the sky?
Brother Stream:
Why do you run and run?
do you dream some day to fill the sea?
Brother Bird:
Why do you sing and sing?
do you dream——

Young Man:
Why do you talk and talk and talk?

CONVENTION

Agnes Lee

The snow is lying very deep,
My house is sheltered from the blast.
I hear each muffled step outside,
I hear each voice go past.

But I'll not venture in the drift
Out of this bright security,
Till enough footsteps tread it down
To make a path for me.

MENDING WALL

ROBERT FROST

Something there is that doesn't love a wall,
That sends the frozen-ground-swell under it,
And spills the upper boulders in the sun;
And makes gaps even two can pass abreast.
The work of hunters is another thing:
I have come after them and made repair
Where they have left not one stone on a stone,
But they would have the rabbit out of hiding,
To please the yelping dogs. The gaps I mean,
No one has seen them made or heard them made,
But at spring mending time we find them there.
I let my neighbor know beyond the hill;
And on a day we meet to walk the line
And set the wall between us once again.
We keep the wall between us as we go.
To each the boulders that have fallen to each.
And some are loaves and some so nearly balls
We have to use a spell to make them balance:
"Stay where you are until our backs are turned!"
We wear our fingers rough with handling them.
Oh, just another kind of outdoor game,
One on a side. It comes to little more:
There where it is we do not need the wall:
He is all pine and I am apple orchard.
My apple trees will never get across
And eat the cones under his pines, I tell him.
He only says, "Good fences make good neighbors."
Spring is the mischief in me, and I wonder

If I could put a notion in his head:
"*Why* do they make good neighbors? Isn't it
Where there are cows? But here there are no cows.
Before I built a wall I'd ask to know
What I was walling in or walling out,
And to whom I was like to give offence.
Something there is that doesn't love a wall,
That wants it down!" I could say "Elves" to him,
But it's not elves exactly, and I'd rather
He said it for himself. I see him there
Bringing a stone grasped firmly by the top
In each hand, like an Old Stone savage armed.
He moves in darkness as it seems to me,
Not of woods only and the shade of trees.
He will not go behind his father's saying,
And he likes having thought of it so well
He says again, "Good fences make good neighbors."

FENCES

REBECCA McCANN

When I consider Time and Space
It fills me with a quiet mirth
To see a human fencing off
A tiny portion of the earth.

THE POET

Mary Sinton Leitch

In the darkness he sings of the dawning;
In the desert he sings of a rose,
Or of limpid and laughing water
That through green meadows flows.

He flings a Romany ballad
Out through his prison bars,
And, deaf, he sings of nightingales
Or, blind, he sings of stars.

And hopeless and old and forsaken,
At last with failing breath
A song of faith and youth and love
He sings at the gates of death.

IN TWO MONTHS NOW

George Dillon

In two months now or maybe one
The sun will be a different sun
And earth that stretches white as straw
With stony ice will crack and thaw
And run in whistling streams and curve
In still blue-shadowed pools. The nerve
Of each pink root will quiver bare
And orchards in the April air
Will show black branches breaking white.
Red roses in the green twilight
Will glimmer ghostly blue and swell
Upon their vines with such a smell
As only floats when the breeze is loud
At dusk from roses in a crowd.
I know that there will be these things,
Remembering them from other springs.
All these and more shall soon be seen,
As beautiful as they have been;
But not so beautiful as they
Seem now to be, a month away.

HOUSEHOLD GODS

J. H. MACNAIR

The baby takes to her bed at night
A one-eyed rabbit that once was white;
A watch that came from a cracker, I think;
And a lidless inkpot that never held ink.
And the secret is locked in her tiny breast
Of why she loves these and leaves the rest.

And I give a loving glance as I go
To three brass pots on a shelf in a row;
To my grandfather's grandfather's loving cup
And a bandy-legged chair I once picked up.
And I can't, for the life of me, make you see
Why just these things are a part of me!

HORIZONS

REBECCA MCCANN

"When I get rich" the children dream
With eyes on some far day.
And when they're old, with eyes turned back:
"When I was rich" they say.

STREET BEGGAR

Anderson M. Scruggs

This is the depth, the end of all despair:
That man for whom the planets toil and sing—
Inheritor of earth and sea and air—
Should come to be this starved, forsaken thing
Whose soft, obsequious words and pleading eye
Invoke the heedless masses of the street,
Hoping that in the crowds that pass him by,
Some fat-faced god may deign to let him eat.
Here is the deepest wrong, the darkest deed
That man must answer in some distant dawn:
That in this fecund earth there should be need
For such as these—the beggars that pass on
Down dim-lit streets and byways of the night,
Asking of man what should be man's by right.

A MAN'S A MAN FOR A' THAT

Robert Burns

Is there for honest poverty
  That hangs his head, an' a' that?
The coward slave—we pass him by;
  We dare be poor for a' that!
For a' that, an' a' that,
  Our toils obscure, an' a' that;
The rank is but the guinea's stamp,
  The man's the gowd for a' that.

What though on hamely fare we dine,
  Wear hodden gray, an' a' that;
Gie fools their silks, and knaves their wine,
  A man's a man for a' that;
For a' that, an' a' that,
  Their tinsel show, an' a' that;
The honest man, though e'er sae poor,
  Is king o' men for a' that.

Ye see yon birkie, ca'd a lord,
  Wha struts, an' stares, an' a' that;
Though hundreds worship at his word,
  He's but a coof for a' that;
For a' that, an' a' that,
  His ribbon, star, an' a' that;
The man o' independent mind,
  He looks and laughs at a' that.

A prince can mak a belted knight,
  A marquis, duke, an' a' that;
But an honest man's aboon his might,
  Guid faith, he mauna fa' that!
For a' that, an' a' that,
  Their dignities, an' a' that;
The pith o' sense an' pride o' worth
  Are higher rank than a' that.

Then let us pray that come it may—
  As come it will for a' that—
That sense and worth o'er a' the earth
  May bear the gree, an' a' that;
For a' that, an' a' that,
  It's coming yet for a' that,
That man to man the warld o'er
  Shall brothers be for a' that.

DISTRIBUTION

Elsie B. Purcell

I trod the mellow earth between the rows
That lay like serpents basking in the sun
And shared the hope of reaping with the one
Who dropped the grain and left it in repose
Securely hidden from marauding crows
And hungry vermin that are not outdone
But clamor for a portion as they run
And gain a livelihood with him who sows.
The summer passed. At harvest time I saw
Earth's children come to share the ample store,
I sensed the justice of God's gracious plan,
For give and live is His omniscient law;
Wild creatures took enough nor sought for more—
In frenzied lust for all, alone came man.

THE DISCOVERY

JOHN COLLINGS SQUIRE

There was an Indian, who had known no change,
Who strayed content along a sunlit beach
Gathering shells. He heard a sudden strange
Commingled noise; looked up; and gasped for speech.
For in the bay, where nothing was before,
Moved on the sea, by magic, huge canoes,
With bellying cloths on poles, and not one oar,
And fluttering colored signs and clambering crews.
And he, in fear, this naked man alone,
His fallen hands forgetting all their shells,
His lips gone pale, knelt low behind a stone,
And stared, and saw, and did not understand,
Columbus's doom-burdened caravels
Slant to the shore, and all their seamen land.

THE WHITE MAN'S ROAD

ARTHUR CHAPMAN

The white man's road is hard for us to follow;
Our feet are bruised and bleeding, but who shall heed our cries?
The white man's code—what has it been but hollow?
No ears have caught our pleading—unheard the red man dies.

The white man's creed is lost in white man's sinning;
Our faith is slowly flagging—no door shall let us in—
None sees our need, though fast our ranks are thinning—
The weary feet are lagging that wear the moccasin.

The white man's word—what has it been but broken?
Our lodge fires low are burning—without the air is cold;
And thus unheard, with sorrows deep, unspoken,
All hopeless are we turning—we who were kings of old!

THE CONGO

A Study of the Negro Race

Being a memorial to Ray Eldred, a Disciple missionary of the Congo River

VACHEL LINDSAY

I. THEIR BASIC SAVAGERY

Fat black bucks in a wine-barrel room,
Barrel-house kings, with feet unstable,
Sagged and reeled and pounded on the table, *A deep rolling bass.*
Pounded on the table,
Beat an empty barrel with the handle of a broom,
Hard as they were able,
Boom, boom, BOOM,
With a silk umbrella and the handle of a broom,
Boomlay, boomlay, boomlay, BOOM.
THEN I had religion, THEN I had a vision.
I could not turn from their revel in derision.
THEN I SAW THE CONGO, CREEPING THROUGH THE BLACK, *More deliberate. Solemnly chanted.*
CUTTING THROUGH THE FOREST WITH A GOLDEN TRACK.
Then along that riverbank
A thousand miles
Tattooed cannibals danced in files;
Then I heard the boom of the blood-lust song
And a thigh bone beating on a tin-pan gong. *A rapidly piling climax of speed and racket.*
And "BLOOD" screamed the whistles and the fifes of the warriors,

"Blood" screamed the skull-faced, lean witch doctors,
"Whirl ye the deadly voodoo rattle,
Harry the uplands,
Steal all the cattle,
Rattle-rattle, rattle-rattle,
Bing.
Boomlay, boomlay, boomlay, Boom,"
A roaring, epic, ragtime tune
From the mouth of the Congo
To the Mountains of the Moon.

With a philosophic pause.

. . . .

Listen to the creepy proclamation,
Blown through the lairs of the forest nation,
Blown past the white ants' hill of clay,
Blown past the marsh where the butterflies play:—
"Be careful what you do,
Or Mumbo Jumbo, God of the Congo,
And all of the other
Gods of the Congo,
Mumbo Jumbo will hoodoo you,
Mumbo Jumbo will hoodoo you,
Mumbo Jumbo will hoodoo you."

All the "o" sounds very golden. Heavy accents very heavy. Light accents very light. Last line whispered.

II. THEIR IRREPRESSIBLE HIGH SPIRITS

Wild crapshooters with a whoop and a call
Danced the juba in their gambling hall
And laughed fit to kill, and shook the town,
And guyed the policemen and laughed them down

Rather shrill and high.

With a boomlay, boomlay, boomlay, Boom.
THEN I SAW THE CONGO, CREEPING THROUGH THE BLACK,
CUTTING THROUGH THE FOREST WITH A GOLDEN TRACK.

Read exactly as in first section.

A negro fairyland swung into view,
A minstrel river
Where dreams come true.
The ebony palace soared on high
Through the blossoming trees to the evening sky.
The inlaid porches and casements shone
With gold and ivory and elephant bone.
And the black crowd laughed till their sides were sore
At the baboon butler in the agate door,
And the well-known tunes of the parrot band
That trilled on the bushes of that magic land.

Lay emphasis on the delicate ideas. Keep as light-footed as possible.

. . . .

The cakewalk royalty then began
To walk for a cake that was tall as a man
To the tune of "Boomlay, boomlay, Boom,"
While the witch men laughed, with a sinister air,
And sang with the scalawags prancing there:—
Walk with care, walk with care,
Or Mumbo Jumbo, God of the Congo,
And all of the other Gods of the Congo,
Mumbo Jumbo will hoodoo you.
Beware, beware, walk with care,

With a touch of negro dialect, and as rapidly as possible toward the end.

Boomlay, boomlay, boomlay, boom.
Boomlay, boomlay, boomlay, boom.
Boomlay, boomlay, boomlay, boom,
Boomlay, boomlay, boomlay,
Boom."
(Oh, rare was the revel, and well worth while
That made those glowering witch men smile.)

Slow, philosophic calm.

III. THE HOPE OF THEIR RELIGION

Heavy bass. With a liter imitation of camp meeting racket, and trance.

A good old negro in the slums of the town
Preached at a sister for her velvet gown.
Howled at a brother for his low-down ways,
His prowling, guzzling, sneak-thief days.
Beat on the Bible till he wore it out
Starting the jubilee revival shout.
And some had visions, as they stood on chairs,
And sang of Jacob, and the golden stairs,
And they all repented, a thousand strong
From their stupor and savagery and sin and
  wrong
And slammed with their hymn books till they
  shook the room
With "glory, glory, glory,"
And "Boom, boom, Boom."

Exactly as the first sectic Begin with te ror and pow end with joy.

THEN I SAW THE CONGO, CREEPING THROUGH
  THE BLACK,
CUTTING THROUGH THE JUNGLE WITH A GOLDEN
  TRACK.
And the gray sky opened like a new-rent veil
And showed the Apostles with their coats of
  mail.

In bright white steel they were seated round
And their fire-eyes watched where the Congo
wound.

. . . .

Redeemed were the forests, the beasts and the
men,
And only the vulture dared again
By the far, lone Mountains of the Moon
To cry, in the silence, the Congo tune:—
"Mumbo Jumbo will hoodoo you,
Mumbo Jumbo will hoodoo you.
Mumbo . . . Jumbo . . . will hoodoo . . .
you."

Dying down into a penetrating, terrified whisper.

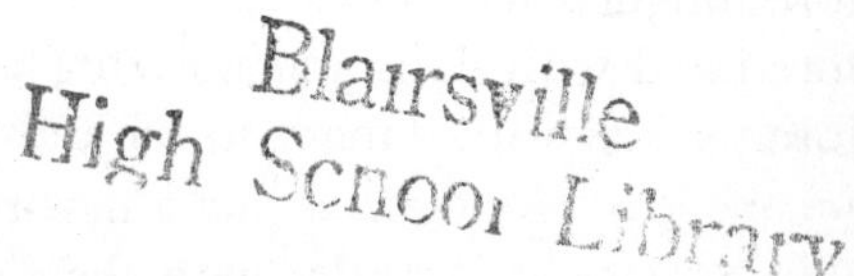

THE MAN WITH THE HOE

God made man in his own image; in the image of God He mad[e] him.—Genesis

EDWIN MARKHAM

Bowed by the weight of centuries he leans
Upon his hoe and gazes on the ground,
The emptiness of ages in his face,
And on his back the burden of the world.
Who made him dead to rapture and despair,
A thing that grieves not and that never hopes,
Stolid and stunned, a brother to the ox?
Who loosened and let down this brutal jaw?
Whose was the hand that slanted back this brow?
Whose breath blew out the light within this brain?

Is this the Thing the Lord God made and gave
To have dominion over sea and land;
To trace the stars and search the heavens for power;
To feel the passion of Eternity?
Is this the dream He dreamed who shaped the suns
And marked their ways upon the ancient deep?
Down all the caverns of hell to their last gulf
There is no shape more terrible than this—
More tongued with cries against the world's blind greed—
More filled with signs and portents for the soul—
More packed with danger to the universe.

What gulfs between him and the seraphim!
Slave of the wheel of labor, what to him
Are Plato and the swing of Pleiades?
What the long reaches of the peaks of song,
The rift of dawn, the reddening of the rose?
Through this dread shape the suffering ages look;
Time's tragedy is in that aching stoop;
Through this dread shape humanity betrayed,
Plundered, profaned and disinherited,
Cries protest to the Powers that made the world,
A protest that is also prophecy.

O masters, lords and rulers in all lands,
Is this the handiwork you give to God,
This monstrous thing distorted and soul-quenched?
How will you ever straighten up this shape;
Touch it again with immortality;
Give back the upward looking and the light;
Rebuild in it the music and the dream;
Make right the immemorial infamies,
Perfidious wrongs, immedicable woes?

O masters, lords and rulers in all lands,
How will the future reckon with this Man?
How answer his brute question in that hour
When whirlwinds of rebellion shake all shores?
How will it be with kingdoms and with kings—
With those who shaped him to the thing he is—
When this dumb terror shall rise to judge the world,
After the silence of the centuries?

THE FACTORIES

MARGARET WIDDEMER

I have shut my little sister in from life and light
  (For a rose, for a ribbon, for a wreath across my hair),
I have made her restless feet still until the night,
  Locked from sweets of summer and from wild spring ai
I who ranged the meadowlands, free from sun to sun,
  Free to sing and pull the buds and watch the far wings fl
I have bound my sister till her playing time was done—
  Oh, my little sister, was it I? Was it I?

I have robbed my sister of her day of maidenhood
  (For a robe, for a feather, for a trinket's restless spark)
Shut from love till dusk shall fall, how shall she know goo
  How shall she go scatheless through the sin-lit dark?
I who could be innocent, I who could be gay,
  I who could have love and mirth before the light went b
I have put my sister in her mating time away—
  Sister, my young sister, was it I? Was it I?

I have robbed my sister of the lips against her breast,
  (For a coin, for the weaving of *my* children's lace and lawn
Feet that pace beside the loom, hands that cannot rest—
  How can she know motherhood, whose strength is gon
I who took no heed of her, starved and labor-worn,
  I, against whose placid heart my sleepy gold-heads lie,
Round my path they cry to me, little souls unborn—
  God of life! Creator! It was I! It was I!

FACTORY WINDOWS ARE ALWAYS BROKEN

VACHEL LINDSAY

Factory windows are always broken.
Somebody's always throwing bricks,
Somebody's always heaving cinders,
Playing ugly Yahoo tricks.

Factory windows are always broken.
Other windows are let alone.
No one throws through the chapel window
The bitter, snarling, derisive stone.

Factory windows are always broken.
Something or other is going wrong.
Something is rotten—I think, in Denmark:
End of the factory-window song.

CALIBAN IN THE COAL MINES

LOUIS UNTERMEYER

God, we don't like to complain.
  We know that the mine is no lark.
But—there's the pools from the rain;
  But—there's the cold and the dark.

God, You don't know what it is—
  You, in Your well-lighted sky,
Watching the meteors whizz;
  Warm, with a sun always by.

God, if You had but the moon
  Stuck in Your cap for a lamp,
Even You'd tire of it soon,
  Down in the dark and the damp.

Nothing but blackness above,
  And nothing that moves but the cars. . . .
God, if You wish for our love,
  Fling us a handful of stars!

LINES WRITTEN IN EARLY SPRING

William Wordsworth

I heard a thousand blended notes
  While in a grove I sat reclined,
In that sweet mood when pleasant thoughts
  Bring sad thoughts to the mind.

To her fair works did Nature link
  The human soul that through me ran;
And much it grieved my heart to think
  What Man has made of Man.

Through primrose tufts, in that sweet bower,
  The periwinkle trailed its wreaths;
And 'tis my faith that every flower
  Enjoys the air it breathes.

The birds around me hopped and played;
  Their thoughts I cannot measure—
But the least motion which they made,
  It seemed a thrill of pleasure.

The budding twigs spread out their fan
  To catch the breezy air;
And I must think, do all I can,
  That there was pleasure there.

If this belief from heaven be sent,
  If such be Nature's holy plan,
Have I not reason to lament
  What Man has made of Man?

REPORT ON THE PLANET, EARTH

JAMES OPPENHEIM

To the Sky-Council on Star, Riga, Milky Way:
I have to report:
That detailed by the Council I fell on a beam of light down through interstellar space
A year and a day,
Dropping through rings of worlds, and past white flakes of suns,
And found at last, in a cranny of the crowded universe,
The Solar System,
And investigated one of its small planets, the Earth.

These are my findings:
The inhabitants thereof are not very game:
They complain and whine a great deal:
They cannot stand pain:
They object to work:
They think of nothing but themselves:
No concern for these crowded heavens around them:
Nor Earth's purpose in the skies:
Quarrelsome, they slaughter each other with ingenious death-dealers:
They bind themselves with strange chains to one another:
They fear the new: they fear the old: they fear birth: they shrink from death:

Those that have visions among them are persecuted:
They applaud anyone who makes them forget what they are and whither they are going:
They are cruel, stupid, childish, undeveloped.

I have to report:
That they even forget that they are merely movable parts of the Earth,
And everything that inheres in Earth inheres in them:
That the little ball that blusters so, spouting its seas in tempest, and sliding its hills,
Smothered in storm and lightning, and plagued with an uncertainty of flood and thirst,
Hot, cold, distempered, risky,
Is repeated in each one of them: they too full of weather and disaster:
Primitive, perilous. . . .
The which forgetting,
Produces a certain surface of calm and harmony:
Yes, for a while:
Then the explosion: then crime, breakage, battle. . . .

I have to report:
That projected by Earth, as Earth by the skies, for large purposes and splendid adventure,
They side-step, try to evade, escape their destinies:
Do their utmost to reduce life to a mechanism that works by itself:

Leaving them free—for what? Communion with Earth?
Vision of heaven? Probing of self?
Why no: free for stupefying stimulants and memory-sponging joys. . . .

I have to report:
That they are very cunning indeed:
They have builded larger than themselves:
Giant cities have sprung from their pygmy hands:
Their engines are excellent:
But to what use do they put their tools?
Tut! peacock feathers, and the well-stuffed gullet!

I have to report:
That though the Earth is rich, yet most of them are very poor:
In bitter want:
Curious, this childish snatching of things from each other!
Greed is their stupidest sin!

I have to report:
That while there is much excellence in the love between man and woman,
And the tender love toward children,
They so clutch and claw one another that love stales into indifference or irritation:
Greed! greed again!

I have to report:
Hypocrisy rampant, and hardly anyone passing for what he really is:
But advertising himself as something quite other:
Yes, anything to succeed!

I have to report:
Slights, rebuffs, insolences unnumbered,
Nothing run right: but everywhere insidious theft and pilfering:
And everyone sentimental: glossing it all over with a call to love for mother, for children, for one's country.

I have to report:
And, Powers, this is what puzzles me:
An Earth so absorbingly interesting, so electric in spite of its dullness, so joyous in spite of its pain,
That, were I not compelled to make my cosmic examinations,
I should love to live there, say, threescore ten years of their life!

THIS MOMENT YEARNING AND THOUGHTFUL

WALT WHITMAN

This moment yearning and thoughtful sitting alone,
It seems to me there are other men in other lands yearning and thoughtful,
It seems to me I can look over and behold them in Germany, Italy, France, Spain,
Or far, far away, in China, or in Russia or Japan, talking other dialects,
And it seems to me if I could know those men I should become attached to them as I do to men in my own lands,
Oh, I know we should be brethren and lovers,
I know I should be happy with them.

RECESSIONAL

RUDYARD KIPLING

God of our fathers, known of old,
  Lord of our far-flung battle line,
Beneath whose awful Hand we hold
  Dominion over palm and pine—
Lord God of Hosts, be with us yet,
Lest we forget—lest we forget!

The tumult and the shouting dies;
  The captains and the kings depart:
Still stands Thine ancient sacrifice,
  An humble and a contrite heart.
Lord God of Hosts, be with us yet,
Lest we forget—lest we forget!

Far-called, our navies melt away;
  On dune and headland sinks the fire:
Lo, all our pomp of yesterday
  Is one with Nineveh and Tyre!
Judge of the nations, spare us yet,
Lest we forget—lest we forget!

If, drunk with sight of power, we loose
  Wild tongues that have not Thee in awe,
Such boastings as the Gentiles use,
  Or lesser breeds without the Law—
Lord God of Hosts, be with us yet,
Lest we forget—lest we forget!

For heathen heart that puts her trust
  In reeking tube and iron shard,
All valiant dust that builds on dust,
  And guarding, calls not Thee to guard,
For frantic boast and foolish word—
Thy mercy on Thy people, Lord!

LOOKING AT LIFE

In that instant I could feel no doubt of man's oneness with the universe. The conviction came that that rhythm was too orderly, too harmonious, too perfect to be a product of blind chance—that, therefore, there must be purpose in the whole and that man was part of that whole and not an accidental offshoot.

—RICHARD E. BYRD

THE GREAT LOVER

RUPERT BROOKE

I have been so great a lover: filled my days
So proudly with the splendor of love's praise,
The pain, the calm, and the astonishment,
Desire illimitable, and still content,
And all dear names men use, to cheat despair,
For the perplexed and viewless streams that bear
Our hearts at random down the dark of life.
Now, ere the unthinking silence on that strife
Steals down, I would cheat drowsy death so far,
My night shall be remembered for a star
That outshone all the suns of all men's days.
Shall I not crown them with immortal praise
Whom I have loved, who have given me, dared with me
High secrets, and in darkness knelt to see
The inenarrable godhead of delight?
Love is a flame—we have beaconed the world's night.
A city:—and we have built it, these and I.
An emperor:—we have taught the world to die.
So, for their sakes I loved, ere I go hence,
And the high cause of love's magnificence,
And to keep loyalties young, I'll write those names
Golden for ever, eagles, crying flames,
And set them as a banner, that men may know,
To dare the generations, burn and blow
Out on the wind of time, shining and streaming. . . .

These I have loved:
White plates and cups, clean-gleaming,
Ringed with blue lines; and feathery, faëry dust;
Wet roofs, beneath the lamplight; the strong crust
Of friendly bread; and many-tasting food;
Rainbows; and the blue bitter smoke of wood;
And radiant raindrops couching in cool flowers;
And flowers themselves, that sway through sunny hours,
Dreaming of moths that drink them under the moon;
Then, the cool kindliness of sheets, that soon
Smooth away trouble; and the rough male kiss
Of blankets; grainy wood; live hair that is
Shining and free; blue-massing clouds; the keen
Unpassioned beauty of a great machine;
The benison of hot water; furs to touch;
The good smell of old clothes; and other such—
The comfortable smell of friendly fingers,
Hair's fragrance, and the musty reek that lingers
About dead leaves and last year's ferns. . . .
Dear names,
And thousand others throng to me! Royal flames;
Sweet water's dimpling laugh from tap or spring;
Holes in the ground; and voices that do sing;
Voices in laughter, too; and body's pain,
Soon turned to peace; and the deep-panting train;
Firm sands; the little dulling edge of foam
That browns and dwindles as the wave goes home;
And washen stones, gay for an hour; the cold
Graveness of iron; moist black earthen mold;
Sleep; and high places; footprints in the dew;
And oaks; and brown horse chestnuts, glossy-new;

And new-peeled sticks; and shining pools on grass;—
All these have been my loves. And these shall pass,
Whatever passes not, in the great hour,
Nor all my passion, all my prayers, have power
To hold them with me through the gate of Death.
They'll play deserter, turn with the traitor breath,
Break the high bond we made, and sell love's trust
And sacramented covenant to the dust.
—Oh, never a doubt but, somewhere, I shall wake,
And give what's left of love again, and make
New friends, now strangers. . . .
But the best I've known,
Stays here, and changes, breaks, grows old, is blown
About the winds of the world, and fades from brains
Of living men, and dies.
Nothing remains.

O dear my loves, O faithless, once again
This one last gift I give: that after men
Shall know, and later lovers, far-removed,
Praise you, "All these were lovely"; say, "He loved."

¿QUIÉN SABE?

RUTH COMFORT MITCHELL

In Córdoba within the drowsing Plaza,
Beyond the sleepy, sun-drenched market place,
Vacant and bare, denuded of its statue,
There stands a scarred and mournful marble base.
The hours are tinkled from the old Cathedral,
Gray-grim against the brilliance of the sky,
And swooping downward in their clumsy circles
The ugly, dun-winged buzzards slowly fly.

They light and struggle fiercely for a foothold;
Their quarrels, shrill, discordant, pierce the air;
The sluggish stream of life within the city
Flows ever onward, calmly unaware.
You ask in vain whose statue used to stand there
A sun-drunk *peon*, dozing out his day,
A grave-eyed priest, a woman with *tortillas*—
The same regretful, velvet "*Yo no sé!*"

There was a scene here once to fit the setting,
If we could pierce the shrouding of the years;
There was a day for reverent unveiling . . .
And swelling hearts, and brimming eyes, and cheers . . .
What patriot, red-blooded, gave it reason?
What martyr marked it with his placid smile?
Who set the pulses leaping for a season,
And held the limelight for a little while?

Who dares believe his laurel is immortal?
Who thinks the marble proof against the years?—
Or dreams the memory of his deed will linger
When stilled the hearts, and dried away the tears?

A fluttered flag, a sudden blare of trumpets,
A path of flowers, a little burst of song . . .
Then withering and fading and the silence . . .
Time dims all luster, and the years are long.

And now, within the hushed and drowsing Plaza,
Beyond the sleepy, sun-drenched market place,
Stained with the years and weathered with the seasons,
There stands a scarred and mournful marble base.
Unheeding round its story flows forever
The lazy current of the dozing town,
And on it, hurtling in their clumsy circles,
The ugly, dun-winged buzzards settle down.

THE DUST

LIZETTE WOODWORTH REESE

The dust blows up and down
Within the lonely town;
Vague, hurrying, dumb, aloof,
On sill and bough and roof.

What cloudy shapes do fleet
Along the parchèd street;
Clerks, bishops, kings go by—
Tomorrow so shall I!

A LITTLE SONG OF LIFE

LIZETTE WOODWORTH REESE

Glad that I live am I;
That the sky is blue;
Glad for the country lanes,
And the fall of dew.

After the sun the rain;
After the rain the sun;
This is the way of life,
Till work be done.

All that we need to do,
Be we low or high,
Is to see that we grow
Nearer the sky.

LEAF AND SOUL

JOHN BANISTER TABB

LEAF

Let go the Limb?
My life in him
  Alone is found.
Come night, come day,
'Tis here I stay
  Above the sapless ground.

SOUL

Let go the warm
Lip-kindled form
  And upward fly?
Come joy, come pain,
I here remain,
  Despite the yearning sky.

A sudden frost—and lo!
Both Leaf and Soul let go.

TO AN ATHLETE DYING YOUNG

A. E. Housman

The time you won your town the race
We chaired you through the market place;
Man and boy stood cheering by,
And home we brought you shoulder-high.

Today, the road all runners come,
Shoulder-high we bring you home,
And set you at your threshold down,
Townsman of a stiller town.

Smart lad, to slip betimes away
From fields where glory does not stay
And early though the laurel grows
It withers quicker than the rose.

Eyes the shady night has shut
Cannot see the record cut,
And silence sounds no worse than cheers
After earth has stopped the ears:

Now you will not swell the rout
Of lads that wore their honors out,
Runners whom renown outran
And the name died before the man.

So set, before its echoes fade,
The fleet foot on the sill of shade,
And hold to the low lintel up
The still-defended challenge-cup.

And round that early-laureled head
Will flock to gaze the strengthless dead,
And find unwithered on its curls
The garland briefer than a girl's.

UPHILL

Christina Rossetti

Does the road wind uphill all the way?
  Yes, to the very end.
Will the day's journey take the whole long day?
  From morn to night, my friend.

But is there for the night a resting place?
  A roof for when the slow dark hours begin.
May not the darkness hide it from my face?
  You cannot miss that inn.

Shall I meet other wayfarers at night?
  Those who have gone before.
Then must I knock, or call when just in sight?
  They will not keep you standing at that door.

Shall I find comfort, travel-sore and weak?
  Of labor you shall find the sum.
Will there be beds for me and all who seek?
  Yea, beds for all who come.

NATURE

HENRY WADSWORTH LONGFELLOW

As a fond mother, when the day is o'er,
Leads by the hand her little child to bed,
Half willing, half reluctant to be led,
And leave his broken playthings on the floor,
Still gazing at them through the open door,
Nor wholly reassured and comforted
By promises of others in their stead,
Which, though more splendid, may not please him more
So Nature deals with us, and takes away
Our playthings one by one, and by the hand
Leads us to rest so gently, that we go
Scarce knowing if we wished to go or stay,
Being too full of sleep to understand
How far the unknown transcends the what we know.

TO MY SON

ANONYMOUS

I will not say to you, "This is the Way; walk in it."
For I do not know your way or where the Spirit may call you;
It may be to paths I have never trod or ships on the sea leading to unimagined lands afar,
Or haply, to a star!
Or yet again
Through dark and perilous places racked with pain and full of fear
Your road may lead you far from me or near—
I cannot guess or guide, but only stand aside.
Just this I'll say:
I know for very truth there is a way for each to walk, a right for each to choose, a truth to use.
And though you wander far, your soul will know that true path when you find it.
Therefore, go!
I will fear nothing for you day or night!
I will not grieve at all because your light is called by some new name;
Truth is the same!
It matters nothing to call it star or sun—
All light is one.

LET ME LIVE OUT MY YEARS

John G. Neihardt

Let me live out my years in heat of blood!
  Let me die drunken with the dreamer's wine!
Let me not see this soul-house built of mud
  Go toppling to the dust—a vacant shrine!

Let me go quickly like a candle light
  Snuffed out just at the heyday of its glow!
Give me high noon—and let it then be night!
  Thus would I go.

And grant me, when I face the grisly Thing,
  One haughty cry to pierce the gray Perhaps!
O let me be a tune-swept fiddlestring
  That feels the Master Melody—*and snaps!*

INVICTUS

WILLIAM ERNEST HENLEY

Out of the night that covers me,
  Black as the Pit from pole to pole,
I thank whatever gods may be
  For my unconquerable soul.

In the fell clutch of circumstance
  I have not winced nor cried aloud.
Under the bludgeonings of chance
  My head is bloody, but unbowed.

Beyond this place of wrath and tears
  Looms but the Horror of the shade,
And yet the menace of the years
  Finds, and shall find, me unafraid.

It matters not how strait the gate,
  How charged with punishments the scroll,
I am the master of my fate:
  I am the captain of my soul.

WITH RUE MY HEART IS LADEN

A. E. Housman

With rue my heart is laden
  For golden friends I had,
For many a rose-lipped maiden
  And many a lightfoot lad.

By brooks too broad for leaping
  The lightfoot boys are laid;
The rose-lipped girls are sleeping
  In fields where roses fade.

AT THE CROSSROADS

Richard Hovey

You to the left and I to the right,
  For the ways of men must sever—
And it well may be for a day and a night,
  And it well may be forever.
But whether we meet or whether we part
  (For our ways are past our knowing),
A pledge from the heart to its fellow heart
  On the ways we all are going!
    Here's luck!
  For we know not where we are going.

Whether we win or whether we lose
   With the hands that life is dealing,
It is not we nor the ways we choose
   But the fall of the cards that's sealing.
There's a fate in love and a fate in fight,
   And the best of us all go under—
And whether we're wrong or whether we're right,
   We win, sometimes, to our wonder.
      Here's luck—
   That we may not yet go under!

With a steady swing and an open brow
   We have tramped the ways together,
But we're clasping hands at the crossroads now
   In the Fiend's own night for weather;
And whether we bleed or whether we smile
   In the leagues that lie before us,
The ways of life are many a mile
   And the dark of fate is o'er us.
      Here's luck!
   And a cheer for the dark before us!

You to the left and I to the right,
   For the ways of men must sever,
And it well may be for a day and a night
   And it well may be forever!
But whether we live or whether we die
   (For the end is past our knowing),
Here's two frank hearts and the open sky,
   Be a fair or an ill wind blowing!
      Here's luck!
   In the teeth of all winds blowing.

MY WAGE

JESSIE B. RITTENHOUSE

I bargained with Life for a penny,
And Life would pay no more,
However I begged at evening
When I counted my scanty store;

For Life is a just employer,
He gives you what you ask,
But once you have set the wages,
Why, you must bear the task.

I worked for a menial's hire,
Only to learn, dismayed,
That any wage I had asked of Life,
Life would have paid.

ON HIS BLINDNESS

John Milton

When I consider how my light is spent,
Ere half my days, in this dark world and wide,
And that one talent which is death to hide
Lodged with me useless, though my soul more bent
To serve therewith my Maker, and present
My true account, lest He returning chide,
"Doth God exact day labor, light denied?"
I fondly ask. But Patience, to prevent
That murmur, soon replies: "God doth not need
Either man's work, or His own gifts. Who best
Bear His mild yoke, they serve Him best. His state
Is kingly; thousands at His bidding speed
And post o'er land and ocean without rest.
They also serve who only stand and wait."

TO A MOUSE

On turning her up in her nest with the plow, November, 1785

Robert Burns

Wee, sleekit, cow'rin', tim'rous beastie,
Oh, what a panic's in thy breastie!
Thou need na start awa sae hasty
  Wi' bickerin' brattle!
I wad be laith to rin an' chase thee
  Wi' murderin' pattle!

I'm truly sorry man's dominion
Has broken nature's social union
An' justifies that ill opinion
  Which makes thee startle
At me, thy poor earthborn companion
  An' fellow mortal!

I doubt na, whyles, but thou may thieve;
What then? poor beastie, thou maun live!
A daimen icker in a thrave
  'S a sma' request;
I'll get a blessin' wi' the lave,
  An' never miss't!

Thy wee bit housie, too, in ruin!
Its silly wa's the win's are strewin'.
An' naething now to big a new ane
  O' foggage green;
An' bleak December's win's ensuin',
  Baith snell an' keen!

Thou saw the fields laid bare an' waste,
An' weary winter comin' fast,
An' cozy here beneath the blast
Thou thought to dwell—
Till crash! the cruel colter passed
Out through thy cell.

That wee bit heap o' leaves an' stibble
Has cost thee mony a weary nibble!
Now thou's turned out, for a' thy trouble,
But house or hald,
To thole the winter's sleety dribble
An' cranreuch cauld!

But, Mousie, thou art no thy lane
In proving foresight may be vain;
The best-laid schemes o' mice an' men
Gang aft agley
An' lea'e us naught but grief an' pain
For promised joy.

Still, thou art blest, compared wi' me!
The present only toucheth thee;
But och! I backward cast my e'e
On prospects drear!
An' forward, though I canna see,
I guess an' fear.

COUNSEL TO GIRLS

ROBERT HERRICK

Gather ye rosebuds while ye may;
  Old Time is still a-flying;
And this same flower that smiles today
  Tomorrow will be dying.

The glorious Lamp of Heaven, the Sun,
  The higher he's a-getting
The sooner will his race be run,
  And nearer he's to setting.

That age is best which is the first,
  When youth and blood are warmer;
But being spent, the worse, and worst
  Times still succeed the former.

Then be not coy, but use your time
  And, while ye may, go marry;
For having lost but once your prime,
  You may forever tarry.

YOUNG AND OLD

CHARLES KINGSLEY

When all the world is young, lad,
  And all the trees are green;
And every goose a swan, lad,
  And every lass a queen;
Then hey for boot and horse, lad,
  And round the world away;
Young blood must have its course, lad,
  And every dog his day.

When all the world is old, lad,
  And all the trees are brown;
And all the sport is stale, lad,
  And all the wheels run down;
Creep home, and take your place there,
  The spent and maimed among:
God grant you find one face there,
  You loved when all was young.

ODE ON A GRECIAN URN

John Keats

Thou still unravished bride of quietness,
  Thou foster child of Silence and slow Time,
Sylvan historian who canst thus express
  A flowery tale more sweetly than our rhyme,
What leaf-ringed legend haunts about thy shape
  Of deities or mortals, or of both,
    In Tempe or the dales of Arcady?
What men or gods are these? What maidens loath?
  What mad pursuit? What struggle to escape?
    What pipes and timbrels? What wild ecstasy?

Heard melodies are sweet, but those unheard
  Are sweeter; therefore, ye soft pipes, play on,
Not to the sensual ear, but, more endeared,
  Pipe to the spirit ditties of no tone.
Fair youth beneath the trees, thou canst not leave
  Thy song, nor ever can those trees be bare.
    Bold lover, never, never canst thou kiss,
Though winning near the goal—yet, do not grieve.
  She cannot fade; though thou hast not thy bliss,
    Forever wilt thou love, and she be fair!

Ah, happy, happy boughs! that cannot shed
  Your leaves, nor ever bid the spring adieu;
And, happy melodist, unwearièd,
  Forever piping songs forever new;
More happy love! more happy, happy love!
  Forever warm and still to be enjoyed,
    Forever panting and forever young,

All breathing human passion far above
  That leaves a heart high-sorrowful and cloyed,
    A burning forehead, and a parching tongue.

Who are these coming to the sacrifice?
  To what green altar, O mysterious priest,
Lead'st thou that heifer lowing at the skies,
  And all her silken flanks with garlands dressed?
What little town by river or sea shore,
  Or mountain-built with peaceful citadel,
    Is emptied of this folk this pious morn?
And, little town, thy streets forevermore
  Will silent be, and not a soul to tell
    Why thou art desolate can e'er return.

O Attic shape! Fair attitude! with brede
  Of marble men and maidens overwrought,
With forest branches and the trodden weed,
  Thou, silent form, dost tease us out of thought
As doth eternity. Cold Pastoral!
  When old age shall this generation waste,
    Thou shalt remain, in midst of other woe
Than ours, a friend to man, to whom thou say'st,
  "Beauty is truth, truth beauty"—that is all
    Ye know on earth, and all ye need to know.

THE GARGOYLE IN THE SNOW

KATHLEEN MILLAY

The gargoyle looked at the snowing town,
Bending lower—bending low—
His old stone elbows reaching high
To touch the early snow.
The gargoyle looked at the sleeping town,
Bending lower—bending down—
And he said: There's nothing new for the world to know.

Four hundred years I've watched the town,
Leaning farther—reaching down—
And there's never another way for a child to grow.
Four hundred years, four hundred years,
Of love and laughter, blood and tears,
Of feast and famine, weal and woe—
And there's never another way for the Seine to flow.

And high and lonely, and cold and lone,
The gargoyle wept a tear of stone—
Four hundred weary years I've leaned
For priest and penitent and fiend,
And there's no new way for man to sin
And no new way to atone.

Spring and summer, winter, fall,
The people cry and the swallows call,
And I am old beneath the empty snow—

Bending lower—bending—bending—low—

RECIPE FOR A HAPPY LIFE

MARGARET OF NAVARRE

Three ounces are necessary, first of Patience,
Then, of Repose & Peace; of Conscience,
A pound entire is needful;
Of Pastimes of all sorts, too,
Should be gathered as much as the hand can hold;
Of Pleasant Memory & of Hope, three good drachms
There must be at least. But they should moistened be
With a liquor made from True Pleasures which rejoice the
heart.
Then of Love's Magic Drops, a few—
But use them sparingly, for they may bring a flame
Which naught but tears can drown.
Grind the whole and mix therewith of Merriment, an ounce
To even. Yet all this may not bring happiness
Except in your Orisons you lift your voice
To Him who holds the gift of health.

THE FLESH IS WEAK

STANTON A. COBLENTZ

The flesh is weak, we say—so weak and frail
A pin may slay it, or a germ prevail.
And yet this pulpy, salt-and-water thing
Outlives great engines sheathed in iron mail.

MIRACLES

WALT WHITMAN

Why, who makes much of a miracle?
As to me I know nothing else but miracles,
Whether I walk the streets of Manhattan,
Or dart my sight over the roofs of houses toward the sky,
Or wade with naked feet along the beach just in the edge
of the water,
Or stand under trees in the woods,
Or talk by day with anyone I love,
Or sit at table at dinner with the rest,
Or look at strangers opposite me riding in the car,
Or watch honeybees busy around the hive of a summer fore-
noon,
Or animals feeding in the fields,
Or birds, or the wonderfulness of insects in the air,
Or the wonderfulness of the sundown, or of stars shining so
quiet and bright,
Or the exquisite delicate thin curve of the new moon in
spring;
These with the rest, one and all, are to me miracles,
The whole referring, yet each distinct and in its place.
To me every hour of the light and dark is a miracle,
Every cubic inch of space is a miracle,
Every square yard of the surface of the earth is spread with
the same,
Every foot of the interior swarms with the same.

To me the sea is a continual miracle,
The fishes that swim—the rocks—the motion of the waves
—the ships with men in them,
What stranger miracles are there?

LAUGHTER AND DEATH

WILFRID SCAWEN BLUNT

There is no laughter in the natural world
Of beast or fish or bird, though no sad doubt
Of their futurity to them unfurled
Has dared to check the mirth-compelling shout.
The lion roars his solemn thunder out
To the sleeping woods. The eagle screams her cry.
Even the lark must strain a serious throat
To hurl his blest defiance at the sky.
Fear, anger, jealousy have found a voice.
Love's pain or rapture the brute bosoms swell.
Nature has symbols for her nobler joys,
Her nobler sorrows. Who has dared foretell
That only man, by some sad mockery,
Should learn to laugh who learns that he must die?

THE PARABOLA

HOOPER REYNOLDS GOODWIN

This curve I'm plotting? A parabola.
This point is called the focus; it's the point—
Oh, no, not an ellipse. Ellipses have two foci:
Here, I'll show you one I've drawn.
You see the difference. These two lines of the parabola,
They stretch out wide and wider,
"World without end," as preachers say.
(I don't know what they mean; perhaps *they* don't;)
But you see how it goes.

There was a man—Sir Isaac Newton, I believe it was—
Who had the notion a parabola was an ellipse,
Its other focus at infinity.
You may not understand just what he meant;
You have to sort of take the thing on faith.
The keenest scholar can't quite picture it, you know.

I've often thought,
It might be called a symbol of man's life:
A curve of ever-widening sweep.
And here in this world
Is the focus we may call, say, temporal interests,
Food and drink and clothes . . .
But yet it cannot be that this is all;
For out beyond the reach of sight must be
Another point, a heavenly focus, see?
'Round which the sweeping curves of human life
Complete the ellipse.
Fantastic? Well, perhaps,
But yet the more I think of it . . .

And here—
Another thing I've often thought about:
Suppose we draw here two parabolas
With axes parallel, and let the arms cross—
"Intersect" the word is—at this point.
Now if there be a focus
Somewhere out beyond the bounds of space,
And these are two ellipses,
As Sir Isaac thought they were,
Why, don't you see, they'll intersect again
Somewhere out there.
Just as two lives that once have crossed,
Then gone their separate ways,
And one has disappeared long since into the void of death
May——but who knows? It's just a thought. . . .

Well, come again; I don't get callers often.
They don't see much in old folks nowadays,
And when a man's not only old, but got his head
Stuck always in a book of "Analyt"!

Young people think I'm queer; they can't see why
A man that doesn't have to study graphs
Should plague his head; don't understand that such
Dry, dull things as a parabolic curve
May bring up mem'ries of a face that's gone.

FAITH

HORTENSE FLEXNER

If on this night of still, white cold,
  I can remember May,
New green of tree and underbrush,
A hillside orchard's mounting flush,
The scent of earth and noon's blue hush,
  A robin's jaunty way;

If on this night of bitter frost,
  I know such things can be,
That lovely May is true—ah, well,
I shall believe the tales men tell,
Wonders of bliss and asphodel,
  And immortality.

A PARTING GUEST

JAMES WHITCOMB RILEY

What delightful hosts are they—
  Life and Love!
Lingeringly I turn away,
  This late hour, yet glad enough
They have not withheld from me
  Their high hospitality.
So, with face lit with delight
  And all gratitude, I stay
  Yet to press their hands and say,
"Thanks.—So fine a time! Good night."

THINGS THAT COUNT

Man doth not live by bread only.

—DEUTERONOMY 8:3

THE HAPPIEST HEART

John Vance Cheney

Who drives the horses of the sun
  Shall lord it but a day;
Better the lowly deed were done,
  And kept the humble way.

The rust shall find the sword of fame,
  The dust will hide the crown;
Ay, none shall nail so high his name
  Time will not tear it down.

The happiest heart that ever beat
  Was in some quiet breast
That found the common daylight sweet,
  And left to Heaven the rest.

DREAM THE GREAT DREAM

FLORENCE EARLE COATES

Dream the Great Dream, though you should dream—you, only,
And friendless follow in the lofty quest.
Though the dream lead you to a desert lonely,
Or drive you, like the tempest, without rest,
Yet, toiling upward to the highest altar,
There lay before the gods your gift supreme,
A human heart whose courage did not falter
Though distant as Arcturus shone the Gleam.

The Gleam?—Ah, question not if others see it,
Who nor the yearning nor the passion share;
Grieve not if children of the earth decree it—
The earth, itself—their goddess—only fair!
The soul has need of prophet and redeemer:
Her outstretched wings against her prisoning bars,
She waits for truth—and truth is with the dreamer—
Persistent as the myriad light of stars!

VITAÏ LAMPADA

HENRY NEWBOLT

There's a breathless hush in the Close to-night—
  Ten to make and the match to win—
A bumping pitch and a blinding light,
  An hour to play and the last man in.
And it's not for the sake of a ribboned coat,
  Or the selfish hope of a season's fame,
But his Captain's hand on his shoulder smote—
  "Play up! play up! and play the game!"

The sand of the desert is sodden red,—
  Red with the wreck of a square that broke;—
The Gatling's jammed and the Colonel dead,
  And the regiment blind with dust and smoke.
The river of death has brimmed his banks,
  And England's far, and Honour, a name,
But the voice of a schoolboy rallies the ranks:
  "Play up! play up! and play the game!"

This is the word that year by year,
  While in her place the School is set,
Every one of her sons must hear,
  And none that hears it dare forget.
This they all with a joyful mind
  Bear through life like a torch in flame,
And falling fling to the host behind—
  "Play up! play up! and play the game!"

IF

Rudyard Kipling

If you can keep your head when all about you
Are losing theirs and blaming it on you,
If you can trust yourself when all men doubt you,
But make allowance for their doubting too;
If you can wait and not be tired by waiting,
Or being lied about, don't deal in lies,
Or being hated don't give way to hating,
And yet don't look too good, nor talk too wise:

If you can dream—and not make dreams your master;
If you can think—and not make thoughts your aim;
If you can meet with Triumph and Disaster
And treat those two impostors just the same;
If you can bear to hear the truth you've spoken
Twisted by knaves to make a trap for fools,
Or watch the things you gave your life to, broken,
And stoop and build 'em up with worn-out tools:

If you can make one heap of all your winnings
And risk it on one turn of pitch-and-toss,
And lose, and start again at your beginnings
And never breathe a word about your loss;
If you can force your heart and nerve and sinew
To serve your turn long after they are gone,
And so hold on when there is nothing in you
Except the will which says to them: "Hold on!"

If you can talk with crowds and keep your virtue,
  Or walk with kings—nor lose the common touch,
If neither foes nor loving friends can hurt you,
  If all men count with you, but none too much;
If you can fill the unforgiving minute
  With sixty seconds' worth of distance run,
Yours is the earth and everything that's in it,
  And—which is more—you'll be a man, my son!

THE WAYS

JOHN OXENHAM

To every man there openeth
A Way, and Ways, and a Way.
And the High Soul climbs the High Way,
And the Low Soul gropes the Low,
And in between, on the misty flats,
The rest drift to and fro.
But to every man there openeth
A High Way, and a Low.
And every man decideth
The Way his soul shall go.

A DREAMER

ARTHUR GUITERMAN

Here lies a little boy who made believe;
  Who found in sea and city, hill and star,
What wise men said were not; who loved to weave
  Dream warp and woof more fair than things that are.
He made believe that heavy toil and stress
  Were only play, and sang the while he wrought;
He made believe that wealth and fame are less
  Than faith and truth—that love cannot be bought;
That honor lives; that far beyond the goal
  That lures our eyes, to nobler ports we steer;
That grief was meant to forge the living soul,
  And death itself is not for men to fear.
At last he made believe his play was played;
  A kindly Hand the darkening curtain drew.
So well he made believe he nearly made
  The world believe his make-believes were true.

WANTED

J. G. Holland

God give us men! A time like this demands
Strong minds, great hearts, true faith, and ready hands;
Men whom the lust ot office does not kill;
Men whom the spoils of office cannot buy;
Men who possess opinions and a will;
Men who have honor—men who will not lie;
Men who can stand before a demagogue,
And damn his treacherous flatteries without winking!
Tall men, sun-crowned, who live above the fog
In public duty, and in private thinking:
For while the rabble, with their thumb-worn creeds,
Their large professions and their little deeds,
Mingle in selfish strife, lo! Freedom weeps,
Wrong rules the land, and waiting Justice sleeps!

WINTER BREATH

Edward Weismiller

A man will need
before his death
a little anger
in his breath,

a little fire
through his day,
lest what he sing
and what he say

be wholly like,
and made to bear
the selfsame color
in the air,

and even love
be somehow thinned
to frosty silence
on the wind.

FRICTION

Esther Pinch

The water in the creek glides by
As quiet as a snake,
A rocky bed is better,
With the song that pebbles make.
A little argument is good,
And better than a dead
And stupid acquiescence,
With everything that's said.

NO WORDS ARE LOST

Margaret Widdemer

No words are lost;
Bright words are shields, high-tossed
Against the weariness of this poor world,
Strong words are spears, high-hurled
Against the wall of life's most feared defeat—

Oh still, my words, be fleet,
Be gay, be gold and silver, white and red,
Be trumpets and be songs till I am dead!

THE THINKER

BERTON BRALEY

Back of the beating hammer
By which the steel is wrought,
Back of the workshop's clamor
The seeker may find the thought,
The thought that is ever master
Of iron and steam and steel,
That rises above disaster
And tramples it under heel!

The drudge may fret and tinker
Or labor with dusty blows,
But back of him stands the thinker,
The clear-eyed man who knows;
For into each plow or saber,
Each piece and part and whole,
Must go the brains of labor,
Which gives the work a soul!

Back of the motors humming,
Back of the belts that sing,
Back of the hammers drumming,
Back of the cranes that swing,
There is the eye which scans them
Watching through stress and strain,
There is the mind which plans them—
Back of the brawn, the brain!

Might of the roaring boiler,
  Force of the engine's thrust,
Strength of the sweating toiler,
  Greatly in these we trust.
But back of them stands the schemer,
  The thinker who drives things through;
Back of the job—the dreamer
  Who's making the dream come true!

WORK

HENRY VAN DYKE

Let me but do my work from day to day,
In field or forest, at the desk or loom,
In roaring market place or tranquil room;
Let me but find it in my heart to say,
When vagrant wishes beckon me astray,
"This is my work; my blessing, not my doom;
Of all who live, I am the one by whom
This work can best be done in the right way."
Then shall I see it not too great, nor small,
To suit my spirit and to prove my powers;
Then shall I cheerful greet the laboring hours,
And cheerful turn, when the long shadows fall
At eventide, to play and love and rest,
Because I know for me my work is best.

PRAYER

Louis Untermeyer

God, though this life is but a wraith,
  Although we know not what we use,
Although we grope with little faith,
  Give me the heart to fight—and lose.

Ever insurgent let me be,
  Make me more daring than devout;
From sleek contentment keep me free,
  And fill me with a buoyant doubt.

Open my eyes to visions girt
  With beauty, and with wonder lit—
But let me always see the dirt,
  And all that spawn and die in it.

Open my ears to music; let
  Me thrill with spring's first flutes and drums—
But never let me dare forget
  The bitter ballads of the slums.

From compromise and things half-done,
  Keep me, with stern and stubborn pride;
And when, at last, the fight is won,
  God, keep me still unsatisfied.

CAT'S EYE

PAUL ENGLE

If suddenly blackness crawled
Over the world and the sun hurtled down
The vast and verge of space until it glowed
No bigger than a cat's eye in the night,
And wind beat the bruised face of the earth with awful
Tornado-clubbing fists, and all the waters
Rose in a leaping body to the heavens
Tidally challenging the moon, and then
With foaming, gibbering mouth went howling over
The shuddering plains and ocean bottoms:
If stars
Splattered and dashed the sky, and the moon wallowed
Dark without the sun, and I were the last
Man moving through the streets of towns the tiny
Pale hands of men had fashioned, and out of the shouting
Air and split space and trembling earth a voice
Asked softly what one thing I wished to see
Before the universe grew tense and cracked
To the core, and burst beyond the farthest gaunt
Galaxies of heaven, I would plead
That through the shadow there would loom the friendly
White magnificence of a human face.

PHILOSOPHER'S GARDEN

JOHN OXENHAM

"*See this my garden,*
Large and fair!"
—Thus, to his friend,
The Philosopher.

"*'Tis not too long,*"
His friend replied,
With truth exact,
"*Nor yet too wide.*
But well compact,
If somewhat cramped
On every side."

Quick the reply—
"*But see how high!—*
It reaches up
To God's blue sky!"

Not by their size
Measure we men
Or things.
Wisdom, with eyes
Washed in the fire,
Seeketh the things
That are higher—
Things that have wings,
Thoughts that aspire.

SILENCE

EDGAR LEE MASTERS

I have known the silence of the stars and of the sea,
And the silence of the city when it pauses,
And the silence of a man and a maid,
And the silence for which music alone finds the word,
And the silence of the woods before the winds of spring
begin,
And the silence of the sick
When their eyes roam about the room.
And I ask: For the depths
Of what use is language?
A beast of the fields moans a few times
When death takes its young:
And we are voiceless in the presence of realities—
We cannot speak.

A curious boy asks an old soldier
Sitting in front of the grocery store,
"How did you lose your leg?"
And the old soldier is struck with silence,
Or his mind flies away,
Because he cannot concentrate it on Gettysburg.
It comes back jocosely
And he says, "A bear bit it off."
And the boy wonders, while the old soldier
Dumbly, feebly, lives over
The flashes of guns, the thunder of cannon,
The shrieks of the slain,
And himself lying on the ground,

And the hospital surgeons, the knives,
And the long days in bed.
But if he could describe it all
He would be an artist.
But if he were an artist there would be deeper wounds
Which he could not describe.

There is the silence of a great hatred,
And the silence of a great love,
And the silence of a deep peace of mind,
And the silence of an embittered friendship.
There is the silence of a spiritual crisis,
Through which your soul, exquisitely tortured,
Comes with visions not to be uttered
Into a realm of higher life.
And the silence of the gods who understand each other
without speech.
There is the silence of defeat.
There is the silence of those unjustly punished;
And the silence of the dying whose hand
Suddenly grips yours.
There is the silence between father and son,
When the father cannot explain his life,
Even though he be misunderstood for it.

There is the silence that comes between husband and
wife.
There is the silence of those who have failed;
And the vast silence that covers
Broken nations and vanquished leaders.
There is the silence of Lincoln,
Thinking of the poverty of his youth.

And the silence of Napoleon
After Waterloo.
And the silence of Jeanne d'Arc
Saying amid the flames, "Blessed Jesus"—
Revealing in two words all sorrow, all hope.
And there is the silence of age,
Too full of wisdom for the tongue to utter it
In words intelligible to those who have not lived
The great range of life.

And there is the silence of the dead.
If we who are in life cannot speak
Of profound experiences,
Why do you marvel that the dead
Do not tell you of death?
Their silence shall be interpreted
As we approach them.

DERRICKS AND RAINBOWS

JOSEPH AUSLANDER

Horizons cannot nourish me,
  Nor dullness in a deacon's hat;
No mathematical certainty
  Ever clothed my bones with fat.

I'd rather lick the empty cup
  That John Keats poured his porridge in
Than wear a cutaway and sup
  With sober folk on terrapin.

I know a derrick excavates
  A culvert, tears a hill in two:
It is as real as addled pates;
  It does the work that derricks do.

It lifts a mountain by the hair;
  It even cracks a mountain's spine;
And yet I know a ghost of air,
  Than gossamer less firm, more fine,

Less actual than light or cloud,
  Child of the drenched and dripping sky,
The hostage given man by God
  That man might see him better by;

A thing as friendly and remote,
  That sets a bridge between them both,
That shakes a man, that grips his throat,
  That binds God by the rainbow oath.

The derrick splits earth wide apart;
  The derrick bites a mountain through;
The rainbow raises up the heart,
  Which derricks want the strength to do.

SIGHT

WILFRID WILSON GIBSON

By the lamplit stall I loitered, feasting my eyes
On colors ripe and rich for the heart's desire—
Tomatoes redder than Krakatoa's fire,
Oranges like old sunsets over Tyre,
And apples golden-green as the glades of Paradise.

And as I lingered lost in divine delight,
My heart thanked God for the goodly gift of sight
And all youth's lively senses keen and quick . . .
When suddenly behind me in the night
I heard the tapping of a blind man's stick.

A PRAYER

THOMAS HARRY BASIL WEBB

Give me a good digestion, Lord,
And also something to digest;
But when or how that something comes
I leave to Thee, Who knowest best.

Give me a healthy body, Lord;
Give me the sense to keep it so;
Also a heart that is not bored
Whatever work I have to do.

Give me a healthy mind, good Lord,
That finds the good that dodges sight,
And, seeing sin, is not appalled,
But seeks a way to put it right.

Give me a point of view, good Lord,
Let me know what it is, and why;
Don't let me worry overmuch
About the thing that's known as "I."

Give me a sense of humor, Lord,
Give me the power to see a joke;
To get some happiness from life,
And pass it on to other folk.

MEMORY

THOMAS BAILEY ALDRICH

My mind lets go a thousand things,
Like dates of wars and deaths of kings,
And yet recalls the very hour—
'Twas noon by yonder village tower,
And on the last blue noon in May—
The wind came briskly up this way,
Crisping the brook beside the road;
Then, pausing here, set down its load
Of pine-scents, and shook listlessly
Two petals from that wild-rose tree.

JENNY KISSED ME

LEIGH HUNT

Jenny kissed me when we met,
  Jumping from the chair she sat in.
Time, you thief, who love to get
  Sweets into your list, put that in!
Say I'm weary, say I'm sad,
  Say that health and wealth have missed me,
Say I'm growing old, but add:
    Jenny kissed me!

THE DAFFODILS

William Wordsworth

I wandered lonely as a cloud
  That floats on high o'er vales and hills,
When all at once I saw a crowd,
  A host of golden daffodils,
Beside the lake, beneath the trees,
Fluttering and dancing in the breeze.

Continuous as the stars that shine
  And twinkle on the Milky Way
They stretched in never-ending line
  Along the margin of a bay:
Ten thousand saw I at a glance
Tossing their heads in sprightly dance.

The waves beside them danced, but they
  Outdid the sparkling waves in glee.
A poet could not but be gay
  In such a jocund company.
I gazed—and gazed—but little thought
What wealth the show to me had brought,

For oft, when on my couch I lie
  In vacant or in pensive mood,
They flash upon that inward eye
  Which is the bliss of solitude;
And then my heart with pleasure fills,
And dances with the daffodils.

ACHIEVEMENT

MORRIS ABEL BEER

The poet is a lazy man,
Instead of building bridges, roads,
He sits back in his easy chair,
And fashions odes.

The poet is a peaceful man,
Who idly dreams from sun to sun;
And what has he accomplished when
His dreams are spun?

Perhaps a book of slender songs
To sweeten life with lilac rhyme,
That may, when roads and bridges crash,
Still cling to time!

FAILURE

ORRICK JOHNS

Five score years the birds have flown
  Back from March to May,
And this land has never known
  A man who made his way.

Flocks have passed of faces here
  Jovial and sour,
And never a single one of them
  Became a man of power.

Year on year these slopes were plowed
  By man and boy and still
Hardly have they yielded more
  Than the burying bill.

Five score years they've risen green
  Almost from the snow;
Now they're beautiful and clean . . .
  Failure made them so.

UNUSUAL THOUGHTS

Imagination is more important than knowledge.

—ALBERT EINSTEIN

INDIFFERENCE

LOUISE DRISCOLL

Over my garden
An airplane flew,
But nothing there
Either cared or knew.

Cabbage butterflies
Chased each other.
A young wren cried
Seeking his mother.

Gay zinnias
With heavy heads
Flaunted yellows
And mauves and reds.

A hummingbird
On the late larkspur
Never knew what
Went over her.

Crickets chirped
And a blinking toad
Watched for flies
On the gravel road.

They don't care
How smart men are—
To go through heaven
In a flying car!

To a yellow bee
  On a marigold
The adventure seems
  A trifle old.

MATHEMATICS

LIONEL WIGGAM

Child, behold the lovely pattern
Mars and Venus draw with Saturn.
Pause upon a hill and see
Celestial geometry.

Bend and carefully observe
The petal's precise fabric curve.
This is mathematics true
Beyond the kind that men construe.

Any vine you gaze upon
Plots a perfect pentagon.
Every ray the sun expels
Fashions faultless parallels.

Where the comet wanes and comes
Are essential axioms.
Gaze upon the sky, and ponder—
Primal algebra is yonder.

STEAM SHOVEL

CHARLES MALAM

The dinosaurs are not all dead.
I saw one raise its iron head
To watch me walking down the road
Beyond our house today.
Its jaws were dripping with a load
Of earth and grass that it had cropped.
It must have heard me where I stopped,
Snorted white steam my way,
And stretched its long neck out to see,
And chewed, and grinned quite amiably.

THERE IS NO FRIGATE LIKE A BOOK

EMILY DICKINSON

There is no frigate like a book
  To take us lands away,
Nor any coursers like a page
  Of prancing poetry.
This traverse may the poorest take
  Without oppress of toll;
How frugal is the chariot
  That bears a human soul!

YOU, ANDREW MARVELL

ARCHIBALD MACLEISH

And here face down beneath the sun
  And here upon earth's noonward height
To feel the always coming on
  The always rising of the night

To feel creep up the curving east
  The earthly chill of dusk and slow
Upon those under lands the vast
  And ever climbing shadow grow

And strange at Ecbatan the trees
  Take leaf by leaf the evening strange
The flooding dark about their knees
  The mountains over Persia change

And now at Kermanshah the gate
  Dark empty and the withered grass
And through the twilight now the late
  Few travelers in the westward pass

And Bagdad darken and the bridge
  Across the silent river gone
And through Arabia the edge
  Of evening widen and steal on

And deepen on Palmyra's street
  The wheel rut in the ruined stone
And Lebanon fade out and Crete
  High through the clouds and overblown

And over Sicily the air
  Still flashing with the landward gulls
And loom and slowly disappear
  The sails above the shadowy hulls

And Spain go under and the shore
  Of Africa the gilded sand
And evening vanish and no more
  The low pale light across that land

Nor now the long light on the sea

  And here face downward in the sun
To feel how swift how secretly
  The shadow of the night comes on . . .

THE TICKET AGENT

Edmund Leamy

Like any merchant in a store
Who sells things by the pound or score,

He deals with scarce perfunctory glance
Small passkeys to the world's romance.

He takes dull money, turns and hands
The roadways to far distant lands.

Bright shining rail and fenceless sea
Are partners to his wizardry.

He calls off names as if they were
Just names to cause no heart to stir.

For listening you'll hear him say
" . . . and then to Aden and Bombay . . . "

Or " . . . 'Frisco first and then to Nome,
Across the Rocky Mountains—home . . . "

And never catch of voice to tell
He knows the lure or feels the spell.

Like any salesman in a store,
He sells but tickets—nothing more.

And casual as any clerk
He deals in dreams, and calls it—work!

HANDS

Wilfrid Wilson Gibson

Tempest without: within, the mellow glow
Of mingling lamp and firelight over all—
Etchings and water colors on the wall,
Cushions and curtains of clear indigo,
Rugs damask-red and blue as Tyrian seas,
Deep chairs, black oaken settles, hammered brass,
Translucent porcelain, and sea-green glass—
Color and warmth and light and dreamy ease:
And I sit wondering where are now the hands
That wrought at anvil, easel, wheel, and loom—
Hands slender, swart, red, gnarled—in foreign lands
Or English shops to furnish this seemly room;
And all the while without the windy rain
Drums like dead fingers tapping at the pane.

SANCTUARY

ELINOR WYLIE

This is the bricklayer; hear the thud
  Of his heavy load dumped down on stone.
His lustrous bricks are brighter than blood,
  His smoking mortar whiter than bone.

Set each sharp-edged, fire-bitten brick
  Straight by the plumb-line's shivering length;
Make my marvelous wall so thick
  Dead nor living may shake its strength.

Full as a crystal cup with drink
  Is my cell with dreams, and quiet, and cool. . . .
Stop, old man! You must leave a chink;
  How can I breathe? *You can't, you fool!*

BLIND

Cumberland Market, London

HARRY KEMP

The Spring blew trumpets of color;
Her green sang in my brain. . . .
I heard a blind man groping
"Tap-tap" with his cane;

I pitied him in his blindness;
But can I boast, "I see"?
Perhaps there walks a spirit
Close by, who pities me—

A spirit who hears me tapping
The five-sensed cane of mind
Amid such unguessed glories
That I am worse than blind!

THUNDERSTORM

ARTHUR GUITERMAN

The smiths of the heavens are mending the weather;
Their hammers are beating the fragments together.
The cumulus mountains with nebulous gorges
Are dazzled with flame of the wind-bellowsed forges;
The cloud-pillared anvils with silvery edges
Resound to the thunderous fall of the sledges;
Till broadening patches of azure are showing
Storm-welded, rain-tempered, and, splendidly glowing,
The rainbow, from valley to valley extended,
Proclaims to the world that the weather is mended.

SOMETIMES

THOMAS S. JONES, JR.

Across the fields of yesterday
  He sometimes comes to me,
A little lad just back from play—
  The lad I used to be.

And yet he smiles so wistfully
  Once he has crept within,
I wonder if he hopes to see
  The man I might have been.

FLAMES

E. Merrill Root

Prisoners in the dark of wood,
Fast in fibered solitude,
Passionate scarlet silken things—
Dancing daggered folk with wings—
Fettered children of the sun
Who would storm the sky and run
Flame-armed, uniformed with light,
Burning death and spurning night,
Exiled and disarmed must lie
Locked in wood until they die . . .
Or until the blazing key
Of a match shall set them free;
Then in a wild flash and maze,
Fiercer for their dungeon days,
Up they quiver integral,
While their cells and fetters fall
Ashes . . . and they leap and run
Upward to their Lord, the sun. . . .

(Pity, pity us who lie
Wooden flames until we die!)

THE DISCOVERER

NATHALIA CRANE

Mystical, sorrowful, stiff and still,
A sparrow stood on a wintry sill.

The night wind laden with icy sleet
Ruffled his feathers and stung his feet,

But his right eye peered through a window pane
And visioned the warmth of a Junetime lane.

He saw the lights from a fireplace fall
Over the patterns on somebody's wall.

His heart was thrilled by a paper rose—
He had found at last where the summer goes.

ARGUMENT

MILDRED WESTON

Two stubborn beaks
Of equal strength
Can stretch a worm
To any length.

LIQUIDS

MERRILL MOORE

Liquids we use have always seemed to me
Stranger even than what we use them for,
Ink is an instance, uncork it with care,
It is astounding when you suddenly see
Words formed of it spread on an empty page
That was only paper before it met the ink
And to know that from it unborn men may drink
The sweet or bitter thought of a perished age.
One may consider, though one may forget,
Mysterious humors of the most daily kind;
Milk, out of which the shapes of our bones are laid,
Or drugs that cut the cords in Memory's net
Allowing the fish-like thoughts to escape and hide
In the thin streams that trickle through the mind.

RADIUM

AGNES LEE

A fateful youngling of the dark and drift,
  Unconscious of its goal,
But giving, giving, eager with the gift,
  Exhaustless as the soul.

ALLENBY ENTERS JERUSALEM!

We hope, by God's Grace, to receive the Holy City of Jerusalem.—
Richard, Coeur de Lion, A.D. 1191

STEPHEN CHALMERS

Wake from thy slumbering, Heart of the Lion!
  Rise from the dream of it, centuries old.
Look ye from Ascalon eastward to Zion,
  Where in the dawning our banners unfold!

Over the domes of the infidel enemy
  Blows the Red Cross of the Crusaders' might;
Over the Sepulcher, over Gethsemane,
  Ay, over Calvary, glowing with light!

Godfrey de Bouillon speeds with the tidings,
  Stirred, too, from dreams in yon Holiest Crypt,
High in his stirrups, the dust of his stridings
  Staining the Crescent from Saladin stripped!

Nay, royal sire!—no mirage of hope dying,
  Fruit of the Dead Sea, or figment of sleep!—
Saladin's slain and his Saracens flying!
  God and St. George o'er Jerusalem sweep!

RETURN

MARY S. HAWLING

On such a day St. Francis walked
And counseled with the birds.
The flowers listened as he spoke,
The tall trees heard his words.

On such a day St. Francis paused
And all around him stood
The soft-furred little trusting things
Who ran within that wood.

The sky was very blue for him
(Perhaps his eyes were blue);
The wind was cool upon his face
(A gentle wind he knew).

On such a day St. Francis walked,
And down each wooded lane
I listen for his footsteps now—
Perhaps he walks again.

TREES THAT SHADE A HOUSE

KATHARINE WORTH

Trees that shade a house have memories
More beautiful than all the starry talk
Of birches etched into a silver frieze
Against a lone black sky where hill winds walk.
They keep their thoughts of little brides in white
Coming with trusting feet across the grass,
And ponder on the first soft candlelight
Striking across a nursery window glass.
Inside their still green hearts they hold a grief
For wistful folk who cried beneath their shade;
They shake green laughter out of every leaf
When oldsters walk where childishly they played—
It's quaint to look on grown-up men and know
They wore pink-flowered rompers long ago!

INFLUENCE

JOHN BANISTER TABB

He cannot as he came depart—
  The Wind that woos the Rose;
Her fragrance whispers in his heart
  Wherever hence he goes.

HAWAIIAN HILLTOP

GENEVIEVE TAGGARD

In Greece the shadows slept as still,
In Rome, the hills were arched as high—
Their wind now blows my hair, and will
Stir other maidens' when I die.

And leaves that print the dust with lines,
And pebbles rubbed and rounded blue,
And burrs like baby porcupines
Looked this way when the Nile was new.

And dust, to Babylonian feet
Was downy soft, and good to tread.
The bees that mumble in this heat
Made the same honey for their bread.

Both early with the sun and late
Crept the same shades and flew the same
White flags of clouds across the straight
Horizon of another name.

Men chipped us messages in stone,
The careful stories of their kings—
But they were dumb about their own
Undying things!

THE HAMMERS

RALPH HODGSON

Noise of hammers once I heard,
Many hammers, busy hammers,
Beating, shaping, night and day,
Shaping, beating dust and clay
To a palace; saw it reared;
Saw the hammers laid away.

And I listened, and I heard
Hammers beating, night and day,
In the palace newly reared,
Beating it to dust and clay:
Other hammers, muffled hammers,
Silent hammers of decay.

DAVID AND GOLIATH

JOHN BANISTER TABB

One word of well-directed wit,
A pebble jest, has often hit
A boastful evil and prevailed
Where many a nobler weapon failed.

HANDS

MARGARET LATHROP LAW

There are jasmine-petaled hands that droop
Upon the manicurist's velvet pad
Or shuffle cards for hours across a table;
And attenuated surgical fingers
That sever pain from a tortured body;
Others that winnow ripened grain
Or beat metal upon anvils.
Some are contrived for chiseling dreams in marble
Or conjuring visions of paradise from a harp.
A soldier's hand must plunge the bayonet
Through a fellow being.
But soon afterwards the hand can fondle a dog
Or a child.
Finally a hand bestows extreme unction.
It matters very little
Whether they are white, like gardenias,
Or black as withered mushrooms.
Creating, driving, grasping,
Clinging or searching,
We live through hands.

AT THE AQUARIUM

MAX EASTMAN

Serene the silver fishes glide,
Stern-lipped, and pale, and wonder-eyed!
As through the agèd deeps of ocean,
They glide with wan and wavy motion!
They have no pathway where they go,
They flow like water to and fro.
They watch with never winking eyes,
They watch with staring, cold surprise,
The level people in the air,
The people peering, peering there,
Who wander also to and fro,
And know not why or where they go,
Yet have a wonder in their eyes,
Sometimes a pale and cold surprise.

THE QUESTION MARK

PERSIS GREELY ANDERSON

Behold the wicked little barb
Which catches fish in human garb
And yanks them back when they feel gay
With "Will it last?" or "Does it pay?"
It fastens neatly in the gills
Of those who have uncertain wills,
But even wily eels are caught
Upon this bent pin of a thought.

THOSE WHO SOAR

MARGARET LATHROP LAW

Scientists have not made known
Progenitors we crave to own:
The butterfly in sunny hour
Caressing each seductive flower;
Experimental bumblebee,
An oriole above his tree;
A moth whose all-consuming aim
Was devoured in scorching flame.
Behind the very birth of time,
Ambition never bred in slime;
Abolish crawling, legless things,
I want forbears boasting wings!

THE WOMAN WITH THE BABY TO THE PHILOSOPHER

FRANCES CORNFORD

How can I dread you, O portentous wise,
When I consider you were once this size?
How cringe before the sage who understands,
Who once had foolish, perfect, waving hands,
As small as these are? How bow down in dread,
When I conceive your warm, domed, downy head
Smelling of soap? O you—from North to South
Renowned—who put your toes inside your mouth.

FUTILITY

Mary S. Hawling

I try to capture rhythm with
The makeshift words that limit me:
The wind has more success than I
By simply bending down a tree.

I seek for color, and must be
Content with some cold, distant name:
Yet swiftly, as the night walks near,
The sky is surging bronze and flame.

I struggle for a single line
To measure an emotion by:
A wild bird, effortless, takes wing
And writes a poem across the sky.

WORD PICTURES

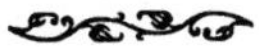

Painting is silent poetry, and poetry is painting with the gift of speech.

—SIMONIDES

WINGS

WILLIAM ROSE BENÉT

The bay was bronze with sunset, and so light
The ripples idled on the gentle tide
That we who swam in silence side by side
Paused; shifted poise; and, floating, lost our sight
In a vast well of blue, benign and bright,
Just ere it faded and the clouds were dyed
Saffron and crimson. With one gasp we cried,
"Thus eagles float, through heavens of pure delight!"
Then, with the splendor of a falling star,
Great wings swept down; a muffled engine whirred;
And, iridescent as a hummingbird,
A biplane swooped upon us, veered, and fled
Chanting Man's realized dream. . . . Yet higher far
We soared, upbuoyed on waters sunset-red!

MOTOR CARS

ROWENA BASTIN BENNETT

From a city window, 'way up high,
I like to watch the cars go by.
They look like burnished beetles, black,
That leave a little muddy track
Behind them as they slowly crawl.
Sometimes they do not move at all
But huddle close with hum and drone
As though they feared to be alone.
They grope their way through fog and night
With the golden feelers of their light.

THE ROUNDHOUSE

William Rose Benét

Rembrandt alone could paint this mammoth shed
Filled with weird hissing like some Hydra's lair,
Where thick smoke eddies through the sunless air
And webs of steel curve upward overhead.
These floors run burning oils. These fires are fed
From pits of Tartarus. Against the glare
High-shouldered, coal-black gryphons crouch and stare.
Their heavy panting wakes a sense of dread.
Yet stranger far, the human ants in hordes
Who swarm like imps in some infernal masque,
Seeming to guide each awful shape of power
As th' elemental spirits' potent lords—
Yet only toiling at their common task,
Bound by a schedule to the clamoring hour!

GENTLE STORM

MARTHA BANNING THOMAS

Through miles of mist the lighthouse candle sweeps
In hazy arcs, and like a sickle, reaps
Dissolving harvest of the windless rain,
And cuts and goes, and leaves the ghostly grain
Upright as ever.

And the single eye
That winks upon the buoy, seeks the sky
With bright impertinence, and hunts a star
Where only rain and heavy storm clouds are.

The foghorn shouts its long and faithful roar
That links a chain of echoes with the shore;
The water moves in one wide whisper then,
As if a giant woke, and turned . . . and slept again.

FOG

CARL SANDBURG

The fog comes
on little cat feet.

It sits looking
over harbor and city
on silent haunches
and then moves on.

SILVER

WALTER DE LA MARE

Slowly, silently, now the moon
Walks the night in her silver shoon;
This way, and that, she peers, and sees
Silver fruit upon silver trees;
One by one the casements catch
Her beams beneath the silvery thatch;
Couched in his kennel, like a log,
With paws of silver sleeps the dog;
From their shadowy cote the white breasts peep
Of doves in a silver-feathered sleep;
A harvest mouse goes scampering by,
With silver claws, and silver eye;
And moveless fish in the water gleam,
By silver reeds in a silver stream.

DAWN

ISABEL BUTCHART

A drifting mist beyond the bar,
  A light that is no light,
A line of gray where breakers are,
  And in the distance—night.

The watching lamps along the coasts
  Shine wanly on the foam,
And silently, like tired ghosts,
  The fishing fleet comes home.

THE WINDMILLS

JOHN GOULD FLETCHER

The windmills, like great sunflowers of steel,
Lift themselves proudly over the straggling houses;
And at their feet the deep blue-green alfalfa
Cuts the desert like the stroke of a sword.

Yellow melon flowers
Crawl beneath the withered peach trees;
A date palm throws its heavy fronds of steel
Against the scoured metallic sky.

The houses, double-roofed for coolness,
Cower amid the manzanita scrub,
A man with jingling spurs
Walks heavily out of a vine-bowered doorway,
Mounts his pony, rides away.

The windmills stare at the sun.
The yellow earth cracks and blisters.
Everything is still.

In the afternoon
The wind takes dry waves of heat and tosses them
Mingled with dust, up and down the streets,
Against the belfry with its green bells:

And, after sunset, when the sky
Becomes a green and orange fan,
The windmills, like great sunflowers on dried stalks,
Stare hard at the sun they cannot follow.

Turning, turning, forever turning
In the chill night wind that sweeps over the valley,
With the shriek and clank of the pumps groaning beneath
them,
And the choking gurgle of tepid water.

NIGHT SHOWER

Brock Milton

Farewell to slumber! Air that has been still
Stirs restlessly. A loosely-flapping shade,
A few first drops, which spurt across the sill,
Contemptuously daring to invade
This sanctuary, and a battered pane,
Stricken with thunder, half alive with sound,
Presage the cataract. At last the rain
Beats on the concrete armor of the ground.
Keen splendor stabs the sky. An ancient fear
Shutters the eyes, but each refulgent spark
Leaps from the heavens like a silver spear,
Piercing the lids and blotting out the dark.
A final patter fades into the deep,
Consuming throb of rediscovered sleep.

APPLES IN NEW HAMPSHIRE

MARIE GILCHRIST

Long poles support the branches of the orchards in New Hampshire,
Each bough fruited closely enough to take a prize;
The apple crop is heavy this year in New Hampshire:
Baldwins, McIntoshes, Winesaps, Northern Spies.
Hay is heaped in cocks on the sloping floors of the orchards,
So that none of the fruit may be lost in the tangled grasses.
Let the sun lie a few weeks more against the boughs of the orchards;
It will not be long before September passes.
The dew stands thickly beaded on the reddening cheeks of apples
When the sluggard autumn sun breaks through the mists;
Even when the moon shines, in the hard green apples
Ivory seeds blacken and ripening persists.
Sound core, wormy core, bruised and bitten,
The farmers' men will harvest them, heap after heap;
They will pick the best for market, they will shake the boughs and gather
Apples for cider, apples to keep.
Dark and cold in the earthy cellar,
Packed in barrels, laid upon shelves,
Filling the darkness with redolence of summer,
Waiting for the children to help themselves,
White teeth piercing the glossy skins of apples—
The juice spurts and the cores are sweet and mellow;
There will be enough to last until March,
When the red skins wither and the pulp turns yellow.

And the bleak trees dreaming in the sharp still moonlight,
Snow nested in the crotches, rotted windfalls on the
  ground,
Will remember apples vaguely like a flood long remembered,
A mighty weight of apples, greedy and round,
Dragging their straining boughs lower and lower,
Sapping roots of their slow honey, stealing the dew.
The apple crop is heavy this year in New Hampshire;
Next year the trees will rest and apples will be few.

THE SKATERS

JOHN GOULD FLETCHER

Black swallows swooping or gliding
In a flurry of entangled loops and curves;
The skaters skim over the frozen river.
And the grinding click of their skates as they impinge upon
  the surface,
Is like the brushing together of thin wing tips of silver.

LONDON SNOW

ROBERT BRIDGES

When men were all asleep the snow came flying,
  In large white flakes falling on the city brown,
Stealthily and perpetually settling and loosely lying,
  Hushing the latest traffic of the drowsy town;
Deadening, muffling, stifling its murmurs failing;
  Lazily and incessantly floating down and down:
Silently sifting and veiling road, roof and railing;
  Hiding difference, making unevenness even,
Into angles and crevices softly drifting and sailing.
  All night it fell, and when full inches seven
It lay in the depth of its uncompacted lightness,
  The clouds blew off from a high and frosty heaven;
And all woke earlier for the unaccustomed brightness
  Of the winter dawning, the strange unheavenly glare:
The eye marveled—marveled at the dazzling whiteness;
  The ear hearkened to the stillness of the solemn air;
No sound of wheel rumbling nor of foot falling,
  And the busy morning cries came thin and spare.
Then boys I heard, as they went to school, calling,
  They gathered up the crystal manna to freeze
Their tongues with tasting, their hands with snowballing;
  Or rioted in a drift, plunging up to the knees;
Or peering up from under the white-mossed wonder,
  "Oh, look at the trees!" they cried. "Oh, look at the trees!"
With lessened load a few carts creak and blunder,
  Following along the white deserted way,
A country company long dispersed asunder:
  When now already the sun, in pale display

Standing by Paul's high dome, spread forth below
His sparkling beams, and awoke the stir of the day.
For now doors open, and war is waged with the snow;
And trains of somber men, past tale of number,
Tread long brown paths, as toward their toil they go:
But even for them awhile no cares encumber
Their minds diverted; the daily word is unspoken,
The daily thoughts of labor and sorrow slumber
At sight of the beauty that greets them, for the charm they have broken.

THE WOLF CRY

LEW SARETT

The Arctic moon hangs overhead;
The wide white silence lies below.
A starveling pine stands lone and gaunt,
Black-penciled on the snow.

Weird as the moan of sobbing winds,
A lone long call floats up from the trail;
And the naked soul of the frozen North
Trembles in that wail.

MOUNTAIN HAMLET

LEW SARETT

Wide-eyed all night in the weatherworn inn,
As the bleak winds rattled on the rain trough's tin,
Deep in a feather bed I tossed in the gloom
That dripped from the walls of the attic room.

There was never a sound in the moldering house
But the wail of the wind and the squeak of a mouse
Eerily scampering under the gable . . .
Over the rafter . . . down on the table.

Never a sound but the slow tick-tock
From the laggard tongue of the grandfather's clock,
The bronchial whirr and the dubious chime
Of the old bronze bells as they croaked the time.

Remote I was from the face of a friend,
In a hamlet tucked where the mountains bend
A gnarly arm round a lonely sweep
So desolate that I could not sleep.

Restless, I crept to the window sill:
The ice-browed cabins under the hill,
Forlorn, abandoned, huddled in a row
Like frozen ptarmigan squat in the snow.

The tavern lamplight, leaning on the blizzard,
Hooded in white, was a hunched-up wizard
With lean yellow fingers that conjured hosts
Of shambling shadows and slim gray ghosts.

I groped my way to the old bedstead
And stared at the portrait over my head:
The long-gone father of my host who was sleeping,
Snoring at ease, while the hours were creeping.

Through Gunflint Pass, with his old oxcart,
He had reached this glade; with a resolute heart
He had swung his ax through these forest halls,
Had hewn the logs of these homestead walls.

Here in the hills, for seventy years,
This gaunt bellwether of the pioneers
Had browsed content, and with placid eye
Had mulled his cud as the world rushed by.

And here, with his paunch and his applelike face,
My host, his son—the last of his race—
Had slept untroubled by the slow tick-tock
And the dull bronze bells of his father's clock;

Had lived content, like his pioneer sire,
With his hickory chair and his wide hearth-fire,
His cobwebbed kegs in the cellar's damp,
His feather beds and his tavern lamp.

I burrowed in my bed when a wintry gust
Clattered on the panes with a brittle white dust,
As the keen wind fumbled the flapping shutter
And moaned like a cat in the loose rain gutter.

Soundless the mountain, soundless the wood,
Except for a lynx in the neighborhood,
Who shivered the night with a frozen wail
When the wind's teeth raked him from muzzle to tail.

Faintly I caught the struggle and strain,
The melancholy cry of a railway train
Climbing the Gunflint, high and higher,
The belly-born tones of the West Coast Flier.

Nearer the grinding clang and rattle
Of the transcontinental streaming to Seattle,
Whistling as she flew: "Make way! Make way!
For another tribe and another day!"—

Laden with vendors of motorcars,
Radio experts and cinema stars,
With railway presidents, governors,
Airplane mechanics and realtors.

Like a red-tailed rocket in the midnight's black,
It crashed through the hamlet; and left in its track
The blinking eye of a signal light
As its cloud of glory vanished in night.

The faint gold tones of the mellow bell—
Like the mumble of the sea held in a shell—
Trembled in the hills, so cupped and hollowed
They echoed the echoes. Silence followed.

Oh, never a sound but the groan of the floor—
Two ghostly feet at the inn-keeper's door . . .
Pacing the room of my host who sighed
And rolled on the bed where his father had died.

Never a sound but a squeak on the rafter,
The windmill's creak and the wind's wild laughter,
The interminable tick, the inevitable tock
Of the thick halt tongue of the grandfather's clock.

SMELLS

CHRISTOPHER MORLEY

Why is it that the poets tell
So little of the sense of smell?
These are the odors I love well:

The smell of coffee freshly ground;
Or rich plum pudding, holly crowned;
Or onions fried and deeply browned.

The fragrance of a fumy pipe;
The smell of apples, newly ripe;
And printers' ink on leaden type.

Woods by moonlight in September
Breathe most sweet; and I remember
Many a smoky campfire ember.

Camphor, turpentine, and tea,
The balsam of a Christmas tree,
These are whiffs of gramarye. . . .
A ship smells best of all to me!

PEOPLE

A wonderful fact to reflect upon, that every human creature is constituted to be that profound secret and mystery to every other.

—CHARLES DICKENS

THE STATISTICIAN

CHARLES WHARTON STORK

He gathers data:
The mathematics of a comet's curve
Or when the oriole nests,
The tensile strength of steel
Or the decline of cholera in the Philippines.
He does not formulate laws
Or institute practical measures
Or touch the kindling spark of imagination
To facts observed;
He counts and sifts and classifies.

He is no architect, inventor, poet;
Yet on his faithfulness we build:
A plumb line wrong,
And all the bricks are tumbling round our heads.
He bent the timbers of Columbus' galleon
And squared the stones of Chartres,
He pounded Titian's colors
And chronicled events that Shakespeare sang.

A slave, some call him.
But is he not—
This man who dares not lose himself in beauty
For fear he miss a fact—
The proofreader of God?

EPITAPH

EDWARD WEISMILLER

It seemed that he would rather hear
The running footfalls of the deer
Than any perfect rhythmic sound
Of wheels turned endlessly around,

And when you saw him you could tell
That he would find the crimson fell
Of autumn maples lovelier far
Than smooth-drawn silver metals are.

He thought sometimes of things like these:
High-drifting birds, and leaf-dark trees;
And all the while his greasy hands
Moved surely over cold steel bands.

PORTRAIT

SYDNEY KING RUSSELL

He knows why certain sycophants adore him
Who bask serenely in reflected glory,
And tolerates a host of friends who bore him
And ladies who . . . but that's another story.
He listens to their troubles when they're down
And charitably lends a helping hand
To those who feebly weather fortune's frown—
The very clouds disperse at his command.
Yet I am certain there are times when he
Would give the world to know what friend might care
Were he in rags, what hospitality
The earth would offer one who faced despair.
Who likes his wealth, his wit, he knows full well—
Who loves him for himself, he cannot tell.

THE FIDDLER OF DOONEY

W. B. Yeats

When I play on my fiddle in Dooney,
Folk dance like a wave of the sea;
My cousin is priest in Kilvarnet,
My brother in Mocharabuiee.

I passed my brother and cousin:
They read in their books of prayer;
I read in my book of songs
I bought at the Sligo fair.

When we come at the end of time
To Peter sitting in state,
He will smile on the three old spirits,
But will call me first through the gate;

For the good are always the merry,
Save by an evil chance,
And the merry love the fiddle,
And the merry love to dance:

And when the folk there spy me,
They will all come up to me,
With "Here is the fiddler of Dooney!"
And dance like a wave of the sea.

COBBLER

PEGGY BACON

He mends the shoes
and watches the feet
of the crowd that goes
along the street.

A basement deep
and a sidewalk high;
along the ceiling
the feet go by;

toeing and heeling
they seem to skim
the top of the larky
world to him

in the musty dark,
whose eyes dilate
as he gazes up
through the dingy grate.

The world hobbles
on feet of clay,
the cobbler cobbles
his days away;

crooked heels
and broken toes
are all he feels,
all he knows.

OLD GRAY SQUIRREL

ALFRED NOYES

A great while ago, there was a schoolboy.
He lived in a cottage by the sea.
And the very first thing he could remember
Was the rigging of the schooners by the quay.

He could watch them, when he woke, from his window,
With the tall cranes hoisting out the freight.
And he used to think of shipping as a sea cook,
And sailing to the Golden Gate.

For he used to buy the yellow penny dreadfuls,
And read them where he fished for conger eels,
And listened to the lapping of the water,
The green and oily water round the keels.

There were trawlers with their shark-mouthed flatfish,
And red nets hanging out to dry,
And the skate the skipper kept because he liked 'em,
And landsmen never knew the fish to fry.

There were brigantines with timber out of Norroway,
Oozing with the syrups of the pine.
There were rusty dusty schooners out of Sunderland,
And the ships of the Blue Cross Line.

And to tumble down a hatch into the cabin
Was better than the best of broken rules;
For the smell of 'em was like a Christmas dinner,
And the feel of 'em was like a box of tools.

And, before he went to sleep in the evening,
The very last thing that he could see
Was the sailormen a-dancing in the moonlight
By the capstan that stood upon the quay.

He is perched upon a high stool in London.
The Golden Gate is very far away.
They caught him, and they caged him, like a squirrel.
He is totting up accounts, and going gray.

He will never, never, never, sail to 'Frisco.
But the very last thing that he will see
Will be sailormen a-dancing in the sunrise
By the capstan that stands upon the quay. . . .

To the tune of an old concertina,
By the capstan that stands upon the quay.

A CONVERSATIONAL NEIGHBOR

RICHARD KIRK

When it was said that she was dead,
We were inclined at first to doubt it;
We felt we knew, if it were true,
That she would have told us all about it.

DISTANCE

BABETTE DEUTSCH

Two pale old men
Sit by a squalid window playing chess.
The heavy air and the shrill cries
Beyond the sheltering pane are less
To them than roof-blockaded skies.
Life flowing past them:
Women with gay eyes,
Resurgent voices, and the noise
Of peddlers showing urgent wares,
Leaves their dark peace unchanged.
They are innocent
Of the street clamor as young children bent
Absorbed over their toys.
The old heads nod;
A parchment-colored hand
Hovers above the intricate dim board.
And patient schemes are woven, where they sit
So still,
And raveled, and reknit with reverent skill.
And when a point is scored
A flickering jest
Brightens their eyes, a solemn beard is raised
A moment, and then sunk on the thin chest.
Heedless as happy children, or maybe
Lovers creating their own solitude,
Or worn philosophers, content to brood
On an intangible reality.
Shut in an ideal universe,
Within their darkened window frame

They ponder on their moves, rehearse
The old designs,
Two rusty skullcaps bowed
Above an endless game.

CAPTAIN'S WALK: SALEM

OLIVER JENKINS

Like some old voyager out of the past,
Standing his lonely watch under the stars,
He half imagines moonlight on a mast
And is bewitched by moving sails and spars,
But there is only the dark moving sea,
Speared by some beacon's solitary eye,
And sound of water breaking on the quay
Whenever little boats go stealing by.
So through the lonely silences of night,
Lost in dark revery, with furrowed brows,
He looks beyond the farthest moonlit ledge
For shadows moving in the ghostly light;
And dreams of sails outspread and dipping prows,
Of clippers anchored at the harbor's edge.

SEEIN' THINGS

EUGENE FIELD

I ain't afeard uv snakes, or toads, or bugs, or worms, or mice,
An' things 'at girls are skeered uv I think are awful nice!
I'm pretty brave, I guess; an' yet I hate to go to bed,
For, when I'm tucked up warm an' snug an' when my prayers are said,
Mother tells me "Happy dreams!" and takes away the light,
An' leaves me lyin' all alone an' seein' things at night!

Sometimes they're in the corner, sometimes they're by the door,
Sometimes they're all a-standin' in the middle uv the floor;
Sometimes they are a-sittin' down, sometimes they're walkin' round
So softly an' so creepylike they never make a sound!
Sometimes they are as black as ink, an' other times they're white—
But color ain't no difference when you see things at night!

Once, when I licked a feller 'at had just moved on our street,
An' Father sent me up to bed without a bite to eat,
I woke up in the dark an' saw things standin' in a row,
A-lookin' at me cross-eyed an' p'intin' at me—so!
Oh, my! I wuz so skeered that time I never slep' a mite—
It's almost alluz when I'm bad I see things at night!

Lucky thing I ain't a girl, or I'd be skeered to death!
Bein' I'm a boy, I duck my head an' hold my breath;
An' I am, oh! *so* sorry I'm a naughty boy, an' then
I promise to be better an' I say my prayers again!
Gran'ma tells me that's the only way to make it right
When a feller has been wicked an' sees things at night!

An' so, when other naughty boys would coax me into sin,
I try to skwush the Tempter's voice 'at urges me within;
An' when they's pie for supper, or cakes 'at's big an' nice,
I want to—but I do not pass my plate f'r them things twice!
No, ruther let starvation wipe me slowly out o' sight
Than I should keep a-livin' on an' seein' things at night!

MY POMPOUS FRIEND

LAWRENCE EMERSON NELSON

His sense of worth is strong;
  To watch him walk is fun.
He marches forth, a long
  Processional of one.

PORTRAIT OF A BOY

STEPHEN VINCENT BENÉT

After the whipping he crawled into bed,
Accepting the harsh fact with no great weeping.
How funny uncle's hat had looked striped red!
He chuckled silently. The moon came, sweeping
A black, frayed rag of tattered cloud before
In scorning; very pure and pale she seemed,
Flooding his bed with radiance. On the floor
Fat motes danced. He sobbed, closed his eyes and dreame

Warm sand flowed round him. Blurts of crimson light
Splashed the white grains like blood. Past the cave's mout
Shone with a large, fierce splendor, wildly bright,
The crooked constellations of the South;
Here the Cross swung; and there, affronting Mars,
The Centaur stormed aside a froth of stars.
Within, great casks, like wattled aldermen,
Sighed of enormous feasts, and cloth of gold
Glowed on the walls like hot desire. Again,
Beside webbed purples from some galleon's hold,
A black chest bore the skull and bones in white
Above a scrawled "Gunpowder!" By the flames,
Decked out in crimson, gemmed with syenite,
Hailing their fellows with outrageous names,
The pirates sat and diced. Their eyes were moons.
"Doubloons!" they said. The words crashed gold. "Doub
loons!"

INCORRIGIBLE

Burges Johnson

I guess I'm bad as I can be,
'Cause after uncle found and yanked me
Out of that old apple tree,
And after Dad came home and spanked me,
And while my teacher told me things
About the narrow path of duty,
And how an education brings
The only truly joy and beauty,
And while she said she didn't doubt
They'd wasted all the good they'd taught me,
I had to grin, to think about
The fun I had before they caught me.

LINEMAN

Gerald Raftery

High on a pole, he labors in the sky
Through wires with humming death in every strand;
A careless moment means that he will die.
He holds his life, and death, in one gloved hand.

THE FARM BOY

KATHARINE ATHERTON GRIMES

My father puzzles me—
He goes about his work so soberly.
He looks down at the ground,
And never seems to hear a single sound,
Or see the grasses stir,
Or how the pasture's blowing edges blur.
He never hears the breeze
Fretting and pulling at the new-green trees.

One morning in the spring,
Across the field I thought I heard him sing;
But when our plow-rounds crossed,
He only fussed about the time I'd lost,
Then hustled up his team
And said, "Now Sonny, don't stand there and dream,
With all this work to do."
But I work better when I dream—don't you?

Sometimes I ask him why
He never stops to watch the windy sky,
Or let his horses rest,
While he goes hunting for a blackbird's nest.
He puckers up his face—
"Someone must make a living at this place!"
He seems to think it's tough—
But these warm days I just can't live enough!

My father puzzles me—
But mother laughs, and says some day I'll see
He just puts all that on
To set a good example for his son;
That, if 'twas not for her,
Sometimes he'd not go near that field—no, sir!
But, if he had his way,
He'd take me fishing every other day.

BALLOON MAN

HAZEL I. DANNECKER

Incongruously gray he sits
Selling ornamental bits;
Flashing pinwheels; gimcracks bright;
Spheres like torches all alight;
Radiance that so belies
Drabness in his sullen eyes.

THE SCHOOLBOY READS HIS ILIAD

DAVID MORTON

The sounding battles leave him nodding still:
The din of javelins at the distant wall
Is far too faint to wake that weary will
That all but sleeps for cities where they fall.
He cares not if this Helen's face were fair,
Nor if the thousand ships shall go or stay;
In vain the rumbling chariots throng the air
With sounds the centuries shall not hush away.
Beyond the window where the spring is new,
Are marbles in a square, and tops again,
And floating voices tell him what they do,
Luring his thought from these long-warring men—
And though the camp be visited with gods,
He dreams of marbles and of tops, and nods.

AN OLD MAN'S WINTER NIGHT

ROBERT FROST

All out of doors looked darkly in at him
Through the thin frost, almost in separate stars,
That gathers on the pane in empty rooms.
What kept his eyes from giving back the gaze
Was the lamp tilted near them in his hand.
What kept him from remembering the need
That brought him to that creaking room was age.
He stood with barrels round him—at a loss.
And having scared the cellar under him
In clomping there, he scared it once again
In clomping off;—and scared the outer night,
Which has its sounds, familiar, like the roar
Of trees and crack of branches, common things,
But nothing so like beating on a box.
A light he was to no one but himself
Where now he sat, concerned with he knew what,
A quiet light, and then not even that.
He consigned to the moon, such as she was,
So late-arising, to the broken moon
As better than the sun in any case
For such a charge, his snow upon the roof,
His icicles along the wall to keep;
And slept. The log that shifted with a jolt
Once in the stove, disturbed him and he shifted,
And eased his heavy breathing, but still slept.
One aged man—one man—can't fill a house,
A farm, a countryside, or if he can,
It's thus he does it of a winter night.

GUNGA DIN

RUDYARD KIPLING

You may talk o' gin and beer
When you're quartered safe out 'ere,
An' you're sent to penny-fights an' Aldershot it;
But when it comes to slaughter
You will do your work on water,
An' you'll lick the bloomin' boots of 'im that's got it.
Now in Injia's sunny clime,
Where I used to spend my time
A-servin' of 'Er Majesty the Queen,
Of all them black-faced crew
The finest man I knew
Was our regimental bhisti, Gunga Din.
  He was "Din! Din! Din!
You limpin' lump o' brick dust, Gunga Din!
  Hi! Slippy *hitherao!*
  Water, get it! *Panee lao*
You squidgy-nosed old idol, Gunga Din."

The uniform 'e wore
Was nothin' much before,
An' rather less than 'arf o' that be'ind,
For a piece o' twisty rag
An' a goatskin water bag
Was all the field equipment 'e could find.
When the sweatin' troop train lay
In a sidin' through the day,
Where the 'eat would make your bloomin' eyebrows craw
We shouted "Harry By!"
Till our throats were bricky-dry,
Then we wopped 'im 'cause 'e couldn't serve us all.

It was "Din! Din! Din!
You 'eathen, where the mischief 'ave you been?
You put some *juldee* in it
Or I'll *marrow* you this minute
f you don't fill up my helmet, Gunga Din!"

E would dot an' carry one
Till the longest day was done;
An' 'e didn't seem to know the use o' fear.
f we charged or broke or cut,
You could bet your bloomin' nut,
E'd be waitin' fifty paces right flank rear.
With 'is mussick on 'is back,
E would skip with our attack,
An' watch us till the bugles made "Retire"
An' for all 'is dirty 'ide
E was white, clear white, inside
When 'e went to tend the wounded under fire!
It was "Din! Din! Din!"
With the bullets kickin' dust spots on the green
When the cartridges ran out,
You could hear the front ranks shout,
Hi! ammunition mules an' Gunga Din!"

sha'n't forgit the night
When I dropped be'ind the fight
With a bullet where my belt plate should 'a' been.
was chokin' mad with thirst,
An' the man that spied me first
Was our good old grinnin', gruntin' Gunga Din.
E lifted up my 'ead,
An' he plugged me where I bled,
An' 'e guv me 'arf-a-pint o' water green.

It was crawlin' and it stunk,
But of all the drinks I've drunk,
I'm gratefulest to one from Gunga Din.
  It was "Din! Din! Din!
'Ere's a beggar with a bullet through 'is spleen;
  'E's chawin' up the ground,
  An' 'e's kickin' all around:
For Gawd's sake git the water, Gunga Din!"

'E carried me away
To where a dooli lay,
An' a bullet came an' drilled the beggar clean.
'E put me safe inside,
An' just before 'e died,
"I 'ope you liked your drink," sez Gunga Din.
So I'll meet 'im later on
At the place where 'e is gone—
Where it's always double drill and no canteen.
'E'll be squattin' on the coals
Givin' drink to poor damned souls,
An' I'll get a swig in hell from Gunga Din!
  Yes, Din! Din! Din!
You Lazarushian-leather Gunga Din!
  Though I've belted you and flayed you,
  By the livin' Gawd that made you,
You're a better man than I am, Gunga Din!

RICHARD CORY

EDWIN ARLINGTON ROBINSON

Whenever Richard Cory went down town,
  We people on the pavement looked at him:
He was a gentleman from sole to crown,
  Clean favored, and imperially slim.

And he was always quietly arrayed,
  And he was always human when he talked;
But still he fluttered pulses when he said,
  "Good morning," and he glittered when he walked.

And he was rich—yes, richer than a king—
  And admirably schooled in every grace:
In fine, we thought that he was everything
  To make us wish that we were in his place.

So on we worked, and waited for the light,
  And went without the meat, and cursed the bread;
And Richard Cory, one calm summer night,
  Went home and put a bullet through his head.

JIM BLUDSO OF THE *PRAIRIE BELLE*

JOHN HAY

Wall, no! I can't tell whar he lives,
Becase he don't live, you see;
Leastways, he's got out of the habit
Of livin' like you and me.
Whar have you been for the last three year
That you haven't heard folks tell
How Jimmy Bludso passed in his checks
The night of the *Prairie Belle?*

He weren't no saint—them engineers
Is all pretty much alike—
One wife in Natchez-under-the-Hill
And another one here, in Pike;
A keerless man in his talk was Jim,
And an awkward hand in a row,
But he never flunked, and he never lied—
I reckon he never knowed how.

And this was all the religion he had—
To treat his engine well;
Never be passed on the river;
To mind the pilot's bell;
And if ever the *Prairie Belle* took fire,
A thousand times he swore,
He'd hold her nozzle agin the bank
Till the last soul got ashore.

All boats has their day on the Mississip,
And her day come at last—

The *Movastar* was a better boat,
  But the *Belle* she wouldn't be passed.
And so she came tearin' along that night—
  The oldest craft on the line—
With a Negro squat on her safety valve,
  And her furnace crammed, rosin and pine.

The fire bust out as she clar'd the bar,
  And burnt a hole in the night,
And quick as a flash she turned, and made
  For that willer-bank on the right.
Thar was runnin' and cursin', but Jim yelled out,
  Over all the infernal roar,
"I'll hold her nozzle agin the bank
  Till the last galoot's ashore."

Through the hot, black breath of the burnin' boat
  Jim Bludso's voice was heard,
And they all had trust in his cussedness,
  And knowed he would keep his word.
And, sure's you're born, they all got off
  Afore the smokestacks fell—
And Bludso's ghost went up alone
  In the smoke of the *Prairie Belle*.

He weren't no saint, but at jedgment
  I'd run my chance with Jim,
'Longside of some pious gentlemen
  That wouldn't shook hands with him.
He seen his duty, a dead-sure thing,
  And went for it thar and then;
And Christ ain't a goin' to be too hard
  On a man that died for men.

THEN AND NOW

GEORGE STERLING

Beyond the desolate expanse of plain
  The sunset like a fiery menace glowed.
  The bones of brutes, along the uncertain road,
Were half a year unvisited of rain.

A woman dug within the river bed,
  Eager to know if water could be found.
  Her breathing filled the space with weary sound;
On those gaunt arms and face the light lay red.

The turbid water gathered in the hole.
  Pausing, she watched the west with steady stare. . . .
  Impatiently the oxen sniffed the air,
Tethered and tired beside the wagon pole.

Above, a hungry child began to push
  Aside the canvas of their prairie-van;
  Near the low bank a grim, impatient man
Tugged, grunting, at a thick and withered bush.

It snapped. He rolled, then rose with angry face.
  The woman stood with gnarly hands on hips,
  As broke in epic music from her lips
The swift, unsparing laughter of the race.

. . . .

Beyond the fenced and many-pastured plain
  The sunset rose like minarets of dream.
  The bridge across the summer-wasted stream
Roared with the passing of the splendid train

And from a shining car whose inmates quaffed
  Their jeweled wines, a girl with ivory hands
  Gazed forth, nor knew that on those very sands,
One sunset time, her mother's mother laughed.

Eastward she hastened to the roofs of kings,
  Her each desire accorded ere 'twas felt—
  She who had never toiled nor borne nor knelt,
She, tired of life and love and human things.

FOR A PESSIMIST

COUNTEE CULLEN

He wore his coffin for a hat,
  Calamity his cape,
While on his face a death's-head sat
And waved a bit of crape.

MARY SHAKESPEARE

William Shakespeare, born on April 23, 1564

ADA JACKSON

It may be that the sun was bright
Upon that long-past April day,
It may be clouds like sheep went by,
And that she watched them where she lay.

It may be, as the scents of spring
Crept in and out her low-ceiled room,
That she was glad her babe was come
In time of song and apple bloom:

That she gave thought to Stratford meads,
Made green and fresh, where he should play,
And took a gentle joy that he
Was born on good Saint George's Day.

Mayhap, his little hand in hers,
No common lot for him she planned—
"A farmer, striding Stratford fields,
Whom men shall speak with, cap in hand—

"Or eke his father's honest trade,
A goodman glover, that were best;
High Bailiff of the town, maybe—"
She dreamed with Genius at her breast.

Nor knew the art that he would ply
Would throne him higher than proud kings;
That his was power to shape and limn
Such lovely, everlasting things

That earth would rise to honor him—
Who in his linen swathings lay
The while she mused "Sheriff, perchance—"
Above him on Saint George's Day.

MILTON

William Wordsworth

Milton! thou shouldst be living at this hour.
England hath need of thee; she is a fen
Of stagnant waters. Altar, sword, and pen,
Fireside, the heroic wealth of hall and bower
Have forfeited their ancient English dower
Of inward happiness. We are selfish men.
Oh! raise us up, return to us again,
And give us manners, virtue, freedom, power.
Thy soul was like a star, and dwelt apart;
Thou hadst a voice whose sound was like the sea.
Pure as the naked heavens, majestic, free—
So didst thou travel on life's common way
In cheerful godliness; and yet thy heart
The lowliest duties on herself did lay.

HOW COULD YOU KNOW?

To John Milton, whose feet never left the ground, upon reading those lines of "Paradise Lost" that describe flying, this sonnet by one who has been a pilot

BEN RAY REDMAN

How could you know—who never rose so high
As lowly wren, or thrush, or linnet bright—
The vasty mazes of the upper sky,
The swift, exalting symphony of flight?
How could you shape such lines as make us feel
Aloft again, our pinions rising far,
As Satan turns "in many an aery wheel,"
And Uriel drops like "a shooting star"?
Milton! you give us back our wings again,
When the Arch Fiend, ridden by black desire,
Spreads wide his "sail-broad vans," or when
He upward springs, "a pyramid of fire."
Folly to think that we have ever flown,
When you dared Hell and God's high gate, alone!

ON A FLYLEAF OF BURNS'S SONGS

FREDERIC LAWRENCE KNOWLES

These are the best of him,
  Pathos and jest of him;
    Earth holds the rest of him.

Passions were strong in him—
  Pardon the wrong in him;
    Hark to the song in him!—

Each little lyrical
  Grave or satirical
    Musical miracle!

BEETHOVEN

EDWARD CARPENTER

Betwixt the actual and unseen, alone,
Companionless, deaf, in dread solitude
Of soul amid the faithless multitude,
He lived, and fought with life, and held his own;
Knew poverty, and shame which is not shown,
Pride, doubt, and secret heart-despair of good,
Insolent praise of men and petty feud:
Yet fell not from his purpose, framed and known.
For, as a lonely watcher of the night,
When all men sleep, sees the tumultuous stars
Move forward from the deep in squadrons bright,
And notes them, he through this life's prison bars
Heard all night long the spheric music clear
Beat on his heart—and lived that men might hear.

CARLYLE AND EMERSON

MONTGOMERY SCHUYLER

A balefire kindled in the night,
By night a blaze, by day a cloud,
With flame and smoke all England woke—
It climbed so high, it roared so loud:

While over Massachusetts' pines
Uprose a white and steadfast star;
And many a night it hung unwatched—
It shone so still, it seemed so far.

But light is fire, and fire is light;
And mariners are glad for these—
The torch that flares along the coast,
The star that beams above the seas.

CRAWFORD LONG AND WILLIAM MORTON

ROSEMARY AND STEPHEN VINCENT BENÉT

"*Oh, whet your saws and shine your knives,*
Ye surgeons, tried and true!
We're going for to operate
In eighteen-forty-two!

"*And, if the patient starts to yell*
And bounce about the floor,
Just tell him Pain is bound to be,
And give him one chop more!"

A doctor down in Georgia,
His name was Crawford Long,
Began to wonder, more or less,
About this little song.

"The words," he said, "are elegant.
I like the gay refrain.
But, mightn't there be something in
Abolishing the pain?"

And, up in windy Boston town,
A dentist, bold but kind,
Named William Morton, felt the same
Idea tease his mind.

They didn't know each other from
An inlay or a pill,
But both found out, without a doubt,
That ether filled the bill.

For once a man's anesthetized
And ether's work begins,
You'll sleep without an ouch, although
They stick you full of pins.

To Long belongs priority
In this historic boon,
But Morton was the man who made
The surgeons change their tune.

At Massachusetts General
He showed it to the nation.
—And everybody gaped to see
A painless operation.

For Man had suffered and endured
And Man had racked his brain.
But, till those two, no creature knew
The knife without the pain.

LINCOLN, THE MAN OF THE PEOPLE

EDWIN MARKHAM

When the Norn Mother saw the Whirlwind Hour
Greatening and darkening as it hurried on,
She left the Heaven of Heroes and came down
To make a man to meet the mortal need,
She took the tried clay of the common road—
Clay warm yet with the genial heat of Earth,
Dashed through it all a strain of prophecy,
Tempered the heap with thrill of human tears,
Then mixed a laughter with the serious stuff.
Into the shape she breathed a flame to light
That tender, tragic, ever-changing face;
And laid on him a sense of the Mystic Powers,
Moving—all hushed—behind the mortal veil.
Here was a man to hold against the world,
A man to match the mountains and the sea.

The color of the ground was in him, the red earth,
The smack and tang of elemental things:
The rectitude and patience of the cliff,
The good will of the rain that loves all leaves,
The friendly welcome of the wayside well,
The courage of the bird that dares the sea,
The gladness of the wind that shakes the corn,
The pity of the snow that hides all scars,
The secrecy of streams that make their way
Under the mountain to the rifted rock,
The tolerance and equity of light
That gives as freely to the shrinking flower

As to the great oak flaring to the wind—
To the grave's low hill as to the Matterhorn
That shoulders out the sky. Sprung from the West,
He drank the valorous youth of a new world.
The strength of virgin forests braced his mind,
The hush of spacious prairies stilled his soul.

Up from log cabin to the Capitol,
One fire was on his spirit, one resolve—
To send the keen ax to the root of wrong,
Clearing a free way for the feet of God,
The eyes of conscience testing every stroke,
To make his deed the measure of a man.
He built the rail pile as he built the State,
Pouring his splendid strength through every blow:
The grip that swung the ax in Illinois
Was on the pen that set a people free.

So came the Captain with the mighty heart;
And when the judgment thunders split the house,
Wrenching the rafters from their ancient rest,
He held the ridgepole up, and spiked again
The rafters of the Home. He held his place—
Held the long purpose like a growing tree—
Held on through blame and faltered not at praise—
Towering in calm rough-hewn sublimity.
And when he fell in whirlwind, he went down
As when a lordly cedar, green with boughs,
Goes down with a great shout upon the hills,
And leaves a lonesome place against the sky.

WILBUR WRIGHT AND ORVILLE WRIGHT

ROSEMARY AND STEPHEN VINCENT BENÉT

Said Orville Wright to Wilbur Wright,
  "These birds are very trying.
I'm sick of hearing them cheep-cheep
  About the fun of flying.
A bird has feathers, it is true.
  That much I freely grant.
But, must that stop us, W?"
  Said Wilbur Wright, "It shan't."

And so they built a glider, first,
  And then they built another.
—There never were two brothers more
  Devoted to each other.
They ran a dusty little shop
  For bicycle repairing,
And bought each other soda pop
  And praised each other's daring.

They glided here, they glided there,
  They sometimes skinned their noses.
—For learning how to rule the air
  Was not a bed of roses—
But each would murmur, afterward,
  While patching up his bro,
"Are we discouraged, W?"
  "Of course we are not, O!"

And finally, at Kitty Hawk
  In nineteen-three (let's cheer it!),
The first real airplane really flew
  With Orville there to steer it!
—And kingdoms may forget their kings
  And dogs forget their bites,
But, not till Man forgets his wings,
  Will men forget the Wrights.

A MODERN COLUMBUS

ELEANOR ROBBINS WILSON

Favored was he as that great Genoese
Given the golden dream to read aright
Of a fair land still hidden from his sight
By the vast wilderness of untried seas;
And so, his iron purpose braved the breeze,
On, on, beyond the harbor's faintest light
To wrest new secrets from the lingering Night
And hail with joy a dream's realities.
Thus Edison went on an untracked way
Toward luring vision that illumed his mind—
The riches of the great electric world;
There like Columbus on a deathless day,
He, too, has dowered lives of all mankind,
And conquering, a victor's flag unfurled.

LOVE

Divine is Love and scorneth worldly pelf,
And can be bought with nothing but with self.

—SIR WALTER RALEIGH

WHEN I PERUSE THE CONQUERED FAME

WALT WHITMAN

When I peruse the conquered fame of heroes and the victories of mighty generals, I do not envy the generals,
Nor the President in his Presidency, nor the rich in his great house,
But when I hear of the brotherhood of lovers, how it was with them,
How together through life, through dangers, odium, unchanging, long and long,
Through youth and through middle and old age, how unfaltering, how affectionate and faithful they were,
Then I am pensive—I hastily walk away filled with the bitterest envy.

SONG

FLORENCE EARLE COATES

For me the jasmine buds unfold
  And silver daisies star the lea,
The crocus hoards the sunset gold,
  And the wild rose breathes for me.
I feel the sap through the bough returning,
  I share the skylark's transport fine,
I know the fountain's wayward yearning,
  I love, and the world is mine!

I love, and thoughts that sometimes grieved,
  Still well remembered, grieve not me;
From all that darkened and deceived
  Upsoars my spirit free.
For soft the hours repeat one story,
  Sings the sea one strain divine;
My clouds arise all flushed with glory—
  I love, and the world is mine!

ALL FOR LOVE

LORD BYRON

Oh, talk not to me of a name great in story;
The days of our youth are the days of our glory.
And the myrtle and ivy of sweet two-and-twenty
Are worth all your laurels, though ever so plenty.

What are garlands and crowns to the brow that is wrinkled?
'Tis but as a dead flower with May dew besprinkled.
Then away with all such from the head that is hoary!
What care I for the wreaths that can *only* give glory?

O Fame!—if I e'er took delight in thy praises,
'Twas less for the sake of thy high-sounding phrases
Than to see the bright eyes of the dear one discover
She thought that I was not unworthy to love her.

There chiefly I sought thee, *there* only I found thee;
Her glance was the best of the rays that surround thee.
When it sparkled o'er aught that was bright in my story,
knew it was love, and I felt it was glory.

LOVE IN THE WINDS

RICHARD HOVEY

When I am standing on a mountain crest,
Or hold the tiller in the dashing spray,
My love of you leaps foaming in my breast,
Shouts with the winds and sweeps to their foray;
My heart bounds with the horses of the sea,
And plunges in the wild ride of the night,
Flaunts in the teeth of tempest the large glee
That rides out Fate and welcomes gods to fight.
Ho, Love, I laugh aloud for love of you,
Glad that our love is fellow to rough weather—
No fretful orchid hothoused from the dew,
But hale and hardy as the highland heather,
Rejoicing in the wind that stings and thrills,
Comrade of ocean, playmate of the hills.

INTERLUDE

Holger Lundbergh

The trees are humming a lazy song,
  The sky is an azure pall,
The wind is fragrant, the sun is strong,
  And joyous the blue jay's call.

My heart is emptied of doubt and fear,
  Content, and utterly gay,
My thoughts, like water, are cool and clear,
  For you, my love, are away.

SONG

Dana Burnet

Love's on the highroad,
Love's in the byroad—
  Love's on the meadow, and Love's in the mart!
And down every byway
Where I've taken my way
  I've met Love a-smiling—for Love's in my heart!

MUSIC I HEARD WITH YOU

Conrad Aiken

Music I heard with you was more than music,
And bread I broke with you was more than bread;
Now that I am without you, all is desolate;
All that was once so beautiful is dead.

Your hands once touched this table and this silver,
And I have seen your fingers hold this glass.
These things do not remember you, beloved—
And yet your touch upon them will not pass.

For it was in my heart you moved among them,
And blessed them with your hands and with your eyes;
And in my heart they will remember always—
They knew you once, O beautiful and wise.

TO MY WIFE

William Rose Benét

Braver than sea-going ships with the dawn in their
sails,
Than the wind before dawn more healing and fragrant
and free,
Fairer than sight of a city all white, from the mountaintop
viewed in the vales,
Or the silver-bright flakes of the moonlight in lakes,
when the moon rides the clouds and the forest awakes,
You are to me!

For you are to me what the bowstring is to the shaft,
Speeding my purpose aloft and aflame and afar.
Through the thick of the fight, in your eyes' steady light
my soul hath seen splendor, and laughed.
Now, however I tend betwixt foeman and friend through
the riddle of Life to Death's light at the end,
I ride for your star!

SUMMER EVENING

SARA HENDERSON HAY

You said, "A sound can never die, you know—
Don't you remember learning that in school?
How the small echoes circle out, as though
You'd flung a stone into a quiet pool
And watched the dreaming surface wake, and fill
With little ripples, widening more and more,
Spreading across in silver arcs, until
They lapped the edges of the farthest shore?"
I thought—How strange, the drowsy droning flight
Of crickets, or the sleepy sound of birds,
A casual footfall, echoing faint and far,
All the incredibly symphonic night
Commingling with your voice, and three small words
Brushing the fringes of some distant star!

TO HIS LOVE

WILLIAM SHAKESPEARE

Shall I compare thee to a summer's day?
Thou art more lovely and more temperate.
Rough winds do shake the darling buds of May,
And summer's lease hath all too short a date.
Sometimes too hot the eye of heaven shines,
And often is his gold complexion dimmed;
And every fair from fair sometime declines,
By chance, or nature's changing course, untrimmed.
But thy eternal summer shall not fade
Nor lose possession of that fair thou owest;
Nor shall Death brag thou wanderest in his shade,
When in eternal lines to time thou growest.
So long as men can breathe, or eyes can see,
So long lives this, and this gives life to thee.

A CONSOLATION

WILLIAM SHAKESPEARE

When in disgrace with fortune and men's eyes
I all alone beweep my outcast state,
And trouble deaf heaven with my bootless cries,
And look upon myself, and curse my fate,
Wishing me like to one more rich in hope,
Featured like him, like him with friends possessed,
Desiring this man's art, and that man's scope,
With what I most enjoy contented least;
Yet in these thoughts myself almost despising,
Haply I think on thee—and then my state
Like to the lark at break of day arising
From sullen earth sings hymns at heaven's gate;
For thy sweet love remembered, such wealth brings
That then I scorn to change my state with kings.

THAT TIME OF YEAR

WILLIAM SHAKESPEARE

That time of year thou may'st in me behold
When yellow leaves, or none, or few do hang
Upon those boughs which shake against the cold,
Bare ruined choirs, where late the sweet birds sang.
In me thou see'st the twilight of such day
As after sunset fadeth in the west,
Which by and by black night doth take away,
Death's second self, that seals up all in rest.
In me thou see'st the glowing of such fire
That on the ashes of his youth doth lie
As the deathbed whereon it must expire,
Consumed with that which it was nourished by—
This thou perceiv'st, which makes thy love more strong
To love that well which thou must leave ere long.

JEAN

ROBERT BURNS

O' a' the airts the wind can blaw
  I dearly lo'e the west,
For there the bonnie lassie lives,
  The lassie I lo'e best.
There wildwoods grow, and rivers row,
  And mony a hill between;
But day and night my fancy's flight
  Is ever wi' my Jean.

I see her in the dewy flowers;
  I see her sweet and fair;
I hear her in the tunefu' birds;
  I hear her charm the air.
There's not a bonnie flower that springs
  By fountain, shaw, or green;
There's not a bonnie bird that sings,
  But minds me o' my Jean.

JOHN ANDERSON MY JO

ROBERT BURNS

John Anderson my jo, John,
  When we were first acquent,
Your locks were like the raven,
  Your bonnie brow was brent.
But now your brow is beld, John;
  Your locks are like the snaw;
But blessings on your frosty pow,
  John Anderson my jo.

John Anderson my jo, John,
  We clamb the hill thegither;
And mony a canty day, John,
  We've had wi' ane anither.
Now we maun totter down, John,
  But hand in hand we'll go,
And sleep thegither at the foot,
  John Anderson my jo.

A RED, RED ROSE

ROBERT BURNS

My love is like a red, red rose
  That's newly sprung in June;
My love is like the melody
  That's sweetly played in tune—

As fair art thou, my bonnie lass,
  So deep in love am I;
And I will love thee still, my dear,
  Till a' the seas gang dry—

Till a' the seas gang dry, my dear,
  And the rocks melt wi' the sun;
And I will love thee still, my dear,
  While the sands o' life shall run.

And fare thee weel, my only love!
  And fare thee weel awhile;
And I will come again, my love,
  Though it were ten thousand mile.

HOW DO I LOVE THEE?

ELIZABETH BARRETT BROWNING

How do I love thee? Let me count the ways.
I love thee to the depth and breadth and height
My soul can reach, when feeling out of sight
For the ends of being and ideal grace.
I love thee to the level of every day's
Most quiet need, by sun and candlelight.
I love thee freely, as men strive for right;
I love thee purely, as they turn from praise.
I love thee with the passion put to use
In my old griefs, and with my childhood's faith.
I love thee with a love I seemed to lose
With my lost saints—I love thee with the breath,
Smiles, tears, of all my life!—and, if God choose,
I shall but love thee better after death.

WHY SO PALE AND WAN?

JOHN SUCKLING

Why so pale and wan, fond lover?
  Prithee, why so pale?
Will, when looking well can't move her,
  Looking ill prevail?
  Prithee, why so pale?

Why so dull and mute, young sinner?
  Prithee, why so mute?
Will, when speaking well can't win her,
  Saying nothing do't?
  Prithee, why so mute?

Quit, quit for shame! This will not move,
  This cannot take her.
If of herself she will not love,
  Nothing can make her—
  The devil take her!

THE CONSTANT LOVER

JOHN SUCKLING

Out upon it, I have loved
  Three whole days together;
And am like to love three more,
  If it prove fair weather.

Time shall molt away his wings
  Ere he shall discover
In the whole wide world again
  Such a constant lover.

But the spite on't is, no praise
  Is due at all to me.
Love with me had made no stays
  Had it any been but she.

Had it any been but she,
  And that very face,
There had been at least ere this
  A dozen dozen in her place.

DUNCAN GRAY

ROBERT BURNS

Duncan Gray cam' here to woo,
  Ha, ha, the wooin' o't,
On blithe Yule night when we were fou,
  Ha, ha, the wooin' o't.
Maggie coost her head fu' high,
Looked asklent an' unco skeigh,
Gart poor Duncan stand abeigh,
  Ha, ha, the wooin' o't.

Duncan fleeched, an' Duncan prayed,
  Ha, ha, the wooin' o't;
Meg was deaf as Ailsa Craig,
  Ha, ha, the wooin' o't.
Duncan sighed baith out and in,
Grat his e'en baith bleart an' blin,
Spak o' lowpin' ower a linn,
  Ha, ha, the wooin' o't.

Time an' chance are but a tide,
  Ha, ha, the wooin' o't;
Slighted love is sair to bide,
  Ha, ha, the wooin' o't.
"Shall I, like a fool," quoth he,
"For a haughty hizzie die?
She may gae to—France for me!"
  Ha, ha, the wooin' o't.

How it comes let doctors tell,
  Ha, ha the wooin' o't;
Meg grew sick—as he grew hale,
  Ha, ha, the wooin' o't.
Something in her bosom wrings,
For relief a sigh she brings,
An' oh, her e'en, they spak sic things!
  Ha, ha, the wooin' o't.

Duncan was a lad o' grace,
  Ha, ha, the wooin' o't;
Maggie's was a piteous case,
  Ha, ha, the wooin' o't.
Duncan could na be her death;
Swelling pity smoored his wrath;
Now they're crouse an' canty baith,
  Ha, ha, the wooin' o't.

PRETENSE

HELEN WELSHIMER

Tomorrow when I go to shop,
I'll buy a painted mask,
The brightest one on any shelf;
And then when people ask

Where have you gone, I'll be so gay
No one will ever guess
That now and then I catch my breath
In sudden loneliness.

And heads will nod, and lips will say,
Once you were out of sight,
Forgetting was an easy thing. . . .
And I'll pretend they're right.

HUMMINGBIRD

VIOLET ALLEYN STOREY

"Be like the hummingbird," they said,
"And drift from flower to flower.
Just see how many blooms he seeks
All in a summer hour!"
They meant—to put it into prose—
"Don't care so much for one
When, oh, there are so many folk
Under the summer sun!"
I went to watch the hummingbird.
How unobservant, they!
He fanned a sprig of heliotrope
Along his petaled way;
He fluttered round delphinium;
He hummed above a pink;
And then he found the salvia,
And then—what do you think?—
He stooped and kissed that crimson flower,
And stayed and stayed and stayed!
I can't do less with one I love;
I can't, I am afraid!

THE BANKS O' DOON

ROBERT BURNS

Ye banks and braes o' bonnie Doon,
  How can ye bloom sae fresh and fair?
How can ye chant, ye little birds,
  And I sae weary, fu' o' care?
Thou'lt break my heart, thou warbling bird
  That wantons through the flowering thorn;
Thou minds me o' departed joys,
  Departed—never to return.

Aft hae I roved by bonnie Doon
  To see the rose and woodbine twine;
And ilka bird sang o' its love,
  And fondly sae did I o' mine.
Wi' lightsome heart I pu'd a rose
  Fu' sweet upon its thorny tree;
And my fause lover staw my rose,
  But ah! he left the thorn wi' me.

THE OUTDOORS

For many years I was self-appointed inspector of snowstorms and rainstorms, and did my duty faithfully.

—HENRY DAVID THOREAU

From

SPRING

RICHARD HOVEY

I said in my heart, "I am sick of four walls and a ceiling.
I have need of the sky.
I have business with the grass.
I will up and get me away where the hawk is wheeling,
Lone and high,
And the slow clouds go by.
I will get me away to the waters that glass
The clouds as they pass,
To the waters that lie
Like the heart of a maiden aware of a doom drawing nigh
And dumb for sorcery of impending joy.
I will get me away to the woods.
Spring, like a huntsman's boy,
Halloos along the hillsides and unhoods
The falcon in my will.
The dogwood calls me, and the sudden thrill
That breaks in apple blooms down country roads
Plucks me by the sleeve and nudges me away.
The sap is in the boles today,
And in my veins a pulse that yearns and goads."

When I got to the woods, I found out
What the Spring was about,
With her gypsy ways
And her heart ablaze,
Coming up from the south
With the wander-lure of witch songs in her mouth.

For the sky
Stirred and grew soft and swimming as a lover's eye
As she went by;
The air
Made love to all it touched, as if its care
Were all to spare;
The earth
Prickled with lust of birth;
The woodland streams
Babbled the incoherence of the thousand dreams
Wherewith the warm sun teems.
And out of the frieze
Of the chestnut trees
I heard
The sky and the fields and the thicket find voice in a bird.
The goldenwing—hark!
How he drives his song
Like a golden nail
Through the hush of the air!
I thrill to his cry in the leafage there;
I respond to the new life mounting under the bark.
I shall not be long
To follow
With eft and bulrush, bee and bud and swallow,
On the old trail.

HERESY FOR A CLASSROOM

Rolfe Humphries

Green willows are for girls to study under
When that green lady, Spring, walks down the street:
Look out the windows, Jean, look out and wonder
About their unseen earth-embedded feet.
Under the dark uncolored moldy clay
Where willow roots are thrust, their life is drawn
Up through the limbs, to burst in bud and sway
Slow-shaken green festoons above the lawn.
So never doubt that gloom turns into light
As winter into April, or as bloom
Breaks on the barren branches overnight.—
Little enough is learned in any room
With blackboard walls, on afternoons like these—
O Jean, look out the window at the trees!

I MEANT TO DO MY WORK TODAY

Richard Le Gallienne

I meant to do my work today—
  But a brown bird sang in the apple tree,
And a butterfly flitted across the field,
  And all the leaves were calling me.

And the wind went sighing over the land,
  Tossing the grasses to and fro,
And a rainbow held out its shining hand—
  So what could I do but laugh and go?

A BALLADE OF SPRING'S UNREST

Bert Leston Taylor

Up in the woodland where Spring
Comes as a laggard, the breeze
Whispers the pines that the King,
Fallen, has yielded the keys
To his White Palace and flees
Northward o'er mountain and dale.
Speed then the hour that frees!
Ho, for the pack and the trail!

Northward my fancy takes wing,
Restless am I, ill at ease.
Pleasures the city can bring
Lose now their power to please.
Barren, all barren, are these,
Town life's a tedious tale;
That cup is drained to the lees—
Ho, for the pack and the trail!

Ho, for the morning I sling
Pack at my back, and with knees
Brushing a thoroughfare, fling
Into the green mysteries:
One with the birds and the bees,
One with the squirrel and quail,
Night, and the stream's melodies—
Ho, for the pack and the trail!

ENVOY

Pictures and music and teas,
Theaters—books even—stale.
Ho, for the smell of the trees!
Ho, for the pack and the trail!

UP! UP! MY FRIEND, AND QUIT YOUR BOOKS

William Wordsworth

Up! up! my friend, and quit your books,
  Or surely you'll grow double;
Up! up! my friend, and clear your looks—
  Why all this toil and trouble?

The sun, above the mountain's head,
  A freshening luster mellow
Through all the long, green fields has spread
  His first sweet evening yellow.

Books! 'tis a dull and endless strife—
  Come, hear the woodland linnet;
How sweet his music! on my life,
  There's more of wisdom in it.

And hark! how blithe the throstle sings!
  He, too, is no mean preacher.
Come forth into the light of things;
  Let Nature be your teacher.

She has a world of ready wealth
  Our minds and hearts to bless—
Spontaneous wisdom breathed by health,
  Truth breathed by cheerfulness.

One impulse from a vernal wood
  May teach you more of man,
Of moral evil and of good,
  Than all the sages can.

Sweet is the lore which Nature brings;
  Our meddling intellect
Misshapes the beauteous forms of things—
  We murder to dissect.

Enough of science and of art;
  Close up those barren leaves;
Come forth, and bring with you a heart
  That watches and receives.

THE MOUNTAINS ARE A LONELY FOLK

HAMLIN GARLAND

The mountains they are silent folk,
  They stand afar—alone,
And the clouds that kiss their brows at night
  Hear neither sigh nor groan.
Each bears him in his ordered place
  As soldiers do, and bold and high
They fold their forests round their feet
  And bolster up the sky.

HILLS

ARTHUR GUITERMAN

I never loved your plains!—
  Your gentle valleys,
Your drowsy country lanes
  And pleachèd alleys.

I want my hills!—the trail
  That scorns the hollow.
Up, up the ragged shale
  Where few will follow,

Up, over wooded crest
  And mossy boulder
With strong thigh, heaving chest,
  And swinging shoulder,

So let me hold my way,
  By nothing halted,
Until, at close of day,
  I stand, exalted,

High on my hills of dream—
  Dear hills that know me!
And then, how fair will seem
  The lands below me,

How pure, at vesper time,
  The far bells chiming!
God, give me hills to climb,
  And strength for climbing!

THE JOY OF THE HILLS

EDWIN MARKHAM

I ride on the mountain tops, I ride;
I have found my life and am satisfied.
Onward I ride in the blowing oats,
Checking the field lark's rippling notes—
   Lightly I sweep
   From steep to steep:
Over my head through the branches high
Come glimpses of a rushing sky;
The tall oats brush my horse's flanks;
Wild poppies crowd on the sunny banks;
A bee booms out of the scented grass;
A jay laughs with me as I pass.

I ride on the hills, I forgive, I forget
Life's hoard of regret—
   All the terror and pain
   Of the chafing chain.
   Grind on, O cities, grind:
   I leave you a blur behind.
I am lifted elate—the skies expand:
Here the world's heaped gold is a pile of sand.
Let them weary and work in their narrow walls:
I ride with the voices of waterfalls!

I swing on as one in a dream—I swing
Down the airy hollows; I shout, I sing!
The world is gone like an empty word:
My body's a bough in the wind, my heart a bird!

TREES

JOYCE KILMER

I think that I shall never see
A poem lovely as a tree.

A tree whose hungry mouth is pressed
Against the earth's sweet flowing breast;

A tree that looks at God all day,
And lifts her leafy arms to pray;

A tree that may in summer wear
A nest of robins in her hair;

Upon whose bosom snow has lain;
Who intimately lives with rain.

Poems are made by fools like me,
But only God can make a tree.

PINES

ANDERSON M. SCRUGGS

These are the trees for hill folk—men that toil
On cabined slopes, men on whose weathered faces
Is carved the story of the flinty soil,
Whose speech is stark like pines in rocky places.
Crowning gaunt hills, where rows of ragged corn
Wrench from earth's scrawny breast the season's yield,
There you will find the pines—tall kings that scorn
The soft, rich lowland and the fertile field.
There are no stancher friends of man on earth
Than these bleak pines whose rugged, stoic arms
Lift up no leaf to greet the summer's mirth,
Who stand unmoved by winter's dark alarms.
Steadfast through all the years, in sun and snow,
It is not strange that hill folk love them so.

STREAMS

CLINTON SCOLLARD

I so love water laughter,
  Its bubbling flecks and gleams,
I pray in the hereafter
  There somewhere may be streams.

I'd have for my companion
  In some celestial nook,
Beneath a spreading banyan,
  The music of a brook.

Its measures would entice me,
  Uncumbered by the clay,
Its melody suffice me
  Till drooped the heavenly day.

Then its all-liquid laughter
  Would murmur through my dreams;
I pray in the hereafter
  There somewhere may be streams.

THE MARSHES OF GLYNN

SIDNEY LANIER

Glooms of the live oaks, beautiful-braided and woven
With intricate shades of the vines that myriad-cloven
Clamber the forks of the multiform boughs—
    Emerald twilights—
    Virginal shy lights,
Wrought of the leaves to allure to the whisper of vows,
When lovers pace timidly down through the green colonnades
Of the dim sweet woods, of the dear dark woods,
Of the heavenly woods and glades,
That run to the radiant marginal sand beach within
The wide sea marshes of Glynn;—

Beautiful glooms, soft dusks in the noonday fire—
Wildwood privacies, closets of lone desire,
Chamber from chamber parted with wavering arras of leaves—
Cells for the passionate pleasure of prayer to the soul that grieves,
Pure with the sense of the passing of saints through the wood,
Cool for the dutiful weighing of ill with good;—

O braided dusks of the oak and woven shades of the vine,
While the riotous noonday sun of the June day long did shine
Ye held me fast in your heart and I held you fast in mine;
But now when the noon is no more, and the riot is rest,
And the sun is await at the ponderous gate of the West,

And the slant yellow beam down the wood aisle doth seem
Like a lane into heaven that leads from a dream—
Ay, now, when my soul all day hath drunken the soul of the oak,
And my heart is at ease from men, and the wearisome sound of the stroke
Of the scythe of time and the trowel of trade is low,
And belief overmasters doubt, and I know that I know,
And my spirit is grown to a lordly great compass within,
That the length and the breadth and the sweep of the marshes of Glynn
Will work me no fear like the fear they have wrought me of yore
When length was fatigue, and when breadth was but bitterness sore,
And when terror and shrinking and dreary unnamable pain
Drew over me out of the merciless miles of the plain—

Oh, now, unafraid, I am fain to face
The vast sweet visage of space.
To the edge of the wood I am drawn, I am drawn,
Where the gray beach glimmering runs, as a belt of the dawn,
    For a mete and a mark
    To the forest-dark:—
    So:
    Affable live oak, leaning low,
Thus—with your favor—soft, with a reverent hand
(Not lightly touching your person, Lord of the land!)

Bending your beauty aside, with a step I stand
On the firm-packed sand,
    Free
By a world of marsh that borders a world of sea.
Sinuous southward and sinuous northward the shimmering band
Of the sand beach fastens the fringe of the marsh to the folds of the land.
Inward and outward to northward and southward the beach lines linger and curl
As a silver-wrought garment that clings to and follows the firm sweet limbs of a girl.
Vanishing, swerving, evermore curving again into sight,
Softly the sand beach wavers away to a dim gray looping of light.
And what if behind me to westward the wall of the woods stands high?
The world lies east: how ample, the marsh and the sea and the sky!
A league and a league of marsh grass, waist-high, broad in the blade,
Green, and all of a height, and unflecked with a light or a shade,
Stretch leisurely off, in a pleasant plain,
To the terminal blue of the main.

Oh, what is abroad in the marsh and the terminal sea?
Somehow my soul seems suddenly free
From the weighing of fate and the sad discussion of sin,
By the length and the breadth and the sweep of the marshes of Glynn.

Ye marshes, how candid and simple and nothing-withholding and free
Ye publish yourselves to the sky and offer yourselves to the sea!
Tolerant plains, that suffer the sea and the rains and the sun,
Ye spread and span like the catholic man who hath mightily won
God out of knowledge and good out of infinite pain
And sight out of blindness and purity out of a stain.

As the marsh hen secretly builds on the watery sod,
Behold I will build me a nest on the greatness of God:
I will fly in the greatness of God as the marsh hen flies
In the freedom that fills all the space 'twixt the marsh and the skies:
By so many roots as the marsh grass sends in the sod
I will heartily lay me a-hold on the greatness of God:
Oh, like to the greatness of God is the greatness within
The range of the marshes, the liberal marshes of Glynn.

And the sea lends large, as the marsh: lo, out of his plenty the sea
Pours fast: full soon the time of the flood tide must be:
Look how the grace of the sea doth go
About and about through the intricate channels that flow
    Here and there,
    Everywhere,
Till his waters have flooded the uttermost creeks and the low-lying lanes,
And the marsh is meshed with a million veins,

That like as with rosy and silvery essences flow
In the rose and silver evening glow.
Farewell, my lord Sun!
The creeks overflow: a thousand rivulets run
'Twixt the roots of the sod; the blades of the marsh grass
  stir;
Passeth a hurrying sound of wings that westward whir;
Passeth, and all is still; and the currents cease to run;
And the sea and the marsh are one.

How still the plains of the waters be!
The tide is in his ecstasy.
The tide is at his highest height:
And it is night.

And now from the Vast of the Lord will the waters of sleep
Roll in on the souls of men,
But who will reveal to our waking ken
The forms that swim and the shapes that creep
Under the waters of sleep?
And I would I could know what swimmeth below when the
  tide comes in
On the length and the breadth of the marvelous marshes of
  Glynn.

WHEN THE FROST IS ON THE PUNKIN

JAMES WHITCOMB RILEY

When the frost is on the punkin and the fodder's in the shock,
And you hear the kyouck and gobble of the struttin' turkey-cock,
And the clackin' of the guineys, and the cluckin' of the hens,
And the rooster's hallylooyer as he tiptoes on the fence;
Oh, it's then's the times a feller is a-feelin' at his best,
With the risin' sun to greet him from a night of peaceful rest,
As he leaves the house, bareheaded, and goes out to feed the stock,
When the frost is on the punkin and the fodder's in the shock.

They's something kind o' harty-like about the atmusfere
When the heat of summer's over and the coolin' fall is here—
Of course we miss the flowers, and the blossoms on the trees,
And the mumble of the hummin'birds and buzzin' of the bees;
But the air's so appetizin'; and the landscape through the haze
Of a crisp and sunny morning of the airly autumn days
Is a pictur' that no painter has the colorin' to mock—
When the frost is on the punkin and the fodder's in the shock

The husky, rusty russel of the tossels of the corn,
And the raspin' of the tangled leaves, as golden as the morn
The stubble in the furries—kind o' lonesome-like, but still
A-preachin' sermuns to us of the barns they growed to fill

The strawstack in the medder, and the reaper in the shed;
The hosses in theyr stalls below—the clover overhead!—
Oh, it sets my hart a-clickin' like the tickin' of a clock,
When the frost is on the punkin and the fodder's in the shock!

Then your apples all is gether'd, and the ones a feller keeps
Is poured around the celler floor in red and yeller heaps;
And your cider-makin's over, and your wimmern-folks is through
With theyr mince and apple butter, and theyr souse and saussage too! . . .
 don't know how to tell it—but ef sich a thing could be
As the Angels wantin' boardin', and they'd call around on *me*—
'd want to 'commodate 'em—all the whole indurin' flock—
When the frost is on the punkin and the fodder's in the shock!

DAYS LIKE THESE

ELLA ELIZABETH EGBERT

I like the tangled brakes and briers,
The hazy smoke of forest fires;

The misty hills' soft robe of brown,
The ravished fields' regretful frown;

The wrinkled road's unconscious snare,
The free, unbreathed and fragrant air.

I like the wide, unworried sky,
The resting wind's contented sigh;

The rustle of the vagrant leaves,
The whisper in the standing sheaves;

The birds' lament for summer lost,
The stinging challenge of the frost.

The sturdy life of stalwart trees
Thrills in my veins on days like these!

A VAGABOND SONG

Bliss Carman

There is something in the autumn that is native to my
  blood—
Touch of manner, hint of mood;
And my heart is like a rhyme,
With the yellow and the purple and the crimson keeping
  time.

The scarlet of the maples can shake me like a cry
Of bugles going by.
And my lonely spirit thrills
To see the frosty asters like a smoke upon the hills.

There is something in October sets the gypsy blood astir;
We must rise and follow her,
When from every hill of flame
She calls and calls each vagabond by name.

DO YOU FEAR THE FORCE OF THE WIND?

HAMLIN GARLAND

Do you fear the force of the wind,
The slash of the rain?
Go face them and fight them,
Be savage again.
Go hungry and cold like the wolf,
Go wade like the crane:
The palms of your hands will thicken,
The skin of your cheek will tan,
You'll grow rugged and weary and swarthy,
But you'll walk like a man!

CHALLENGE

John Drinkwater

You fools behind the panes who peer
At the strong black anger of the sky,
Come out and feel the storm swing by,
Aye, take its blow on your lips, and hear
The wind in the branches cry.

No. Leave us to the day's device,
Draw to your blinds and take your ease,
Grow peak'd in the face and crook'd in the knees;
Your sinews could not pay the price
When the storm goes through the trees.

THERE IS SHRILL MUSIC IN HIGH WINDS AT NIGHT

JESSE STUART

There is shrill music in high winds at night
That break dead limbs and shake the pine-tree cones.
And it is life to walk in gray starlight
And hear winds snap the dead brush like dead bones;
To slip through brush and let one's footsteps fall;
Lighter than autumn rain falls on dead leaves,
Slier than snakes that writhe close to the earth,
Quieter than dead leaves falling from the trees.
Shrill music that sinks to the heart and bone
And buries in the blood and brain and flesh.
Such night as this was made for man alone;
The stars and wind and pine-tree cones and brush;
Alone for him to worship gods and trees,
And hear the music of the wind and trees.

ODE TO THE WEST WIND

PERCY BYSSHE SHELLEY

O wild West Wind, thou breath of autumn's being,
Thou, from whose unseen presence the leaves dead
Are driven, like ghosts from an enchanter fleeing,
Yellow, and black, and pale, and hectic red,
Pestilence-stricken multitudes; O thou
Who chariotest to their dark wintry bed
The wingèd seeds, where they lie cold and low,
Each like a corpse within its grave, until
Thine azure sister of the spring shall blow
Her clarion o'er the dreaming earth, and fill
(Driving sweet buds like flocks to feed in air)
With living hues and odors plain and hill;
Wild Spirit, which art moving everywhere,
Destroyer and Preserver: Hear, oh, hear!

Thou on whose stream, 'mid the steep sky's commotion,
Loose clouds like earth's decaying leaves are shed,
Shook from the tangled boughs of heaven and ocean,
Angels of rain and lightning! there are spread
On the blue surface of thine airy surge,
Like the bright hair uplifted from the head
Of some fierce Maenad, even from the dim verge
Of the horizon to the zenith's height
The locks of the approaching storm; thou dirge
Of the dying year, to which this closing night
Will be the dome of a vast sepulcher
Vaulted with all thy congregated might
Of vapors from whose solid atmosphere
Black rain, and fire, and hail, will burst: Oh, hear!

Thou who didst waken from his summer dreams
The blue Mediterranean, where he lay
Lulled by the coil of his crystalline streams
Beside a pumice isle in Baiae's bay,
And saw in sleep old palaces and towers
Quivering within the wave's intenser day,
All overgrown with azure moss and flowers
So sweet the sense faints picturing them; thou
For whose path the Atlantic's level powers
Cleave themselves into chasms, while far below
The sea blooms and the oozy woods which wear
The sapless foliage of the ocean know
Thy voice and suddenly grow gray with fear
And tremble and despoil themselves: Oh, hear!

If I were a dead leaf thou mightest bear;
If I were a swift cloud to fly with thee,
A wave to pant beneath thy power and share
The impulse of thy strength, only less free
Than thou, O uncontrollable! if even
I were as in my boyhood and could be
The comrade of thy wanderings over heaven,
As then, when to outstrip thy skyey speed
Scarce seemed a vision, I would ne'er have striven
As thus with thee in prayer in my sore need.
Oh! lift me as a wave, a leaf, a cloud!
I fall upon the thorns of life! I bleed!
A heavy weight of hours has chained and bowed
One too like thee, tameless, and swift, and proud.

Make me thy lyre, even as the forest is.
What if my leaves are falling like its own!
The tumult of thy mighty harmonies
Will take from both a deep autumnal tone,
Sweet though in sadness. Be thou, Spirit fierce,
My spirit! be thou me, impetuous one!
Drive my dead thoughts over the universe,
Like withered leaves, to quicken a new birth;
And, by the incantation of this verse,
Scatter, as from an unextinguished hearth
Ashes and sparks, my words among mankind!
Be through my lips to the unawakened earth
The trumpet of a prophecy! O Wind,
If winter comes, can spring be far behind?

From

THE PRELUDE

WILLIAM WORDSWORTH

And in the frosty season when the sun
Was set, and visible for many a mile
The cottage windows blazed through twilight gloom,
I heeded not the summons. Happy time
It was indeed for all of us; for me
It was a time of rapture! Clear and loud
The village clock tolled six—I wheeled about,
Proud and exulting like an untired horse
That cares not for his home. All shod with steel
We hissed along the polished ice in games
Confederate, imitative of the chase
And woodland pleasures: the resounding horn,
The pack loud chiming, and the hunted hare.
So through the darkness and the cold we flew,
And not a voice was idle. With the din
Smitten the precipices rang aloud;
The leafless trees and every icy crag
Tinkled like iron; while far-distant hills
Into the tumult sent an alien sound
Of melancholy not unnoticed, while the stars
Eastward were sparkling clear, and in the west
The orange sky of evening died away.

THANKSGIVING

CHARLES HANSON TOWNE

Lord, life is good!
When the first crocus lifts its golden cup,
To drink the beauty up,
And the pink hyacinth smiles in its green bed,
And the long winter is dead,
Ah! life is good,
And even my poor, frail heart has understood.

Then, when the Maytime turns
To summer, and on every hill there burns
The loveliness that seems too great to bear:
Lush grass, ripe fruit, and the blue noons that stare
On earth and sea,
Suddenly comes to me
The wonder in this world; while over my house
Hang the green heavy boughs;
And under me starred meadows; and round about
Bees with their happy murmur, and the thin shout
Of insects speeding over broken walls.
Oh, how the glory falls!
Lord, life is good!

And life is good when autumn's tapestries
Hang on the walls of the hills,
And there is a tang in the breeze,
And a roar in the rills.
And when the first snow shakes the trembling boughs,
And makes the world a tremulous white house,

I lean to look with wonder, lest I miss
Some of the beauty, as the winter's delicate kiss
Touches the roadways with a lover's bliss.

Give thanks, O heart, O soul,
As the bright year doth roll
To a perfect end, like a perfect scroll.
Lord, life is good!

THE SPIRIT OF ADVENTURE

The day shall not be up so soon as I
To try the fair adventure of tomorrow.

—WILLIAM SHAKESPEARE

From

SONG OF THE OPEN ROAD

WALT WHITMAN

Afoot and lighthearted I take to the open road,
Healthy, free, the world before me,
The long brown path before me leading wherever I choose.

Henceforth I ask not good fortune, I myself am good fortune,
Henceforth I whimper no more, postpone no more, need nothing,
Done with indoor complaints, libraries, querulous criticisms,
Strong and content I travel the open road.

ROAD SONG

MARGARET E. SANGSTER

An open road and a wide road
That leads, at last, to the sea—
This is the meaning of summertime,
And the meaning of life, to me!

For I am weary of cities
When the sunlight slants from the west,
And I think of an ocean singing
To the little ships on her breast;
And I think of a road that beckons—
Beckons and lures and calls—
And I think of the dim horizon
When the shadow of nighttime falls!

Give me the dust of the highway
And a breeze that kisses my face—
For, oh, I am tired of hurry,
Of traffic and market place!
Give me a spring by the wayside,
Give me a tree for shade—
An open road and a wide road,
And a heart that is unafraid!

Give me the courage for tramping,
And a soul that bids me follow
The path that winds to the hilltop
After it leaves each hollow.
Give me a glimpse of ocean,
Blue as the gleam of truth—
Give me the urge to find a world
Before I have lost my youth!

An open road and a wide road—
And somewhere the far-flung sea!
This is the meaning of summertime,
And the meaning of life, to me.

ADVENTURE

T. W. Earp

In those great days adventure called
  And men rowed out to sea,
To find the city golden-walled,
  Where the sun's house might be.

Not knowing what their quest would bring,
  They urged their painted ships,
And drowned upon that wayfaring
  With laughter on their lips.

But now we keep the guarded town,
  Secure against surprise,
And watch the royal sun go down,
  With unadventurous eyes.

Hurl back the cautious words men say,
  Renew the ancient quest,
The path lies blue across the bay,
  Beyond, the flaming West!

Oh, come, while still the galley waits,
  Escape the languid hours,
Defy your comfortable fates,
  The prow is crowned with flowers,

The oar is hungry for the wave,
  The sail invites the breeze,
And gloriously the breakers rave
  Within uncharted seas!

It may be we shall sink and know
  Our quest superbly vain,
Or win where gates of sunset glow,
  Adventurers again.

SPANISH WATERS

JOHN MASEFIELD

Spanish waters, Spanish waters, you are ringing in my ears
Like a slow sweet piece of music from the gray forgotte
  years;
Telling tales, and beating tunes, and bringing wear
  thoughts to me
Of the sandy beach at Muertos, where I would that I coul
  be.

There's a surf breaks on Los Muertos, and it never stops t
  roar,
And it's there we came to anchor, and it's there we wen
  ashore,
Where the blue lagoon is silent amid snags of rotting trees
Dropping like the clothes of corpses cast up by the seas.

We anchored at Los Muertos when the dipping sun wa
  red,
We left her half-a-mile to sea, to west of Nigger Head;
And before the mist was on the Cay, before the day wa
  done,
We were ashore on Muertos with the gold that we had wor

We bore it through the marshes in a half-score battere
  chests,
Sinking, in the sucking quagmires, to the sunburn on ou
  breasts,
Heaving over tree trunks, gasping, damning at the flies an
  heat,
Longing for a long drink, out of silver, in the ship's coc
  lazareet.

The moon came white and ghostly as we laid the treasure down,
There was gear there'd make a beggarman as rich as Lima Town,
Copper charms and silver trinkets from the chests of Spanish crews,
Gold doubloons and double moidores, louis d'ors and portagues,

Clumsy yellow-metal earrings from the Indians of Brazil,
Uncut emeralds out of Rio, bezoar stones from Guayaquil,
Silver, in the crude and fashioned, pots of old Arica bronze,
Jewels from the bones of Incas desecrated by the Dons.

We smoothed the place with mattocks, and we took and blazed the tree,
Which marks yon where the gear is hid that none will ever see,
And we laid aboard the ship again, and south away we steers,
Through the loud surf of Los Muertos which is beating in my ears.

I'm the last alive that knows it. All the rest have gone their ways
Killed, or died, or come to anchor in the old Mulatas Cays,
And I go singing, fiddling, old and starved and in despair,
And I know where all that gold is hid, if I were only there.

It's not the way to end it all. I'm old, and nearly blind,
And an old man's past's a strange thing, for it never leaves his mind.

And I see in dreams, awhiles, the beach, the sun's disk dipping red,
And the tall ship, under topsails, swaying in past Nigger Head.

I'd be glad to step ashore there. Glad to take a pick and go
To the lone blazed coco-palm tree in the place no others know,
And lift the gold and silver that has moldered there for years
By the loud surf of Los Muertos which is beating in my ears.

THE VAGABOND

Robert Louis Stevenson

Give to me the life I love,
  Let the lave go by me,
Give the jolly heaven above
  And the byway nigh me.
Bed in the bush with stars to see,
  Bread I dip in the river—
There's the life for a man like me,
  There's the life forever.

Let the blow fall soon or late,
  Let what will be o'er me;
Give the face of earth around
  And the road before me.
Wealth I seek not, hope nor love,
  Nor a friend to know me:
All I seek, the heaven above
  And the road below me.

Or let autumn fall on me
  Where afield I linger,
Silencing the bird on tree,
  Biting the blue finger:
White as meal the frosty field—
  Warm the fireside haven—
Not to autumn will I yield,
  Not to winter even!

Let the blow fall soon or late,
  Let what will be o'er me;
Give the face of earth around,
  And the road before me.
Wealth I ask not, hope nor love,
  Nor a friend to know me.
All I ask the heaven above,
  And the road below me.

THE UNCONQUERED AIR

FLORENCE EARLE COATES

Others endure Man's rule: he therefore deems
I shall endure it—I, the unconquered Air!
Imagines this triumphant strength may bear
His paltry sway! yea, ignorantly dreams,
Because proud Rhea now his vassal seems,
And Neptune him obeys in billowy lair,
That he a more sublime assault may dare,
Where blown by tempest wild the vulture screams!
Presumptuous, he mounts: I toss his bones
Back from the height supernal he has braved:
Aye, as his vessel nears my perilous zones,
I blow the cockleshell away like chaff
And give him to the Sea he has enslaved.
He founders in its depths; and then I laugh!

Impregnable I held myself, secure
Against intrusion. Who can measure Man?
How should I guess his mortal will outran
Defeat so far that danger could allure
For its own sake?—that he would all endure,
All sacrifice, all suffer, rather than
Forego the daring dreams Olympian
That prophesy to him of victory sure?
Ah, tameless courage!—dominating power
That, all attempting, in a deathless hour
Made earthborn Titans godlike, in revolt!—
Fear is the fire that melts Icarian wings:
Who fears nor Fate, nor Time, nor what Time brings,
May drive Apollo's steeds, or wield the thunderbolt!

THE GYPSY HEART

HARRY NOYES PRATT

When I was just a tiny chap long years ago, they say
The gypsies rode away with me across the sunlit day;
Across the moor of yellow furze, out through the day, beyond
The purpling of the distant hills; with me, a vagabond.

We loitered lazy on the road that led afar from town.
We made the gypsy patteran for those who followed down.
The wind that came across the moor blew salty from the sea;
The stars above the drowsy stream smiled friendly down on me.

Through summer days we rode and far, and far the free road ran;
But every road must find its end, and every caravan
Must creak and pause and roll to rest when summer days have gone—
And so they brought me home again and left me in the dawn.

The brick-walled days that hold me here run wearily and slow;
The sun is like a brazen ball with brazen streets below.
I smell the gorse upon the moor, and winds from off the sea—
The gypsies stole my heart, and gave a gypsy heart to me.

ELDORADO

EDGAR ALLAN POE

Gaily bedight,
A gallant knight,
In sunshine and in shadow,
Had journeyed long,
Singing a song,
In search of Eldorado.

But he grew old,
This knight so bold,
And o'er his heart a shadow
Fell as he found
No spot of ground
That looked like Eldorado.

And, as his strength
Failed him at length,
He met a pilgrim shadow.
"Shadow," said he,
"Where can it be—
This land of Eldorado?"

"Over the Mountains
Of the Moon,
Down the Valley of the Shadow,
Ride, boldly ride,"
The shade replied,
"If you seek for Eldorado!"

WANDER-THIRST

GERALD GOULD

Beyond the East the sunrise, beyond the West the sea,
And East and West the wander-thirst that will not let me be.
It works in me like madness, dear, to bid me say good-by;
For the seas call and the stars call, and oh! the call of the sky.

I know not where the white road runs, nor what the blue hills are,
But a man can have the sun for friend, and for his guide a star;
And there's no end of voyaging when once the voice is heard,
For the river calls and the road calls, and oh! the call of a bird!

Yonder the long horizon lies, and there by night and day
The old ships draw to home again, the young ships sail away;
And come I may, but go I must, and if men ask you why,
You may put the blame on the stars and the sun and the white road and the sky.

REVEILLE

A. E. Housman

Wake: the silver dusk returning
  Up the beach of darkness brims,
And the ship of sunrise burning
  Strands upon the eastern rims.

Wake: the vaulted shadow shatters,
  Trampled to the floor it spanned,
And the tent of night in tatters
  Straws the sky-pavilioned land.

Up, lad, up, 'tis late for lying:
  Hear the drums of morning play;
Hark, the empty highways crying
  "Who'll beyond the hills away?"

Towns and countries woo together,
  Forelands beacon, belfries call;
Never lad that trod on leather
  Lived to feast his heart with all.

Up, lad: thews that lie and cumber
  Sunlit pallets never thrive;
Morns abed and daylight slumber
  Were not meant for man alive.

Clay lies still, but blood's a rover;
  Breath's a ware that will not keep.
Up, lad: when the journey's over
  There'll be time enough to sleep.

THE SEA

The sea never changes, and its works, for all the talk of men, are wrapped in mystery.

—JOSEPH CONRAD

HE WHO LOVES THE OCEAN

MARY SINTON LEITCH

He who loves the ocean
And the ways of ships
May taste beside a mountain pool
Brine on his lips:

May feel in the desert
The parched day long
The slow camels swaying
To the sea's song.

A meadow in the moonlight,
However dry it be,
Is slippery with seaweed,
Smells of the sea.

He who is banished
From marshes and weirs,
Who has for sea savor
The salt of his tears,

To him the dust of hoofbeats
On a windless plain
Shall be spindrift flying
Before the hurricane.

In cornfield or wheatfield,
Wherever he may go,
He hears water sobbing
Low . . . low . . .

He hears water calling
Till a prairie mist is thinned
To skysails and royals
Proud in the wind.

Whom the sea has summoned,
Whom the ocean claims her own,
He finds in clouds a caravel
And coral in a stone:

He looks toward lost horizons
Till any city street
May dance and dip and curvet
Under his feet.

Who lives a salt sea lover,
Though inland far he dies,
Feels sea wind on his pillow,
Has the North Star in his eyes.

SEA FEVER

JOHN MASEFIELD

must go down to the seas again, to the lonely sea and the sky,
nd all I ask is a tall ship and a star to steer her by,
nd the wheel's kick and the wind's song and the white sail's shaking,
nd a gray mist on the sea's face and a gray dawn breaking.

must go down to the seas again, for the call of the running tide
s a wild call and a clear call that may not be denied;
nd all I ask is a windy day with the white clouds flying,
nd the flung spray and the blown spume, and the sea gulls crying.

must go down to the seas again to the vagrant gypsy life,
o the gull's way and the whale's way where the wind's like a whetted knife;
nd all I ask is a merry yarn from a laughing fellow rover,
nd quiet sleep and a sweet dream when the long trick's over.

SEA LONGING

Harold Vinal

You who are inland born know not the pain
Of one who longs for gray dunes and the seas
And sound of ebbing tide and windy rain
And sea mews crying down immensities.
You who are inland born know not the urge
Of rapt tides beating passionate and wild,
Nor have you thrilled with wonder at the surge
Of drifting water, wayward as a child.
Impetuous I seek the eager sea,
Imperious for joy and wind-blown spray;
You, who are city beaten every day,
What do you know of mirth and ecstasy?
No thirsty wind has journeyed from the South—
And laid a cool, wet finger on your mouth!

MARINERS

DAVID MORTON

Men who have loved the ships they took to sea,
Loved the tall masts, the prows that creamed with foam,
Have learned, deep in their hearts, how it might be
That there is yet a dearer thing than home.
The decks they walk, the rigging in the stars,
The clean boards counted in the watch they keep—
These, and the sunlight on the slippery spars.
Will haunt them ever, waking and asleep.
Ashore, these men are not as other men;
They walk as strangers through the crowded street,
Or, brooding by their fires, they hear again
The drone astern, where gurgling waters meet,
Or see again a wide and blue lagoon,
And a lone ship that rides there with the moon.

THREE TARRY MEN

EDMUND LEAMY

They came from only God knows where,
  Three tarry, blue-eyed men.
They blundered through the swaying train
  To empty seats, and then—
Forgotten talk of long ago
  I listened to again.

They spoke of rising storm and tides,
  Of heaving decks and seas,
Of Port Sudan and Port-au-Prince,
  Seychelles and Hebrides,
Of lonely hours in doldrum calm,
  And unsolved mysteries.

Their talk was thick with briny oaths,
  And some of it was lies;
They yarned of captains, crews and ships,
  Far seas and ports and skies—
But splendid peace and happiness
  Shone deep in their blue eyes.

And each one knew, whate'er his talk,
  Though cursed as fiend and foe,
The sea was dearer to them all—
  And at her word would go
Each mother's son, for none could fail
  When she lured, sighing low.

So from the train they lumbered off
With worn and battered grips,
With curses they were leaving port,
But smiles upon their lips,
Down, down the twisting ways to where
There lay the waiting ships.

SEA URGE

ANONYMOUS

Oh, to feel the tremble of a ship beneath my feet again,
Now that April's urge is running riot in the tide,
Where gray gull dips to white gull and the salt spray leaps to meet them
Out across blue water where the tall ships ride.

Freshets in the mountain streams and floods along the river
Go rushing down to join the tossing tumult of the sea.
And the April urge that drives them sets the sailor's heart aquiver
With the joy of ocean madness when the sails flap free.

A WET SHEET AND A FLOWING SEA

ALLAN CUNNINGHAM

A wet sheet and a flowing sea,
  A wind that follows fast
And fills the white and rustling sail
  And bends the gallant mast;
And bends the gallant mast, my boys,
  While like the eagle free
Away the good ship flies and leaves
  Old England on the lee.

"Oh, for a soft and gentle wind!"
  I heard a fair one cry;
But give to me the snoring breeze
  And white waves heaving high;
And white waves heaving high, my boys,
  The good ship tight and free—
The world of waters is our home,
  And merry men are we.

There's tempest in yon hornèd moon,
  And lightning in yon cloud;
But hark the music, mariners!
  The wind is piping loud;
The wind is piping loud, my boys,
  The lightning flashing free—
While the hollow oak our palace is,
  Our heritage the sea.

CAPTIVE

John Richard Moreland

The wind is a teasing hunger,
  The sea is a quenchless thirst,
And I am a moon-marked dreamer
  By wind and wave accursed;

With never a place to linger
  Or hide from the seeking sea,
But the curve of a thin, blue finger
  Continually beckons me.

With never a hill or hollow
  To harbor me safe and sure,
But the wind, houndlike, will follow
  And sniff at my bolted door:

Or set the casement shaking
  Till quiet or rest is vain,
Till the sound of water . . . breaking . . .
  Makes me its slave again.

THE FISHER'S WIDOW

ARTHUR SYMONS

The boats go out and the boats come in
Under the wintry sky;
And the rain and foam are white in the wind,
And the white gulls cry.

She sees the sea when the wind is wild
Swept by the windy rain;
And her heart's a-weary of sea and land
As the long days wane.

She sees the torn sails fly in the foam,
Broad on the sky line gray;
And the boats go out and the boats come in,
But there's one away.

NO GULL'S WINGS

(O. E. Rölvaag)

PAUL ENGLE

Here he can sleep, far inland from the sea,
Where the wind's sweet with clover and wild hay
And cooled in blowing over water free
From the wave's salty tang of shattered spray;
Here may a sea-forsaken man find rest,
Where he can hear no sound but the soft tune
Of homesick birds that fly into the west,
Where no tides leap and lapse against the moon.
He would not find repose where the world's rim
Is a thin line of water edged with sky;
But here amid the wheat is peace for him,
Where he can see no ships dock and depart,
Where he can hear no startled cormorant's cry,
Where no gull's wings go beating through his heart.

SAY THAT HE LOVED OLD SHIPS

DANIEL WHITEHEAD HICKY

Say that he loved old ships; write nothing more
Upon the stone above his resting place;
And they who read will know he loved the roar
Of breakers white as starlight, shadow lace
Of purple twilights on a quiet sea,
First ridge of daybreaks in a waiting sky,
The wings of gulls that beat eternally
And haunt old harbors with their silver cry.
Speak softly now, his heart has earned its rest,
This heart that knew each alien star by name,
Knew passion of the waves against his breast
When clouds swept down the sea and lightning's flame
Tore skies asunder with swift finger tips;
Write nothing more; say that he loved old ships.

LOVE OF COUNTRY

We hope there is a patriotism founded on something better than prejudice; that our country may be dear to us without injury to our philosophy; that in loving and justly prizing all lands, we may prize justly and yet love before all others our own stern Motherland.

—THOMAS CARLYLE

I HEAR AMERICA SINGING

WALT WHITMAN

hear America singing, the varied carols I hear,
hose of mechanics, each one singing his as it should be blithe and strong,
he carpenter singing his as he measures his plank or beam,
he mason singing his as he makes ready for work, or leaves off work,
he boatman singing what belongs to him in his boat, the deckhand singing on the steamboat deck,
he shoemaker singing as he sits on his bench, the hatter singing as he stands,
he woodcutter's song, the plowboy's on his way in the morning, or at the noon intermission or at sundown,
he delicious singing of the mother, or of the young wife at work, or of the girl sewing or washing,
ach singing what belongs to him or her and to none else,
he day what belongs to the day—at night the party of young fellows, robust, friendly,
nging with open mouths their strong melodious songs.

THE SOLDIER

RUPERT BROOKE

If I should die, think only this of me:
That there's some corner of a foreign field
That is forever England. There shall be
In that rich earth a richer dust concealed;
A dust whom England bore, shaped, made aware,
Gave, once, her flowers to love, her ways to roam,
A body of England's, breathing English air,
Washed by the rivers, blest by suns of home.
And think, this heart, all evil shed away,
A pulse in the eternal mind, no less
Gives somewhere back the thoughts by England given;
Her sights and sounds; dreams happy as her day;
And laughter, learnt of friends; and gentleness,
In hearts at peace, under an English heaven.

THE HARBOR

Winifred M. Letts

I think if I lay dying in some land
  Where Ireland is no more than just a name,
My soul would travel back to find that strand
    From whence it came.

I'd see the harbor in the evening light,
  The old men staring at some distant ship,
The fishing boats they fasten left and right
    Beside the slip.

The sea wrack lying on the wind-swept shore,
  The gray thorn bushes growing in the sand;
Our Wexford coast from Arklow to Cahore—
    My native land.

The little houses climbing up the hill,
  Sea daisies growing in the sandy grass,
The tethered goats that wait large-eyed and still
    To watch you pass.

The women at the well with dripping pails,
  Their men colloguing by the harbor wall,
The coils of rope, the nets, the old brown sails,
    I'd know them all.

And then the Angelus—I'd surely see
  The swaying bell against a golden sky,
So God, Who kept the love of home in me,
    Would let me die.

THE ANCESTRAL DWELLINGS

HENRY VAN DYKE

Dear to my heart are the ancestral dwellings of America
Dearer than if they were haunted by ghosts of roy
splendor;
They are simple enough to be great in their friend
dignity—
Homes that were built by the brave beginners of a natio

I love the old white farmhouses nestled in New Englar
valleys,
Ample and long and low, with elm trees feathering ov
them:
Borders of box in the yard, and lilacs, and old-fashion
roses,
A fanlight above the door, and little square panes in t
windows,
The woodshed piled with maple and birch and hicko
ready for winter,
The gambrel roof with its garret crowded with househo
relics—
All the tokens of prudent thrift and the spirit of self-relianc

I love the weather-beaten, shingled houses that front t
ocean;
They seem to grow out of the rocks, there is somethir
indomitable about them:
Their backs are bowed, their sides are covered with lichen
Soft in their color as gray pearls, they are full of a patie
courage.

Facing the briny wind on a lonely shore they stand undaunted,
While the thin blue pennant of smoke from the square-built chimney
Tells of a haven for man, with room for a hearth and a cradle.

I love the stately Southern mansions with their tall white columns,
They look through avenues of trees, over fields where the cotton is growing;
I can see the flutter of white frocks along their shady porches,
Music and laughter float from the windows, the yards are full of hounds and horses.
Long since the riders have ridden away, yet the houses have not forgotten,
They are proud of their name and place, and their doors are always open,
For the thing they remember best is the pride of their ancient hospitality.

In the towns I love the discreet and tranquil Quaker dwellings,
With their demure brick faces and immaculate marble doorsteps;
And the gabled houses of the Dutch, with their high stoops and iron railings,
(I can see their little brass knobs shining in the morning sunlight);
And the solid self-contained houses of the descendants of the Puritans,

Frowning on the street with their narrow doors and dormer windows;
And the triple-galleried, many-pillared mansions of Charleston,
Standing open sideways in their gardens of roses and magnolias.
Yes, they are all dear to my heart, and in my eyes they are beautiful;
For under their roofs were nourished the thoughts that have made the nation;
The glory and strength of America come from her ancestral dwellings.

EEN NAPOLI

T. A. Daly

Here een Noo Yorka, where am I
Seence I am landa las' July,
All gray an' ogly ees da sky,
  An' cold as eet can be.
But steell so long I maka mon',
So long ees worka to be done,
I can forgat how shines da sun
  Een Napoli.

But oh, w'en pass da boy dat sal
Da violets, an' I can smal
How sweet dey are, I can not tal
  How seeck my heart ees be.
I no can work, how mooch I try,
But only seet an' wondra why
I could not justa leeve an' die
  Een Napoli.

WHERE A ROMAN VILLA STOOD, ABOVE FREIBURG

Mary Elizabeth Coleridge

On alien ground, breathing an alien air,
  A Roman stood, far from his ancient home,
And gazing, murmured, "Ah, the hills are fair,
  But not the hills of Rome!"

Descendant of a race to Romans kin,
  Where the old son of Empire stood, I stand.
The selfsame rocks fold the same valley in,
  Untouched of human hand.

Over another shines the selfsame star,
  Another heart with nameless longing fills,
Crying aloud, "How beautiful they are,
  But not our English hills!"

EXPATRIATE

MARY BROWN ONSTOTT

All night he sits and plays at solitaire,
A king upon an ace and then a queen,
And sips a little wine his games between
Or strolls out on the balcony for air.
Without, the foreign chatter in the square;
Within, rich foreign silks of rose and green,
Venetian glass, old bronze, an Orient screen,
And for his cards a teakwood stand and chair.
And time has mellowed his calm, unlined face
But cannot quite conceal the look of dread
That comes upon him. . . . Black upon the red
And red upon the black, with easy grace
He plays his cards—and drives back in his brain
The thought of maple trees and snow in Maine.

WAR

Would you end war? Create great Peace.

—JAMES OPPENHEIM

I HAVE A RENDEZVOUS WITH DEATH

ALAN SEEGER

I have a rendezvous with Death
At some disputed barricade,
When Spring comes back with rustling shade
And apple blossoms fill the air—
I have a rendezvous with Death
When Spring brings back blue days and fair.

It may be he shall take my hand
And lead me into his dark land
And close my eyes and quench my breath—
It may be I shall pass him still.
I have a rendezvous with Death
On some scarred slope of battered hill,
When Spring comes round again this year
And the first meadow flowers appear.

God knows 'twere better to be deep
Pillowed in silk and scented down,
Where love throbs out in blissful sleep,
Pulse nigh to pulse, and breath to breath,
Where hushed awakenings are dear . . .
But I've a rendezvous with Death
At midnight in some flaming town,
When Spring trips north again this year,
And I to my pledged word am true,
I shall not fail that rendezvous.

THE VOICES

Written on leave in a Kentish garden

ANONYMOUS

Slow breaks the hushed June dawn:
The pearl-soft light
Strikes from the dew-wet lawn
Diamonds bright,
And, out of sight,
Poised in the limpid blue on quivering wings,
A lark pours out his soul to God and sings
Of hope and faith and love and homely things.
Each dew-kissed rose
Lifts to the ardent Sun her velvet lip.
The splendor grows,
And every jeweled tip
Flashes a myriad, golden, mimic suns.
Then—on the stilled air,
Sullen and sinister,
Mutter the Voices—the Guns.

Noon lifts his flaming crown:
Faint in the heat
The blue hills burn, and down
The village street
On laggard feet,
A carter walks beside his sweating team,
Pausing to let them water at the stream.
On the white road the purple shadows dream,
And like a bell
Tolled faint in fairyland, a cuckoo's note
Rings from the dell.

Clad in his emerald coat
Across the dusty road a lizard runs.
Then—through the heat,
With dull menacing beat,
Mutter the Voices—the Guns.

Soft falls night's star-hung veil:
In the warm gloom
The roses sigh and fill
With rich perfume
The lighted room,
With wave on wave of incense like a prayer.
The candles burn straight in the windless air,
And there is sound of laughter, free from care.
Softly the light
Falls upon gleaming silver and thin glass
And damask white.
But—as the moments pass
And the talk dies to silence and hushed tones,
With shuddering breath,
Chanting their song of death,
Mutter the Voices—the Guns.

ATTACK

SIEGFRIED SASSOON

At dawn the ridge emerges massed and dun
In the wild purple of the glowering sun,
Smoldering through spouts of drifting smoke that shroud
The menacing scarred slope; and, one by one,
Tanks creep and topple forward to the wire.
The barrage roars and lifts. Then, clumsily bowed
With bombs and guns and shovels and battle gear,
Men jostle and climb to meet the bristling fire.
Lines of gray, muttering faces, masked with fear,
They leave their trenches, going over the top,
While time ticks blank and busy on their wrists,
And hope, with furtive eyes and grappling fists,
Flounders in mud. O Jesu, make it stop!

THE SPIRES OF OXFORD

Seen from a train

WINIFRED M. LETTS

I saw the spires of Oxford
  As I was passing by,
The gray spires of Oxford
  Against a pearl-gray sky;
My heart was with the Oxford men
  Who went abroad to die.

The years go fast in Oxford,
  The golden years and gay;
The hoary Colleges look down
  On careless boys at play,
But when the bugles sounded—War!
  They put their games away.

They left the peaceful river,
  The cricket field, the quad,
The shaven lawns of Oxford,
  To seek a bloody sod.
They gave their merry youth away
  For country and for God.

God rest you, happy gentlemen,
  Who laid your good lives down,
Who took the khaki and the gun
  Instead of cap and gown.
God bring you to a fairer place
  Than even Oxford town.

SPORTSMEN IN PARADISE

T. P. Cameron Wilson

They left the fury of the fight,
  And they were very tired.
The gates of Heaven were open, quite
  Unguarded, and unwired.
There was no sound of any gun;
  The land was still and green:
Wide hills lay silent in the sun,
  Blue valleys slept between.

They saw far off a little wood
  Stand up against the sky.
Knee-deep in grass a great tree stood . . .
  Some lazy cows went by. . . .
There were some rooks sailed overhead—
  And once a church bell pealed.
"God! but it's England," someone said,
  "And there's a cricket field!"

IN FLANDERS FIELDS

JOHN McCRAE

In Flanders fields the poppies blow
Between the crosses, row on row,
  That mark our place; and in the sky
  The larks, still bravely singing, fly
Scarce heard amid the guns below.

We are the Dead. Short days ago
We lived, felt dawn, saw sunset glow,
  Loved and were loved, and now we lie
    In Flanders fields.

Take up our quarrel with the foe:
To you from failing hands we throw
  The torch; be yours to hold it high!
  If ye break faith with us who die
We shall not sleep, though poppies grow
    In Flanders fields.

GRASS

CARL SANDBURG

Pile the bodies high at Austerlitz and Waterloo.
Shovel them under and let me work—
  I am the grass; I cover all.

And pile them high at Gettysburg
And pile them high at Ypres and Verdun.
Shovel them under and let me work.
Two years, ten years, and passengers ask the conductor:
  What place is this?
  Where are we now?

  I am the grass.
  Let me work.

STORIES

An honest tale speeds best being plainly told.

—WILLIAM SHAKESPEARE

HE FELL AMONG THIEVES

HENRY NEWBOLT

'Ye have robbed," said he, "ye have slaughtered and made
 an end,
 Take your ill-got plunder, and bury the dead:
Vhat will ye more of your guest and sometime friend?"
 "Blood for our blood," they said.

Ie laughed: "If one may settle the score for five,
 I am ready; but let the reckoning stand till day:
 have loved the sunlight as dearly as any alive."
 "You shall die at dawn," said they.

Ie flung his empty revolver down the slope,
 He climbed alone to the Eastward edge of the trees;
ll night long in a dream untroubled of hope
 He brooded, clasping his knees.

Ie did not hear the monotonous roar that fills
 The ravine where the Yassin river sullenly flows;
Ie did not see the starlight on the Laspur hills,
 Or the far Afghan snows.

Ie saw the April noon on his books aglow,
 The wistaria trailing in at the window wide;
Ie heard his father's voice from the terrace below
 Calling him down to ride.

Ie saw the gray little church across the park,
 The mounds that hide the loved and honoured dead;
'he Norman arch, the chancel softly dark,
 The brasses black and red.

He saw the School Close, sunny and green,
  The runner beside him, the stand by the parapet wall,
The distant tape, and the crowd roaring between
  His own name over all.

He saw the dark wainscot and timbered roof,
  The long tables, and the faces merry and keen;
The College Eight and their trainer dining aloof,
  The Dons on the daïs serene.

He watched the liner's stem ploughing the foam,
  He felt her trembling speed and the thrash of her screw
He heard her passengers' voices talking of home,
  He saw the flag she flew.

And now it was dawn. He rose strong on his feet,
  And strode to his ruined camp below the wood;
He drank the breath of the morning cool and sweet;
  His murderers round him stood.

Light on the Laspur hills was broadening fast,
  The blood-red snow-peaks chilled to a dazzling white:
He turned, and saw the golden circle at last,
  Cut by the Eastern height.

"O glorious Life, Who dwellest in earth and sun,
  I have lived, I praise and adore Thee."
                                        A sword swept.
Over the pass the voices one by one
  Faded, and the hill slept.

IN HARDIN COUNTY, 1809

LULU E. THOMPSON

With flintlock guns and polished stocks,
Knee breeches and long homespun socks,
On morning of St. Valentine
Two hunters met in 1809
Across the line from Illinois;
They stopped their mules and voiced their joy.

"Why, Ben, it's been a quite a spell
Since I've seen you. The folks all well?
Bring any news from up near town?"

"Why, yes. D'you know John Ezry Brown?
They say that he's a-goin' down
To Washington in all the din
To see Jim Madison sworn in.
And this young feller Bonaparte
That's fightin' 'cross the sea
Is slicin' Europe all to bits—
Or so they're tellin' me."

"Wal, wal, nice day, but kinda breezy—
This mule's a-gettin' quite uneasy.
Now come and see us some time, do,
And bring the gals and Hepsy, too."

"Yes, some fine day we'll be along.
Got any news to send along?"

"No, nothin' worth a tinker's song.
There's nothin' happens here near me,
Doggondest place you ever see.
Tom Lincoln lives right over there
In that log cabin, bleak and bare.
They say they have a little babe;
I understand they've named him 'Abe.'
Yes, Sally said just t'other day
That nothin' happens down this way."

ACHILLES DEATHERIDGE

EDGAR LEE MASTERS

"Your name is Achilles Deatheridge?
How old are you, my boy?"
"I'm sixteen past and I went to the war
From Athens, Illinois."

"Achilles Deatheridge, you have done
A deed of dreadful note."
"It comes of his wearing a battered hat,
And a rusty, wrinkled coat."

"Why, didn't you know how plain he is?
And didn't you ever hear,
He goes through the lines by day or night
Like a sooty cannoneer?

"You must have been half dead for sleep,
For the dawn was growing bright."
"Well, Captain, I had stood right there
Since six o'clock last night.

"I cocked my gun at the swish of the grass,
And how am I at fault
When a dangerous-looking man won't stop
When a sentry hollers halt?

"I cried out halt and he only smiled,
And waved his hand like that.
Why, any Johnnie could wear the coat,
And any fellow the hat.

"I hollered halt again and he stopped,
And lighted a fresh cigar.
I never noticed his shoulder badge,
And I never noticed a star."

"So you arrested him? Well, Achilles,
When you hear the swish of the grass,
If it's General Grant inspecting the lines
Hereafter let him pass."

THE CHRYSANTHEMUM LEGEND

Arthur Davison Ficke

There is a tale, beloved of Old Japan.—
Once in Kyoto—so the story ran—
Dwelt a great noble who was lord and warden
Of a renowned and beauty-haunted garden.
But of all glories that his garden showed
None, 'twas reported, in such splendor glowed
As the chrysanthemums which here in fall
Were massed in cohorts of majestical
Vast blooms of purple, crimson, white and gold.
Such tales of this miraculous sight were told
That even to the Emperor's ears at last
The rumor of the great chrysanthemums passed.

Whereupon to the honorable lord
The Emperor dispatched commanding word
That on the morrow with his retinue
He would himself adventure forth to view
That glory of chrysanthemums in fall
Now hidden by the noble's garden wall.

The Emperor next day in pomp of state
Arrived before the noble's massive gate
Where, waiting solemnly, attendants stood
Awed by the coming of the royal blood.
The lord himself strode forth and knelt before
The Imperial One now honoring his door—
And in the robes of ceremonial dressed
Conducted through the gates his mighty guest.

Into the garden then he straightway led
The Heaven-born One, the Sacred Lord of Dread.
The Emperor glanced about—and swift surprise
Spoke in the indignation of his eyes.
His lips closed tight into the lines of wrath
For here about him every garden path
Was like a waste of desolation, strown
With thousands of chrysanthemums, newly mown
And lying dead upon the encumbered ground.
It was as if a whirlwind here had found
Rich plunder for its fury to deface
And left a desolate and ruined place.

"What means this insult?" Thus the Emperor spoke.
The garden's lord with a slow gesture broke
His silence—pointing to one single flower
That rose in perfect beauty, there to tower
Alone in isolate splendor. And he said:
"There is the one, the chosen, perfect head
Of all my flowers. That you might view it best
I ordered to destruction all the rest.
For beauty, perfect, must be viewed alone
In that brief moment ere it too is gone."

The Emperor in meditative mood
Before the single great chrysanthemum stood,
When he departed, it was silentwise
With pools of deep reflection in his eyes.

THE GLOVE AND THE LIONS

LEIGH HUNT

King Francis was a hearty king and loved a royal sport,
And one day as his lions fought sat looking on the cour
The nobles filled the benches, with the ladies in their pride
And 'mongst them sat the Count de Lorge with one for whom he sighed.
And truly 'twas a gallant thing to see that crowning show
Valor and love, and a king above, and the royal beasts below.

Ramped and roared the lions with horrid laughing jaws;
They bit, they glared, gave blows like beams; a wind wen with their paws.
With wallowing might and stifled roar they rolled on one another
Till all the pit with sand and mane was in a thunderous smother.
The bloody foam above the bars came whisking throug the air;
Said Francis then, "Faith, gentlemen, we're better here than there."

De Lorge's love o'erheard the king, a beauteous, lively dame
With smiling lips and sharp bright eyes, which always seemed the same.
She thought, "The Count, my lover, is brave as brave can be;
He surely would do wondrous things to show his love of me

Kings, ladies, lovers, all look on; the occasion is divine.
I'll drop my glove to prove his love; great glory will be mine."

She dropped her glove to prove his love, then looked at him and smiled.
He bowed, and in a moment leaped among the lions wild.
The leap was quick, return was quick; he has regained his place,
Then threw the glove—but not with love—right in the lady's face.
"By heaven," said Francis, "rightly done!" and he rose from where he sat.
"No love," quoth he, "but vanity sets love a task like that."

ANGUS McGREGOR

LEW SARETT

Angus McGregor lies brittle as ice,
With snow tucked up to his jaws,
Somewhere tonight where the hemlocks moan
And crack in the wind like straws.

Angus went cruising the woods last month,
With a blanket roll on his back,
With never an ax, a dirk, a gun,
Or a compass in his pack.

"The hills at thirty below have teeth;
McGregor," I said, "you're daft
To tackle the woods like a simple child."
But he looked at me and laughed.

He flashed his teeth in a grin and said:
"The earth is an open book;
I've followed the woods for forty years,
I know each cranny and crook.

"I've battled her weather, her winds, her brutes;
I've stood with them toe to toe;
I can beat them back with my naked fist
And answer them blow for blow."

Angus McGregor sleeps under the stars,
With an icicle gripped in his hand,
Somewhere tonight where the grim-lipped peaks
Brood on a haggard land.

Oh, the face of the moon is dark tonight,
And dark the gaunt wind's sigh;
And the hollow laughter troubles me
In the wild wolves' cry.

THE HIGHWAYMAN

ALFRED NOYES

PART ONE

The wind was a torrent of darkness among the gusty trees,
The moon was a ghostly galleon tossed upon cloudy seas,
The road was a ribbon of moonlight over the purple moor,
And the highwayman came riding—
    Riding—riding—
The highwayman came riding, up to the old inn door.

He'd a French cocked hat on his forehead, a bunch of lace at his chin,
A coat of the claret velvet, and breeches of brown doeskin;
They fitted with never a wrinkle: his boots were up to the thigh!
And he rode with a jeweled twinkle,
    His pistol butts a-twinkle,
His rapier hilt a-twinkle, under the jeweled sky.

Over the cobbles he clattered and clashed in the dark innyard,
And he tapped with his whip on the shutters, but all was locked and barred;

He whistled a tune to the window, and who should be waiting there
But the landlord's black-eyed daughter,
    Bess, the landlord's daughter,
Plaiting a dark red love knot into her long black hair.

And dark in the dark old innyard a stable wicket creaked
Where Tim the ostler listened; his face was white and peaked;

His eyes were hollows of madness, his hair like moldy hay,
But he loved the landlord's daughter,
    The landlord's red-lipped daughter,
Dumb as a dog he listened, and he heard the robber say—

"One kiss, my bonnie sweetheart, I'm after a prize tonight,
But I shall be back with the yellow gold before the morning light;
Yet, if they press me sharply, and harry me through the day,
Then look for me by moonlight,
    Watch for me by moonlight,
I'll come to thee by moonlight, though hell should bar the way."

He rose upright in the stirrups; he scarce could reach her hand,
But she loosened her hair i' the casement! His face burnt like a brand
As the black cascade of perfume came tumbling over his breast;
And he kissed its waves in the moonlight,
    (Oh, sweet black waves in the moonlight!)
Then he tugged at his rein in the moonlight, and galloped away to the West.

PART TWO

He did not come in the dawning; he did not come at noon;
And out o' the tawny sunset, before the rise o' the moon,
When the road was a gypsy's ribbon, looping the purple moor,
A redcoat troop came marching—
    Marching—marching—
King George's men came marching, up to the old inn door.

They said no word to the landlord, they drank his ale instead,
But they gagged his daughter and bound her to the foot of her narrow bed;
Two of them knelt at her casement, with muskets at their side!
There was death at every window;
And hell at one dark window;
For Bess could see, through her casement, the road that *he* would ride.

They had tied her up to attention, with many a sniggering jest;
They had bound a musket beside her, with the barrel beneath her breast!
"Now keep good watch!" and they kissed her.
She heard the dead man say—
Look for me by moonlight;
Watch for me by moonlight;
I'll come to thee by moonlight, though hell should bar the way!

She twisted her hands behind her; but all the knots held good!
She writhed her hands till her fingers were wet with sweat or blood!
They stretched and strained in the darkness, and the hours crawled by like years,
Till, now, on the stroke of midnight,
Cold, on the stroke of midnight,
The tip of one finger touched it! The trigger at least was hers!

The tip of her finger touched it; she strove no more for the rest!
Up, she stood to attention, with the barrel beneath her breast,
She would not risk their hearing; she would not strive again;
For the road lay bare in the moonlight;
    Blank and bare in the moonlight;
And the blood of her veins in the moonlight throbbed to her love's refrain.

Tlot-tlot; tlot-tlot!—Had they heard it? The horse hoofs ringing clear;
Tlot-tlot, tlot-tlot, in the distance? Were they deaf that they did not hear?
Down the ribbon of moonlight, over the brow of the hill,
The highwayman came riding,
    Riding, riding!
The redcoats looked to their priming! She stood up, straight and still!

Tlot-tlot, in the frosty silence! *Tlot-tlot,* in the echoing night!
Nearer he came and nearer! Her face was like a light!
Her eyes grew wide for a moment; she drew one last deep breath,
Then her finger moved in the moonlight,
    Her musket shattered the moonlight,
Shattered her breast in the moonlight and warned him —with her death.

He turned; he spurred to the west; he did not know who stood
Bowed, with her head o'er the musket, drenched with her own red blood!
Not till the dawn he heard it, his face grew gray to hear
How Bess, the landlord's daughter,
    The landlord's black-eyed daughter,
Had watched for her love in the moonlight, and died in the darkness there.

Back, he spurred like a madman, shrieking a curse to the sky,
With the white road smoking behind him and his rapier brandished high!
Blood-red were his spurs i' the golden noon; wine-red was his velvet coat,
When they shot him down on the highway,
    Down like a dog on the highway,
And he lay in his blood on the highway, with the bunch of lace at his throat.

. . . .

And still of a winter's night, they say, when the wind is in the trees,
When the moon is a ghostly galleon tossed upon cloudy seas,
When the road is a ribbon of moonlight over the purple moor,
A highwayman comes riding—
    Riding—riding—
A highwayman comes riding, up to the old inn door.

Over the cobbles he clatters and clangs in the dark innyard;
He taps with his whip on the shutters, but all is locked and barred;
He whistles a tune to the window, and who should be waiting there
But the landlord's black-eyed daughter,
    Bess, the landlord's daughter,
Plaiting a dark red love knot into her long black hair.

SIR PATRICK SPENS

ANONYMOUS

The king sits in Dumferling town
Drinking the bluid-red wine:
"Oh, whar will I get a guid sailor
To sail this ship of mine?"

Up and spak an eldern knicht
Sat at the king's richt knee:
"Sir Patrick Spens is the best sailor
That sails upon the sea."

The king has written a braid letter
And signed it wi' his hand,
And sent it to Sir Patrick Spens
Was walking on the sand.

The first line that Sir Patrick read,
A loud lauch lauched he;
The next line that Sir Patrick read,
The tear blinded his e'e.

"Oh, wha is this has done this deed,
This ill deed done to me:
To send me out this time o' the year
To sail upon the sea?

"Mak haste, mak haste, my mirry men all;
Our good ship sails the morn."
"Oh, say na sae, my master dear,
For I fear a deadly storm.

"Late, late yestreen I saw the new moon
Wi' the auld moon in her arm;
And I fear, I fear, my dear master,
That we will come to harm."

Oh, our Scots nobles were richt laith
To weet their cork-heeled shoon,
Bot lang e'er a' the play were played
Their hats they swam aboon.

Oh, lang, lang may their ladies sit
Wi' their fans in their hand
Or e'er they see Sir Patrick Spens
Come sailing to the land.

Oh, lang, lang may their ladies stand
Wi' their gold kems in their hair
Waiting for their ain dear lords
For they'll see them na mair.

Half ower, half ower to Aberdour
It's fifty faddom deep;
And there lies guid Sir Patrick Spens
Wi' the Scots lords at his feet.

THE TWO SISTERS

ANONYMOUS

There lived an old lord by the Northern Sea,
  Bow'e down!
There lived an old lord by the Northern Sea,
  Bow and balance to me!
There lived an old lord by the Northern Sea
And he had daughters, one, two, three.
  I'll be true to my love
  If my love will be true to me.

A young man came a-courting there,
And he fell in love with the youngest fair.

He bought the youngest a beaver hat,
The oldest sister didn't like that.

The sisters walked down to the river brim
The oldest pushed the youngest in.

Sister, O sister, lend me your hand
I'll give to you my house and land.

She floated down to the miller's dam.
The miller pulled her safe to land.

From off her finger he took five gold rings,
And then he threw her back in again.

They hanged the miller on a gallows so high
The oldest sister standing close by.

THE GOL-DARNED WHEEL

Anonymous

I can take the wildest bronco in the tough old woolly Wes
I can ride him, I can break him, let him do his level bes
I can handle any cattle ever wore a coat of hair,
And I've had a lively tussle with a tarnel grizzly bear.
I can rope and throw the longhorn of the wildest Tex brand,
And in Indian disagreements I can play a leading hand,
But at last I got my master and he surely made me sque
When the boys got me a-straddle of that gol-darned whee

It was at the Eagle Ranch, on the Brazos,
When I first found that darned contrivance that upset m in the dust.
A tenderfoot had brought it, he was wheeling all the wa
From the sunrise end of freedom out to San Francisco Ba
He tied it up at the ranch for to get outside a meal,
Never thinking we would monkey with his gol-darned wheel.

Arizona Jim begun it when he said to Jack McGill
There was fellows forced to limit bragging on their ridin skill,
And he'd venture the admission the same fellow that h meant
Was a very handy cutter far as riding broncos went;
But he would find that he was bucking 'gainst a differe kind of deal
If he threw his leather leggins 'gainst a gol-darned wheel.

uch a slam against my talent made me hotter than a mink,
nd I swore that I would ride him for amusement or for chink.
nd it was nothing but a plaything for the kids and such about,
nd they'd have their ideas shattered if they'd lead the critter out.
hey held it while I mounted and gave the word to go;
he shove they gave to start me warn't unreasonably slow.
ut I never spilled a cuss word and I never spilled a squeal—
was building reputation on that gol-darned wheel.

loly Moses and the Prophets, how we split the Texas air,
nd the wind it made whipcrackers of my same old canthy hair,
nd I sorta comprehended as down the hill we went
here was bound to be a smash-up that I couldn't well prevent.
h, how them punchers bawled, "Stay with her, Uncle Bill!
tick your spurs in her, you sucker! turn her muzzle up the hill!"
ut I never made an answer, I just let the cusses squeal,
was finding reputation on that gol-darned wheel.

he grade was mighty sloping from the ranch down to the creek
nd I went a-galliflutin' like a crazy lightning streak—
Vent whizzing and a-darting first this way and then that,
he darned contrivance sort o' wobbling like the flying of a bat.

I pulled upon the handles, but I couldn't check it up,
And I yanked and sawed and hollowed but the darne
thing wouldn't stop.
Then a sort of a meachin' in my brain began to steal,
That the devil held a mortgage on that gol-darned whee

I've a sort of dim and hazy remembrance of the stop,
With the world a-goin' round and the stars all tangled u
Then there came an intermission that lasted till I found
I was lying at the ranch with the boys all gathered roun
And a doctor was a-sewing on the skin where it was rippe
And old Arizona whispered, "Well, old boy, I guess you'
whipped,"
And I told him I was busted from sombrero down to hee
And he grinned and said, "You ought to see that go
darned wheel."

CERELLE

MARGARET BELL HOUSTON

There was a score of likely girls
Around the prairieside,
But I went down to Galveston
And brought me home a bride.

A score or more of handsome girls,
Of proper age and size,
But the pale girls of Galveston
Have seashine in their eyes.

As pale as any orange flower,
Cerelle. The gold-white sands
Were like her hair, and drifting shells,
White fairy shells, her hands.

I think she liked my silver spurs,
A-clinking in the sun.
She'd never seen a cowboy till
I rode to Galveston.

She'd never known the chaparral,
Nor smell of saddle leather,
Nor seen a roundup or a ranch,
Till we rode back together.

Shall I forget my mother's eyes?
"Is this the wife you need?
Is this the way to bring me rest
From forty men to feed?"

Cerelle—I think she did her best
All year. She'd lots to learn.
Dishes would slip from out her hands
And break. The bread would burn.

And she would steal away at times
And wander off to me.
And when the wind was in the south
She'd say, "I smell the sea!"

She changed. The white and gold grew dull
As when a soft flame dies,
And yet she kept until the last
The seashine in her eyes.

. . . .

There are (I make a husband's boast)
No stronger arms than Ann's.
She has a quip for all the boys,
And sings among the pans.

At last my mother takes her rest.
And that's how things should be.
But when the wind is in the south
There is no rest for me.

WASHINGTON'S LAST BIRTHDAY

On Washington's last birthday his young kinswoman, Nelly Custis, was married to his nephew

Alfred Noyes

"My birthday, Nelly, and your wedding day!
  Give me your hands, and let me look at you.
I have no doubt you love him, as you say.
  He is my sister's son. I love him, too.
We had great games together, long ago.
When he was—eight; and I—threescore or so;
And, for you both, I've just one prayer to pray:
  Be true to one another, still be true."—

"Dear Uncle George"—and Nelly's frank gray eyes
  Smiled up at that grim mouth, that bent gray head—
"We're young, I know; but very, very wise!"
  A chime rang out; and, blushing rosy red,
She cried, "But you must hurry; you must wear
Your *best* new uniform from France, my dear—
Frogs, epaulettes, and gold embroideries!
  Promise!"—He smiled—"My *very* best," he said.

The guests were gathering at the sunlit door.
  She heard his footstep echoing through the hall,
She turned to see the splendor that he wore;
  And saw—a shadow that outshone them all.
This was his "best" indeed! He had spoken true!
He stood there in the worn old buff and blue,
Faded in great campaigns, long, long, before;
  And her heart leapt, as at a bugle call.

Faded the colors of that warworn host
   Who took for their new flag God's ancient sky;
Faded like those, half sentry and half ghost,
   That guard dark aisles of agelong memory . . .
Her arm slipped round his neck. His grizzled head
Bent down to her.—"Oh, best by far," she said.
"I did not know the way I loved you most;
   But we shall not forget now, he or I."

FIVE PEAS ON A BARRELHEAD

LEW SARETT

The warden spoke of him as "Ninety-four,
The Mystery," and swore no man could plumb
His murky depths, his thinking. The prisoners,
Shunning him always for his sullenness,
Dubbed him "the loco Finn," and they would mutter
Stark tales of Waino's brawls in logging camp—
Of the autumn night when Waino, swaggering,
Reeling with rotgut gin, gone berserker,
Lifted his ax and split three heads wide open
As pretty as a knife could cleave three apples.
That drunken hour forever shut from him
The lovely sweep of Lake Superior's blue,
The surge and lapse of breakers on her crags,
The dulcet talk of rambling brooks and firs
Marching upon her shores.

Little enough
There was about the Finnish lumberjack
To show the hot black lava in his breast.
Power he radiated, from his fists,
Iron and gnarled, his huge gorilla arms,
The granite of his block of head set square
And squat upon his bulging granite shoulders;
But power unfired, stagnant as a ditch.
Never a gleam lit up his slate-gray eyes;
His broad flat face was as shallow as a plate,
As empty of emotion. And when one dusk
He crept away and clambered to the roof
Of the power building, catapulted himself

Flat on the air like any flying squirrel,
Clutched at a cable and scrambled down its length
Hand over hand till he crossed the prison wall
And there dropped twenty feet to earth, to dash
For the freedom of the hills—only to crumple
Under the slugs that whistled from the towers—
The desperado took our breath away.

"To think the stolid Finn," cried Hobbs, the warden,
"Could hold a hunger terrible enough
To breed such recklessness!" He shrugged his arms.
"And yet a black bear sleeping in his den
Seems droll enough and harmless; but who can say
When bears will run amuck and gut a township."

For this they clamped the logger in solitary,
And later in the warehouse, in cellar gloom;
Here, where the stone walls dripped with chilly slime
And melancholy, month on month the Finn
Shifted his bales and boxes, rolled his barrels;
Burrowing underground like a sightless mole
Month upon month, he brooded and fell to bone
And pallid flesh.

Regiments of mice
Began to levy on his sacks of barley,
His prunes, his corn and peas. MacDonald flung
A dozen traps before the blinking Finn
And told him to make an end of all the rodents.
Furtively Waino tucked the string of traps
Under his cot and never set a spring.
Something he liked about the squealing mice,
Something about their merrymaking, their sharp

And gusty delight in the high affairs of mice;
Something—somehow they brought him lively news
Of the pregnant earth six feet beyond the walls
They tunneled under: news of the clover roots
Swollen with April rains, of bugs and birds
Stirring with bright new life, of dandelions
Spreading their buttered crowns to the green and gold
Of soft spring showers; somehow they brought him news.

One morning a slim wan finger of the sun
That wriggled through the single-grated window
High in the cellar, scrawled upon the floor
A slow gold syllable and fell aslant
A sack of parched green peas. A rill of peas
Dribbled from one torn corner, where mice,
Prowling at night, had gnawed the gunny bag.
The stoic Waino held his empty eyes
An hour upon the peas; then, moved by a whim,
He rolled a keg of pickled fish, salt herring,
Into the sunlight and set it on an end.
He scraped his fingers on a barrel that held,
Thick on one broken hoop, a crust of mud
Scooped from the rain-soaked soil of the prison yard
When it had fallen in loading; by patient clawing
He gathered handful on handful of the soil
And piled it on the floor. From a shattered box
He salvaged a scanty pound of fine-ground cork,
And from a bale a fistful of excelsior.
Puddling the whole with water in a pail,
He poured the synthetic earth upon the keg
Of pickled fish and formed a plot of soil
Bound by the jutting staves and a strip of tin
He lashed around the barrelhead to form a wall.

He gathered from the dribbling sack five peas;
Stabbing his thumb upon the dirt, he drew
The pattern of a cross, and solemnly
Into the form he poked his five parched peas,
Covered them firmly, and went about his work.

Each morning he drenched the rounded plot of earth
And scrutinized it eagerly for life.
One day he marked upon the black a cloud
Of thick soft green no larger than his palm.
He bent on it and knew the cloud of frail
Green spears at once as grass, a catch from beyond
The walls. He speculated on the passing bird
Whose bill had taken up the seeds, whose droppings
Had yielded him this gift of swelling life.
And when the blades of green were tall and thick
As fur on a gopher's back, he broke the clump
And patiently transplanted spear on spear
Over his barrel garden to form a sod
Around his seeds.

Another morning his eyes
Gleamed suddenly and wetly when they fell
On five white succulent stems that pierced the soil
And hungrily stretched for the wisp of passing sun.
Eagerly, day on day, he marked their growth:
The first faint lancing green that stabbed the soil,
The slow unfurling patch of velvet leaf,
The pea vines eager to climb a little sky—
These glinted his eyes with the luster of a dream
And put in Waino's throat a quiet laughter
Like bubbles in the bottom of a well.

ne Sunday morning Waino, loath to go
o hear the belching of the prison chaplain,
alked in his cellar and worshiped at his shrine
f blossoming peas; bent on his barrel plot,
e found delight in pruning the roving stems,
n sniffing at the new-blown crinkled petals,
nd training the vines on tiny trellises.
he clatter of the cellar door, the creak
f coming footsteps, brought him up alert.

e shambled out to meet a dim black figure
roping among the bales—the half-breed, Fillion,
he bluffest voyageur on Lac la Croix,
Vhose hot French blood had driven him to sink
thirsty dagger to the ficklc heart
f Rose Labrie, the village courtesan;
is Indian strain of philosophic calm
nd taciturnity had won for him
he freedom of a trusty.

"Those cook, La Plante,"
he Frenchman mumbled, "she's want one keg from
herring.
I'sieu, you got one keg from fish in here?
ome place in cellar—yes?"

The eyes of Waino
luttered a moment; he drew his gnarled red hand
ully across his forehead.

"No," he rasped,
That fish—that keg of fish ain't here in warehouse."

"Bah Gar!" the Frenchman muttered, as the Finn
Shuffling, retreated to a dusky corner,
"Those cook M'sieu La Plante, she's got it down
On inventory barrel from herring fish
It's deliver it last fall. I look around—
Me—I am look around; I find it—maybe."

Fumbling among the boxes, methodically
The mixed-blood penetrated every corner;
Furtively Waino stepped across the floor,
Planted his burly frame before the keg
To shelter it, and waited. Fillion came
At last and faced him, puzzled.

"Sacré! That's funny"—
Scratching his head—"those fish she ain't in here."

He turned to go, but as he wheeled, his eyes
Fell on a splash of green, a spray of leaves
That peeped around the elbow of the Finn.

"Ho-ho!" he laughed, "you got it posies here?
She's pretty—yes?"

The white-faced Finn dropped back,
Trembling from crown to toe. The voyageur
Stepped forward to survey the patch of green
And sniff the blossoms.

"Mon Calvary!" he cried,
"That's keg from fish!—those keg she's growing on!"

Gorillalike the Finn crouched sullenly
Beside the barrel and tensed the huge bunched hands
That dangled at his sides.

"That's fish all right
La Plante she's got it on those inventory!
Almost I'm thinking—me—she's lost, those fish!"
Cried Fillion as he stooped to tilt the keg
And roll it to a truck.

The Finn crouched down;
Sharp fury flickered from his squinting eyes
Raggedly, hotly as the darting tongue
Of any badgered snake; his raw red throat
Rattled with stony syllables:

"Don't!—
Don't touch that fish! You take that keg, by Christ,
I break—I break your goddam back in two!"

Fillion glanced up an instant at the Finn,
Snorted, and wrapped his arms about the staves.
With a desperate roar the Finn flung up his head
And shattered the cold gray granite of his posture;
Lifting his groping hands above his head,
He clutched from on a shelf a syrup jug
And crashed its huge black bulk on Fillion's skull.

The voyageur collapsed and sank to earth
Like an ox that drops beneath a butcher's sledge.
Minute on minute he sprawled upon the floor,

Stone-cold and stunned; a steaming crimson river
Spurted and dribbled from his severed scalp—
A ragged wound from his cowlick to his ear.
Slowly his eyelids fluttered open; he gasped,
Rose to his knees and tottered to his feet—
Only to crumple like a hamstrung doe.
He struggled to his knees again and crawled
Blindly and dizzily across the floor
And up the steps to safety—while Waino huddled
Over his keg and shook with guttural sobs
That racked his ribs and rocked his huge broad back.

The warden, flanked by Clancy and Moran,
Came on him thus a dozen minutes later.
Hobbs fixed his cold gray eyes upon the Finn,
Slowly remarked his quivering shoulders, his head
Shaggy and wet with sweat, and driven deep
Into the vines upon the keg of fish.
Grimly he turned his interest to the plot—
The pulsing green of stem, the satin-white
Of petal, the rich cool pungence of the earth.
Slowly the iron of his jaw relaxed;
Gently and dubiously he wagged his head.
With something of a smile, a quizzical grin,
He muttered to Moran:

"Go tell La Plante
There is no keg of herring in the warehouse;
He must have been mistaken. And tell him, too,
To strike the item from the inventory."

Clancy, amazed, let down his lantern jaw
And stared; the warden was too much for him.

ANIMAL LIFE

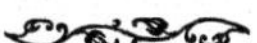

Animals are such agreeable friends—they ask no questions, they pass no criticisms.

—GEORGE ELIOT.

OLD HOUND

FLORENCE RIPLEY MASTIN

With paws in firelight dipped, and drowsy ears
He disregards the calling of the night.
The small fox runs, the hare his shadow fears,
Below the moon the wild geese wing their flight.
But under shelter now he seems content
With serene breath to lie in silken ease.
Back from the lonely forest's ferny scent,
His trail has ended at his master's knees.
He nods his proud head through a night of frost,
His twitching feet alone reveal his dream:
The whirling autumn cloud, the clear track lost,
The antlers gleaming in the mountain stream . . .
No inch of him betrays to morning skies
That hour—except his melancholy eyes.

A MONGREL PUP

NANCY BYRD TURNER

Here lies at rest, unknown to fame,
Of dark descent and doubtful name,
One Binks. Here lie his treasures, too—
A ball, a bone, a worried shoe.

Nay, stranger, shed no idle tears:
He loved one small lad all his years.

UNSATISFIED YEARNING

RICHARD KENDALL MUNKITTRICK

Down in the silent hallway
Scampers the dog about,
And whines, and barks, and scratches,
In order to get out.

Once in the glittering starlight,
He straightway doth begin
To set up a doleful howling
In order to get in.

LONE DOG

IRENE RUTHERFORD McLEOD

I'm a lean dog, a keen dog, a wild dog, and lone;
I'm a rough dog, a tough dog, hunting on my own;
I'm a bad dog, a mad dog, teasing silly sheep;
I love to sit and bay the moon, to keep fat souls from sleep.

I'll never be a lap dog, licking dirty feet,
A sleek dog, a meek dog, cringing for my meat,
Not for me the fireside, the well-filled plate,
But shut door, and sharp stone, and cuff, and kick, and hate.

Not for me the other dogs, running by my side;
Some have run a short while, but none of them would bide.
Oh, mine is still the lone trail, the hard trail, the best,
Wide wind, and wild stars, and the hunger of the quest!

THE TOMCAT

DON MARQUIS

At midnight in the alley
A tomcat comes to wail,
And he chants the hate of a million years
As he swings his snaky tail.

Malevolent, bony, brindled,
Tiger and devil and bard,
His eyes are coals from the middle of hell
And his heart is black and hard.

He twists and crouches and capers
And bares his curved sharp claws,
And he sings to the stars of the jungle nights
Ere cities were, or laws.

Beast from a world primeval,
He and his leaping clan,
When the blotched red moon leers over the roofs
Give voice to their scorn of man.

He will lie on a rug tomorrow
And lick his silky fur,
And veil the brute in his yellow eyes
And play he's tame, and purr.

But at midnight in the alley
He will crouch again and wail,
And beat the time for his demon's song
With the swing of his demon's tail

IN HONOR OF TAFFY TOPAZ

CHRISTOPHER MORLEY

Taffy, the topaz-colored cat,
Thinks now of this and now of that,
  But chiefly of his meals.
Asparagus, and cream, and fish,
Are objects of his Freudian wish;
  What you don't give, he steals.

His gallant heart is strongly stirred
By clink of plate or flight of bird,
  He has a plumy tail;
At night he treads on stealthy pad
As merry as Sir Galahad
  A-seeking of the Grail.

His amiable amber eyes
Are very friendly, very wise;
  Like Buddha, grave and fat,
He sits, regardless of applause,
And thinking, as he kneads his paws,
  What fun to be a cat!

KRAZY: REFLECTION NO. 5

BARON IRELAND

Krazy, they tell me you're not really chummy.
That in you real affection does not stir.
That when you settle down upon my tummy
And purr

And wiggle round to make yourself more cozy
And stretch your forepaws out upon my chest
To make between them for your twitching nosey
A nest,

I'm just an object you have found to serve you
Whereon to snooze a dreamy hour away.
No warmer feeling comes within your purview,
Sneer they.

They tell me if I think it is affection
Which thus inspires your visits to my lap
That I'm (to put it stripped of indirection)
A sap.

They may be right. Perhaps I'm self-deceiving
To sentimentalize about you there.
No doubt I *am* a softy for believing
You care.

Tush! Let them sneer. Their armor's fatal joint is:
It makes no odds if all their jibes be true.
What matter *why* you cuddle up? . . . The point is:
You do.

THE LAST ANTELOPE

Edwin Ford Piper

Behind the board fence at the banker's house
The slender, tawny-gray creature starves and thirsts
In agony of fear. A dog may growl,
It cowers; the cockcrow shakes it with alarm.

White frost lay heavy on the buffalo grass
That winter morning when three graceful shapes
Slipped by the saddleback across the ridge
Along the rutted pathway to the creek.
In former years the track was bare, and worn
With feet of upland creatures every day.
A boy spied these three outlaws. Two hours' chase,
Fifty pursuers, and the ways all stopped—
Guns, dogs, and fences. Torn by the barbed wire,
Drilled by a dozen buckshot, one; the next,
O'erheaped by snapping jaws, cried piteously
An instant; but the last on treacherous ice
Crashed through, a captive.

Ropes—the jolting wagon—
Its heart was audible as you touched its fur.

Behind the board fence at the banker's house—
Oh, once it capered wild on dewy grass
In grace and glee of dancing, arrowy bounds!—
At the banker's house, behind the high board fence
The last slim pronghorn perishes of fear.

THE DONKEY

G. K. Chesterton

When fishes flew and forests walked
And figs grew upon thorn,
Some moment when the moon was blood
Then surely I was born.

With monstrous head and sickening cry
And ears like errant wings,
The devil's walking parody
On all four-footed things.

The tattered outlaw of the earth,
Of ancient crooked will;
Starve, scourge, deride me: I am dumb,
I keep my secret still.

Fools! For I also had my hour;
One far fierce hour and sweet:
There was a shout about my ears,
And palms before my feet.

FOUR LITTLE FOXES

LEW SARETT

peak gently, Spring, and make no sudden sound;
or in my windy valley, yesterday I found
ewborn foxes squirming on the ground—
Speak gently.

alk softly, March, forbear the bitter blow;
er feet within a trap, her blood upon the snow,
he four little foxes saw their mother go—
Walk softly.

o lightly, Spring, oh, give them no alarm;
hen I covered them with boughs to shelter them from harm
he thin blue foxes suckled at my arm—
Go lightly.

tep softly, March, with your rampant hurricane;
uzzling one another, and whimpering with pain,
he new little foxes are shivering in the rain—
Step softly.

ALL GOATS

ELIZABETH COATSWORTH

All goats have a wild-brier grace
They are as elegant as thorns
With little bells beneath their chins
And pointed horns.

So quick are they upon their feet,
So light and gaily do they prance
Their hoofs seem sportive castanets
To which they dance.

And as they raise sagacious heads
Disturbed by some crude passer-by
They gaze upon him with a most
Satiric eye.

THE DROMEDARY

ARCHIBALD Y. CAMPBELL

In dreams I see the Dromedary still,
As once in a gay park I saw him stand.
A thousand eyes in vulgar wonder scanned
His hump and hairy neck, and gazed their fill
At his lank shanks and mocked with laughter shrill.
He never moved; and if his Eastern land
Flashed on his eye with stretches of hot sand,
It wrung no mute appeal from his proud will.
He blinked upon the rabble lazily;
And still some trace of majesty forlorn
And a coarse grace remained. His head was high,
Though his gaunt flanks with a great mange were worn;
There was not any yearning in his eye,
But on his lips and nostril infinite scorn.

CLIPPED WINGS

LEW SARETT

Why do you flutter in my arms and scream,
O frenzied bird, as my poised blue scissors gleam
Above your outstretched wings, and wait to clip
From your shining mallard plumes each buoyant tip?

As I prepare to groom you for the stool
Of shorn decoys who swim my barnyard pool,
Do you by some vague intuition sense
The subtle coming of your impotence?

Never again will you rapturously tilt
Your wings to the sun to wash them in its gilt,
To wheel, and dizzily eddy down the expanse
Of blue earth like a whistling fiery lance.

And ended the nights when the bayou lies asleep
And stars like silver minnows swim its deep—
Of breathless waiting, as your wild mate swings
Over your head and spreads her satin wings.

O wildling, the rebellion in your blood and bone
Doubles the constant anguish of my own—
Your fear of dark earth-fettered days to be,
Of a world whose sky lines are a mockery;

A world of shallow barricaded ponds
That holds for you no shining blue beyonds,
No flaming high horizons to fire your breast
And send you bugling on a lofty quest.

Find comfort in this: if your proud wings are shorn
By my faltering blades, you shall wax fat with corn,
Drowse in the sun, and never know the bite
Of adversity again in day or night.

Shielded from every stealthy fox and hawk,
Contented on your puddle, you shall squawk
And find among my pens of placid geese,
Even as I, a soft seductive peace.

But when wild mallards stretch their vibrant throats
Against the moon and fling their brazen notes
Earthward to challenge and stop the hearts of all
Who grovel on earth, in a deep strong trumpet call;

And when the frosted silver bell of sky
Rings with the rush of wings and the joyous cry
Of mallards streaming home, home again—
What then, O wretched sky-born bird, what then!

THE EAGLE

Alfred Lord Tennyson

He clasps the crag with crooked hands;
Close to the sun in lonely lands,
Ringed with the azure world, he stands.

The wrinkled sea beneath him crawls;
He watches from his mountain walls,
And like a thunderbolt he falls.

THE BLACK VULTURE

George Sterling

Aloof upon the day's immeasured dome,
He holds unshared the silence of the sky.
Far down his bleak, relentless eyes descry
The eagle's empire and the falcon's home—
Far down, the galleons of sunset roam;
His hazards on the sea of morning lie;
Serene, he hears the broken tempest sigh
Where cold sierras gleam like scattered foam.
And least of all he holds the human swarm—
Unwitting now that envious men prepare
To make their dream and its fulfillment one,
When, poised above the caldrons of the storm,
Their hearts, contemptuous of death, shall dare
His roads between the thunder and the sun.

AN AUGUST MIDNIGHT

THOMAS HARDY

I

A shaded lamp and a waving blind,
And the beat of a clock from a distant floor:
On this scene enter—winged, horned, and spined—
A longlegs, a moth, and a dumbledore;
While 'mid my page there idly stands
A sleepy fly, that rubs its hands . . .

II

Thus meet we five, in this still place,
At this point of time, at this point in space.
—My guests besmear my new-penned line,
Or bang at the lamp and fall supine.
"God's humblest, they!" I muse. Yet why?
They know earth-secrets that know not I.

From

SONG OF MYSELF

WALT WHITMAN

I think I could turn and live with animals, they are so placid and self-contained,
I stand and look at them long and long.
They do not sweat and whine about their condition,
They do not lie awake in the dark and weep for their sins,
They do not make me sick discussing their duty to God,
Not one is dissatisfied, not one is demented with the mania of owning things,
Not one kneels to another, nor to his kind that lived thousands of years ago,
Not one is respectable or unhappy over the whole earth.

THE MOLLUSK

JAMES J. MONTAGUE

Wherever may the mollusk roam
He takes along his own sweet home,

And though he goes from bay to bay
And every day is moving day,

He has no furniture to pack,
No old and precious Sèvres to crack,

And nothing with him does he take
That moving men could ever break.

Wherever he can find a meal
Becomes the mollusk's domicile.

Around him he is sure to find
Congenial creatures of his kind,

Who never gossip, never pry,
But in the mud contented lie;

Who never seek to put on airs
But sternly mind their own affairs.

The mollusk does not need to mix
In any sort of politics.

He does not need a radio
To tell him how elections go,

Nor has he any bonds or stocks
Which may perhaps go on the rocks.

Aloof from worry, care and strife,
It has its points, the mollusk's life.

THE RABBITS' SONG OUTSIDE THE TAVERN

ELIZABETH COATSWORTH

We, who play under the pines,
We, who dance in the snow
That shines blue in the light of the moon,
Sometimes halt as we go—
Stand with our ears erect,
Our noses testing the air,
To gaze at the golden world
Behind the windows there.

Suns they have in a cave,
Stars, each on a tall white stem,
And the thought of a fox or an owl
Seems never to trouble them.
They laugh and eat and are warm,
Their food is ready at hand,
While hungry out in the cold
We little rabbits stand.

But they never dance as we dance!
They haven't the speed nor the grace.
We scorn both the dog and the cat
Who lie by their fireplace.
We scorn them licking their paws
Their eyes on an upraised spoon—
We who dance hungry and wild
Under a winter's moon.

HUMOR

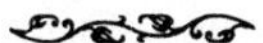

A merry heart doeth good like a medicine.

—PROVERBS 17:22

THE UNTUTORED GIRAFFE

OLIVER HERFORD

A child at school who fails to pass
Examination in his class
Of Natural History will be
So shaky in Zoology,
That, should he ever chance to go
To foreign parts, he scarce will know
The common *Mus Ridiculus*
From *Felis* or *Caniculus*.
And what of boys and girls is true
Applies to other creatures, too,
As you will cheerfully admit
When once I've illustrated it.

Once on a time a young Giraffe
(Who when at school devoured the chaff,
And trampled underneath his feet
The golden grains of Learning's wheat)
Upon his travels chanced to see
A Python hanging from a tree,
A thing he'd never met before.
All neck it seemed and nothing more;
And, stranger still, it was bestrown
With pretty spots much like his own.
Well, well! I've often heard," he said,
"Of foolish folk who lose their head;
But really it's a funnier joke
To meet a head that's lost its folk.

"Dear me! Ha! ha! It makes me laugh.
Where *has* he left his other half?
If he could find it he would be
A really fine Giraffe, like me."

The Python, waking with a hiss,
Exclaimed, "What kind of snake is this?
Your spots are really very fine,
Almost as good in fact as mine,
But with those legs I fail to see
How you can coil about a tree.
Take away half, and you would make
A very decent sort of snake—
Almost as fine a snake as I;
Indeed, it's not too late to try."

A something in the Python's eye
Told the Giraffe 'twas best to fly,
Omitting all formality.
And afterward, when safe at home,
He wrote a very learned tome,
Called, "What I Saw beyond the Foam."
Said he, "The strangest thing one sees
Is a Giraffe who hangs from trees,
And has—(right here the author begs
To state a *fact*) and has *no legs!*"

The book made a tremendous hit.
The public all devoured it,
Save one, who, minding how he missed
Devouring the author—*hissed.*

THE RICH MAN

FRANKLIN P. ADAMS

The rich man has his motorcar,
  His country and his town estate.
He smokes a fifty-cent cigar
        And jeers at Fate.

He frivols through the livelong day;
  He knows not Poverty her pinch.
His lot seems light, his heart seems gay,
        He has a cinch.

Yet though my lamp burns low and dim,
  Though I must slave for livelihood—
Think you that I would change with him?
        You bet I would!

LINES TO DR. DITMARS

By one who observed him filling out his customs declaration in th
lounge of the *S.S. Nerissa*, September 6

KENNETH ALLAN ROBINSON

Here between lunch and teatime, and days and hour
between
The wash from the Orinoco and the vast Sargasso green,
As I watch you sitting and brooding, fitfully biting your pen
I wonder: Are you, too, tempted, even as other men?

Is it thoughts like these you are thinking, here on the ocea
plain,
Far from the wave-washed Bocas, distant from Port o
Spain,
When the last of the loveless Virgins has vanished into th
sea:
"How many boa constrictors can I take in duty-free?

"Touching those fer-de-lances I found in that little place
—Why am I always chasing more than I meant to chase?—
Is it wrong to forget to declare them; would anyone count i
amiss?
I could carry them in my pockets if only they wouldn't hiss

"And my coral snakes, capital fellows"—your brow i
creased in a frown—
"I fear I've exceeded my quota; do I *have* to put them down?
Why couldn't some of us *wear* them? Is anyone bound t
know
That we didn't have them with us when we sailed three
weeks ago?

"My vampire bats are no trouble"—your dark frown lightens and lifts—
"Touristy trifles, I'll grant you, but they *do* make excellent gifts.
And I hope that the chaps at Customs who rummage among my things
Will keep if they can from mussing my bushmaster's loops and rings."

The trade winds stir at the curtains; the dark is beginning to fall,
But your features are firm with a purpose: "No, I'll declare them *all*.
I never was good at deceiving, and what excuse could I make
If the man reached into my luggage and pulled out a nine-foot snake?

"Conscience is always conscience; if there's some slight duty to pay,
One doesn't come back from a journey with a bushmaster every day."
So you write out your declaration, with a firm, deliberate pen,
Down to the last little lizard, even as other men.

THE COURTSHIP OF MILES STANDISH

William F. Kirk

Miles Standish ban having a courtship
Ven all of his fighting ban tru;
Maester Longfaller tal me about it,
And so ay skol tal it to yu.
He say to his roommate, Yohn Alden:
"Yu know dis Priscilla, ay s'pose.
Last veek, ven ay try to get busy,
Priscilla yust turn op her nose."

Yohn Alden ban nervy young faller.
So Standish yust tal him: "Old pal,
Pleese boost me to dis har Priscilla,
Yu know ay can't talk wery val.
Pleese tal her ay ban a gude soldier,
And say ay have money in bank.
Ay'd do dis myself, but, ay tal yu,
My manners in parlor ban rank."

So Yohn go and call on Priscilla,
And happen to finding her in;
He sit close beside her on sofa,
And give her gude lots of his chin.
"Miles Standish," he say, "ban gude faller,
Hot stuff vith his pistol and knife;
And so ay ban coming to tal yu
He'd lak yu, Priscilla, for vife."

Priscilla, she listen to Alden,
And den give him a cute little venk,
And say: "Vy not speak for yureself, Yohn?
Miles Standish ban lobster, ay tenk."
So Standish get double-crossed planty;
And dat's yust vat *ay* vant, by yee,
Ef ever ay get any faller
To doing my sparking for me!

THOUGHT FOR A SUNSHINY MORNING

DOROTHY PARKER

It costs me never a stab nor squirm
To tread by chance upon a worm.
"Aha, my little dear," I say,
"Your clan will pay me back one day."

THE AMBIGUOUS DOG

ARTHUR GUITERMAN

The Dog beneath the Cherry-tree
Has ways that sorely puzzle me:

Behind, he wags a friendly tail;
Before, his Growl would turn you pale!

His meaning isn't wholly clear—
Oh, is the Wag or Growl sincere?

I think I'd better not descend—
His Bite is at the Growly End.

THE CENTIPEDE

MRS. EDWARD CRASTER

The centipede was happy quite,
  Until a toad in fun
Said, "Pray, which leg comes after which?"
That worked her mind to such a pitch,
She lay distracted in a ditch
  Considering how to run.

ENIGMA IN ALTMAN'S

PHYLLIS McGINLEY

It is a strange, miraculous thing
About department stores,
How elevators upward wing
By twos and threes and fours,

How pale lights gleam, how cables run
All day without an end,
Yet how reluctant, one by one,
The homing cars descend.

They soar to Furniture, or higher,
They speed to Gowns and Gifts,
But when the bought weighs down the buyer,
Late, late, return the lifts.

Newton, himself, beneath his tree,
Would ponder this and frown:
How what goes up so frequently
So seldom cometh down.

BETWEEN TWO LOVES

T. A. Daly

I gotta love for Angela,
I love Carlotta, too.
I no can marry both o' dem,
So w'at I gona do?

Oh, Angela ees pretta girl,
She gotta hair so black, so curl,
An' teeth so white as anytheeng.
An' oh, she gotta voice to seeng,
Dat mak' your hearta feel eet must
Jomp up an' dance or eet weell bust.
An' alla time she seeng, her eyes
Dey smila like Italia's skies,
An' makin' flirtin' looks at you—
But dat ees all w'at she can do.

Carlotta ees no gotta song,
But she ees twice so big an' strong
As Angela, an' she no look
So beautiful—but she can cook.
You oughta see her carry wood!
I tal you w'at, eet do you good.
W'en she ees be som'body's wife
She worka hard, you bat my life!
She nevva gattin' tired, too—
But dat ees all w'at she can do.

Oh, my! I weesh dat Angela
Was strong for carry wood,
Or else Carlotta gotta song
An' looka pretta good.
I gotta love for Angela,
I love Carlotta, too.
I no can marry both o' dem,
So w'at I gona do?

THE LAZY WRITER

BERT LESTON TAYLOR

In summer I'm disposed to shirk,
As summer is no time to work.

In winter inspiration dies
For lack of outdoor exercise.

In spring I'm seldom in the mood,
Because of vernal lassitude.

The fall remains. But such a fall!
We've really had no fall at all.

THE STREET OF DOCTORS

THOMAS WALSH

In old Pekin a monarch reigned
Who in a high decree ordained—
"Each Doctor must a lamp provide
For every patient that has died,
No matter how they're multiplied;
On pain of death do we enact
That by his door each prophylact
Shall keep his score of lamps exact."
Then straightway with a blaze of lights
The Street of Doctors shone by nights;
The world of fashion more and more
Strolled up and down before their door,
And blessed the shrewd old monarch's cue
For such a brilliant rendezvous.

While "Feasts of Lanterns" shamed the sun
Around the porticoes of one,
His neighbors filled a lamp or two,
Rejoicing patients were so few;
Or else when things looked bright and bad
Brought on the case some likely lad,
And called in consultation him
Whose rival lamps looked all too dim—
(A game, though hardly after Hoyle,
Of how to save the midnight oil).
Yet while all Chinaland grew bright,
With spirit lamps, alas, what plight!
Dyspepsia fastened more and more
Upon their dear old emperor,

Until with tonsils, blue and furry,
He bade the mandarins to hurry,
And fetch, to ease his gripes and cramps,
The doctor with the fewest lamps.

By north and south and east and west
They journeyed on their slippered quest;
And made their census of the lights
Through glasses smoked to save their sights;
Or, wisdom-lighted, far would prowl
Through dismal haunts of bat and owl,
Cursing the darkened doors in wrath
Of osteo- and hydro-path;
Not knowing as they barked their shin
That every ill was cured within.
At last into the sacred door
They ushered to the emperor
A most tremendous, strange M.D.
Whose porch lamps numbered only three—
Who called for fire and called for ice,
For plover's eggs, and purple mice,
Nux vomica, and mermaids' toes
And chutney sauce, which he boiled and froze
And shook into a salmon tint,
And decked the cup with a sprig of mint.
The Son of Heaven was heard to gulp
As he tossed it down to the very pulp;
His eyes bulged out, and he muttered, "My, sir,
You certainly pour an appetizer!
But tell me, now, while your balm is working
How long have you been so darkly lurking?"

The M.D. stiffened down to his cue
As he noticed the emperor turning blue—
"O, Son of Glory, but yesterday
I got my practice under way;
Three lamps I lighted to make my score,
For the market was short of any more—
I mean no wrong to professional brothers,
So I hope tonight to display some others."

TO A POET

By Spring

CAROLYN WELLS

Yes, Poet, I am coming down to earth,
  To spend the merry months of blossomtime;
But don't break out in paeans of glad mirth
  (Expressed in hackneyed rhyme.)

For once, dear Poet, won't you kindly skip
  Your ode of welcome? It is such a bore;
I am no chicken, and I've made the trip
  Six thousand times or more.

And as I flutter earthward every year,
  You must admit that it grows rather stale
When I arrive, repeatedly to hear
  The same old annual "Hail!"

Time was when I enjoyed the poet's praise,
  Will Shakespeare's song, or Mr. Milton's hymn;
Or even certain little twittering lays
  By ladies quaint and prim.

Chaucer and Spenser filled me with delight—
  And how I loved to hear Bob Herrick woo!
Old Omar seemed to think I was all right,
  And Aristotle, too.

But I am sated with this fame and glory,
  Oh, Poet, leave Parnassian heights unscaled;
This time let me be spared the same old story,
  And come for once unhailed!

THE TWINS

HENRY S. LEIGH

In form and feature, face and limb,
  I grew so like my brother
That folks got taking me for him
  And each for one another.
It puzzled all our kith and kin;
  It reached an awful pitch;
For one of us was born a twin,
  And not a soul knew which.

One day (to make the matter worse),
  Before our names were fixed,
As we were being washed by Nurse,
  We got completely mixed.
And thus, you see, by Fate's decree
  (Or rather Nurse's whim),
My brother John got christened *me*,
  And I got christened *him*.

This fatal likeness even dogged
  My footsteps when at school;
And I was always getting flogged,
  For John turned out a fool.
I put this question hopelessly
  To everyone I knew:
"What *would* you do, if you were me,
  To prove that you were *you?*"

Our close resemblance turned the tide
   Of my domestic life,
For somehow my intended bride
   Became my brother's wife.
In short, year after year the same
   Absurd mistakes went on;
And when I died—the neighbors came
   And buried brother John!

SALLY AND MANDA

Alice B. Campbell

Sally and Manda are two little lizards
Who gobble up flies in their two little gizzards.
They live by a toadstool near two little hummocks
And crawl all around on their two little stomachs.

AUTUMN LEAVES

By a poet who counts

W. Hodgson Burnet

The leaves are falling, falling,
The trees are getting bare,
To me its just appalling
That no one seems to care!

In parks and open spaces
In rusty heaps they lie,
And men with vacant faces
Unheeding pass them by.

The numbers keep on mounting
By thousands every day,
But no one thinks of counting
Before they're swept away.

To High-brows and to Mystics
Numbers have no appeal,
But lovers of statistics
Will know just how I feel.

But what's the use of grumbling?
I'll never know, I fear,
How many leaves come tumbling
From London's trees each year!

ECHO

MILDRED WESTON

You
Over there
Beyond the hill
Have nothing to say
Yet can't keep still—
Have nothing to do
But mimic me
And double the words
That I set free.
Garrulous ghost!
Garrulous ghost.

Maybe you'd say
In your defence
No echo practices
Reticence,
And the repartee
Of a voice's ghost
Makes conversation
As good as most!
As good as most.

A SCOT'S FAREWELL TO HIS GOLF BALL

James J. Montague

Guid-by, auld ba'! Fu' mony a year
  I've sent ye sailin' yon an' hither;
But, puir, wee friend, I sairly fear
  We'll play nae mair at gowf thegither.
Ye willna last the summer through,
  As I ha' airnestly been hopin',
For ye are bidin' here the noo,
  A' bruk wide open.

I swung at ye wi' might an' main,
  I thocht to send ye fairly flyin'.
I didna see the ledge o' stane
  Beneath the sand whaur ye were lyin'.
I was owerhasty, for I meant
  To stand a wee bit closer to ye,
But pressin' juist a mite I sent
  My niblick through ye.

Ye bore fu' mony a dent an' scar
  An' cut an mashie mairk aboot ye,
But mon! ye'd travel fast an' far
  Whenever I wad brawly cloot ye.
Fu' aft's the time ye've hid yersel
  Amang the gorse an' broom around ye,
But I ha' hunted lang an' well
  An' always found ye.

A bonnie time for gowf, the fa';
  But noo—an' sairly I deplore it—
I needs maun buy anither ba'
  An' gie a precious shillin' for it.
The game is my ane lane delight,
  But it grows costly past a' reason—
Puir, broken ba', I hoped ye might
  Last oot the season.

A TIMELY WARNING

ANONYMOUS

If your nose is close to the grindstone rough,
And you hold it down there long enough,
In time you'll say there's no such thing
As brooks that babble and birds that sing.
These three will all your world compose:
Just You, the Stone, and your own old Nose.

TO A VERY YOUNG GENTLEMAN

CHRISTOPHER MORLEY

My child, what painful vistas are before you!
  What years of youthful ills and pangs and bumps—
Indignities from aunts who "just adore" you,
  And chicken pox and measles, croup and mumps!
I don't wish to dismay you—it's not fair to,
  Promoted now from bassinet to crib—
But, O my babe, what troubles flesh is heir to
  Since God first made so free with Adam's rib!

Laboriously you will proceed with teething;
  When teeth are here, you'll meet the dentist's chair;
They'll teach you ways of walking, eating, breathing,
  That stoves are hot, and how to brush your hair;
And so, my poor, undaunted little stripling,
  By bruises, tears, and trousers you will grow,
And, borrowing a leaf from Mr. Kipling,
  I'll wish you luck, and moralize you so:

If you can think up seven thousand methods
  Of giving cooks and parents heart disease;
Can rifle pantry shelves, and then give death odds
  By water, fire, and falling out of trees;
If you can fill your every boyish minute
  With sixty seconds' worth of mischief done,
Yours is the house and everything that's in it,
  And, which is more, you'll be your father's son!

A PURE MATHEMATICIAN

ARTHUR GUITERMAN

Let Poets chant of Clouds and Things
  In lonely attics!
A Nobler Lot is his, who clings
  To Mathematics.

Sublime he sits, no Worldly Strife
  His Bosom vexes,
Reducing all the Doubts of Life
  To Y's and X's.

And naught to him's a Primrose on
  The river's border;
A Parallelepipedon
  Is more in order.

Let Zealots vow to do and dare
  And right abuses!
He'd rather sit at home and square
  Hypotenuses.

Along his straight-ruled paths he goes
  Contented with 'em,
The only Rhythm that he knows,
  A Logarithm!

THE MUSIC OF THE FUTURE

OLIVER HERFORD

The politest musician that ever was seen
Was Montague Meyerbeer Mendelssohn Green.
So extremely polite he would take off his hat
Whenever he happened to meet with a cat.

"It's not that I'm partial to cats," he'd explain;
"Their music to me is unspeakable pain.
There's nothing that causes my flesh so to crawl
As when they perform a G-flat caterwaul.

"Yet I cannot help feeling—in spite of their din—
When I hear at a concert the first violin
Interpret some exquisite thing of my own,
If it were not for *cat gut* I'd never be known.

"And so, when I bow as you see to a cat,
It isn't to *her* that I take off my hat;
But to fugues and sonatas that possibly hide
Uncomposed in her—well—in her tuneful inside!"

THE DINOSAUR

BERT LESTON TAYLOR

Behold the mighty Dinosaur,
Famous in prehistoric lore,
Not only for his weight and strength
But for his intellectual length.
You will observe by these remains
The creature had two sets of brains—
One in his head (the usual place),
The other at his spinal base.
Thus he could reason *a priori*
As well as *a posteriori*.
No problem bothered him a bit:
He made both head and tail of it.
So wise he was, so wise and solemn,
Each thought filled just a spinal column.
If one brain found the pressure strong,
It passed a few ideas along;
If something slipped his forward mind
'Twas rescued by the one behind;
And if in error he was caught
He had a saving afterthought.
As he thought twice before he spoke
He had no judgments to revoke;
For he could think, without congestion,
Upon both sides of every question.

Oh, gaze upon this model beast,
Defunct ten million years at least.

RELATIVITY

KATHLEEN MILLAY

"The world is such a funny place,"
  Remarked a topsy-turvy Ace,
    A-sliding down a curve in space,

"But, from this angle I can see
  No gently sloping theory,
    I am inclined toward Gravity,

"And even Einstein would compute
  That Time and Space are both *Acute*
    When dropping in a parachute!"

A GUIDE TO POETRY

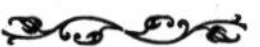

GETTING ACQUAINTED WITH POETRY

POETRY is the airplane of the mind, for it takes us on imaginary flights. We visit places both strange and familiar, meet all kinds of people, and sometimes catch glimpses of uncharted lands.

"But," someone may ask, "can't we have imaginary experiences just as well by reading prose?" Although we can, they are not likely to be the same. Prose might be compared to the automobile. Excellent as the automobile is, we cannot obtain from it the broad views of landscape and the unusual angle of vision that we can from an airplane. Similarly, we may read a chapter of prose, yet not find as much to arouse the imagination as we find in a few lines of poetry.

Getting acquainted with poetry is like learning to fly—the method of procedure is important. Imagine an inexperienced pilot taking off in a ship he does not understand. The intricate controls bother him, the numerous instruments puzzle him; and if in addition he flies over strange territory, the consequences may not be entirely pleasant.

The inexperienced reader has the same sort of difficulties when he begins to read some kinds of poetry. Unusual wording confuses him, strange figures of speech bewilder him, unfamiliar references make him feel lost. No wonder he often ends in a mental tailspin.

Of course no inexperienced pilot, if he is sensible, puts himself in the awkward position described. On the contrary, he chooses a plane with fairly simple controls and stay close to his own landing field. In like manner, the persor who is not accustomed to reading poetry does well to begir with poems which are simply worded and about things h understands.

The Subject Matter of Poetry

The subjects for the poet are unlimited, for there ar probably no thoughts or ideas which cannot be expresse in poetry. Thomas Carlyle said, "Wherever there is a sk above him, and a world around him, the poet is in his place for here too is man's existence, with its infinite longings an small acquirings." He may be on a lonely island. Here h observes the warmth and cheer of the sun, the unceasin rise and fall of the tides, the habits of the birds and animals On the other hand, he may be in the city. Here he sees th beauty and ugliness of the buildings, the behavior of man i intimate contact with his fellows, the humor and tragedy o events. These are but a few of the countless things which th poet, with his observant eye and his gift of expression, put into his poems.

A Definition of Poetry

There are various definitions of poetry, chiefly becaus authorities do not agree on one as being satisfactory in ever respect. Some people even go so far as to say that it canno be defined. However, we may get an idea of its nature if w say: *Poetry is the expression of emotion in picturesque, rhythmica language.*

We must realize at the beginning that poetry is no "something that rhymes." Of course much poetry doe rhyme, but by no means all. Familiar examples of unhymed poetry are Shakespeare's plays, Longfellow's 'Evangeline," and Arnold's "Sohrab and Rustum."

Poetry may be classified as narrative, lyric, dramatic, or epic.

A *narrative* poem is one that tells a story.

A *lyric* poem expresses the poet's emotions rather than ncidents or events.

A *dramatic* poem is a picture of human life designed to be acted on a stage.

An *epic* poem is one of considerable length celebrating the deeds of a national hero.

The definition of poetry which is given here fits all kinds of poems, narrative, dramatic, epic, and lyric, for the emotional quality and picturesque language are characteristic of them all.

Emotion

The emotion, or feeling, which the poet expresses is his reaction to his surroundings. His impressions come to him in the same way that they come to everyone—through sight, hearing, touch, taste, and smell; but his feelings are more sensitive, and he is more skillful in using words. Therefore, he is able to put his feelings into effective language. For instance, when an ordinary person observes a skyscraper, he has rather matter-of-fact thoughts: "It is a fine-looking building," or "I wonder how many people are in it," or "Its owner must be making money."

However, when the poet observes the skyscraper, his imagination is stirred, and his mind is filled with unusual thoughts. These thoughts he is able to put into a poem which also arouses the feelings and imaginations of those who read or hear what he has written. An illustration of the poet's point of view may be found in "Skyscraper" by Carl Sandburg, page 58. Here the poet thinks of the building in terms of what it means to the people who use it—their labors, their ambitions, their sorrows; and also in terms of those who built it—some of them dead, some out of work, some in prison. But because the souls of these living and dead are so closely associated with it, he declares that the skyscraper has a soul.

Picturesque Language

Any expressions, either literal or figurative, which produce mental pictures may be described as picturesque language.

Literal expressions are those in which the words have exact or ordinary meaning. The poet uses literal expressions that are vivid, as "bleak buildings," "white stars," "the signaling lanterns rise and fall," "a radio that blares and squeaks," "dawn is a smoke-thick gray."

Figurative expressions are those in which the words take on unusual meanings because of relationships which they suggest. If we say "The man is energetic," the expression is literal. If we say "The man is a dynamo," the expression is figurative. It would, of course, be absurd to take this latter expression literally because a man is not actually a dynamo. The word does, however, suggest his energy by calling up a picture of a machine which gives forth a great amount of energy.

Daily speech is full of figurative language: "as quick as lightning," "a manner that froze us," "a two-faced person," "a lion in the fight." Taken literally such expressions are ridiculous. Many of them have been used so much that they have lost their original vividness, and we scarcely think of them as figurative.

Figurative language is sometimes called "the language of poetry." The poet uses it to give in a few words a vivid impression of something he has seen or heard or felt. Such language starts from the poet's imagination and appeals to the imagination of others. In the following lines John Gould Fletcher uses figurative language to describe the skaters.

Black swallows swooping or gliding
In a flurry of entangled loops and curves;
The skaters skim over the frozen river.
And the grinding click of their skates as they impinge upon
  the surface,
Is like the brushing together of thin wing tips of silver.

There are various forms of figurative language known as *figures of speech*. Definitions and illustrations of some of the main ones follow.

A *simile* is a comparison of two things which are essentially unlike but which have some characteristic in common. "The man is like his energetic friend" is not a simile because *man* and *friend* are not different enough, both being members of the human race. "The man is like a dynamo" is a simile because *man* and *dynamo*, though different in practically every respect, have, in this instance, one characteristic in common, namely abundant energy. In a simile, the comparison is definitely expressed, usually by *like* or *as*.

Similes occur frequently in poetry, for the poet seeing one thing imagines another like it and makes a striking comparison between the two things.

Clusters of electric bulbs
Like giant chrysanthemums
Paint the black cavern

With streaks and blots
Of faded yellow.

Examples of other interesting similes may be found in "Apartment House," page 35; "Filling Station," page 39; "Nature," page 126; and "The Windmills," page 204.

A *metaphor* is a compressed simile, compressed in the sense that the comparison between two unlike things is implied rather than fully stated by *like*, *as*, or some other word. The point of similarity between the two is emphasized by speaking as if one thing were the other. "The man is a dynamo" implies that the man is like a dynamo in some respect, obviously in having great energy.

The comparison may be suggested by an adjective, as in "a man of iron will," that is, a will like iron. Again, it may be suggested by a verb, as in "His troubles evaporated." *Evaporated* suggests complete disappearance, as of a liquid.

Sometimes a whole expression suggests the comparison:

They [cars] grope their way through fog and night
With the golden feelers of their light.

The cars are spoken of as if they were insects, the thought being that as an insect gropes its way with its feelers, so automobiles seen from a height appear to grope their way, using their headlights as feelers.

Often entire poems are metaphors. Examples are: "Waterfalls of Stone," page 51; "No Words Are Lost," page 157; "Steam Shovel," page 177; and "Thunderstorm," page 184.

The metaphor and the simile are the figures of speech most commonly used.

A metaphor may be converted into a simile by putting in the word to express the comparison; a simile may be converted into a metaphor by taking it out. For example, Alfred Noyes used a metaphor when he said, "the road was a gypsy's ribbon." If he had said "the road was *like* a gypsy's ribbon," he would have been using a simile. On the other hand, John Gould Fletcher chose a simile to express his idea in "The windmills, like great sunflowers of steel." Had he said, "The windmills are great sunflowers of steel," he would have used a metaphor to convey his idea.

Metonymy is the use of one word in place of another which it suggests by close association, as *flag* for *country*.

> Winnipeg and Florida and Spain
> Met Norway and Brazil at breakfast time
> Upon the table.

These places suggest such articles as bread, oranges, grapes, herring, coffee.

Personification gives human qualities to things or ideas, as "Fortune smiled on him." Personifications are used with great effectiveness in poetry.

> Great towers of steel, which stride
> Across the countryside.

Entire poems may be personification as "The Secret of the Machines," page 6; "Chant of the Box Cars," page 16; "The Gargoyle in the Snow," page 140; "Trees That Shade a House," page 190; and "The Unconquered Air," page 322.

Apostrophe is direct address to the Deity, an absent person, or something inanimate.

Brother Tree:
Why do you reach and reach?

Poems may be largely or entirely apostrophe, as "Great Towers of Steel," page 18; "Ode to Machines," page 45 and "Autumn, Forsake These Hills," page 68.

Hyperbole is obvious exaggeration. Thomas Babington Macaulay wrote: "Somebody has said of the boldest figure in rhetoric, the hyperbole, that it lies without deceiving." Hyperbole is used to emphasize a point or to produce humorous effects. Daily speech is full of hyperbole, as "This suitcase weighs a ton."

Irony is the use of words whose real meaning is the opposite of that intended, as "Dropping a watch is a fine way to make it run." Sometimes entire poems are ironical in tone, as "A Pure Mathematician," page 441, or the following poem entitled "Parlor Car":

What a comfort! through conditioned air
  A radio that blares and squeaks;
Beyond the glass (if one should care)
  The thunderous silence of the peaks.

Onomatopoeia is the use of words which produce sound images. That is, the sounds of the words suggest the sense, as *buzz*, *splash*, *clatter*.

The dull-booming rumble
Of scampering traffic.

Whole poems are very seldom written in this type of figurative language, but onomatopoeic words and phrases are frequently used in poetry.

Rhythmical Language

Another distinguishing characteristic of poetry, as the definition suggests, is rhythm. *Rhythm* is the more or less regular recurrence of accents or ideas. Deep in us all is a feeling for rhythm. We hear it in the traffic noises on a busy street, in the blowing of the wind, and in the beat of the rain. It is so fundamental in man that his speech tends to become rhythmical when he expresses emotion. Rhythm, then, is fundamental to poetry, for poetry expresses the emotion of the poet.

The rhythmical lines of poetry, known as *verse*, may take one of two forms: the *measured* (*metrical*) based on a regular succession of accents, and the *free* based on a regular succession and balance of ideas in the natural rhythm of speech.

Metrical verse, the rhythm of regularly repeated accents, is like the rhythm of most running machinery: the tick of a clock, the slap of a belt on a pulley, the puff of a locomotive, the click of car wheels on the rails.

All language consists of a mixture of accented syllables (louder sounds) and unaccented syllables (softer sounds). English words of more than one syllable nearly always have their syllables unequally stressed. One-syllable words are accented or unaccented according to their importance. In the following illustrations the accented syllables are marked.

> Two thóusand féet benéath our whéels
> The cíty spráwls acróss the lánd.

Free verse, as the name indicates, is free from the restraint of regularly repeated accents. Instead, it has a rhythm of ideas and phrases like the rhythm of waves breaking on a shore. As wave follows wave, the interval between them i not always equal, yet the effect is rhythmical. In the illus tration below it is evident that the accents do not fal regularly, as they do in the preceding one.

By day the skyscraper looms in the smoke and sun and ha
  a soul
Prairie and valley, streets of the city, pour people into it anc
  they mingle among its twenty floors and are poured ou
  again back to the streets, prairies and valleys.
It is the men and women, boys and girls so poured in anc
  out all day that give the building a soul of dreams anc
  thoughts and memories.

The term *verse* includes both measured verse and free verse, although it is often used to mean only the former When free verse is meant, it is usually specified by name.

Though all poetry is verse, all verse is not poetry. Fo instance, if directions for performing an experiment or fo baking a cake were written in verse, the resulting lines woulc not be poetry because they would not express emotion.

Reading Poetry Aloud

Many people believe that the way to enjoy poetry most is to read it aloud because its rhythm as well as part of its emotional effect depends on the sound of words. The rhythm resembles the rhythm of music, for both are based on sound. Songs, which are words set to music or music set to words, show the close relationship between the two forms of expression. We know that music is composed to be heard, and we may assume that poetry because of its rhythmical sound is also meant to reach the ear.

Rhythmical speech has a fascination which children are quick to discover. They delight in saying nursery rhymes, game rhymes, and counting-out rhymes. This early, instinctive liking for the sound of verse also suggests that poetry is more effective when heard.

It is significant that poetry in its beginnings was linked with speech. Poetry began early in the languages of the human race, probably in connection with the other forms of rhythmical expression, music and dancing. As language developed, poetry naturally underwent changes in form, but it was still spoken or sung. Much of this early poetry was doubtless lost, but some of it was written down and so has been preserved. For example, the Psalms of the Bible were originally sung by choirs; the poems of the Anglo-Saxons were recited by their gleemen, or minstrels; and the old English and Scottish ballads were sung by the people themselves. For centuries, then, until the invention of printing made books plentiful, poetry was addressed almost entirely to the ear.

Reading poetry aloud effectively is a matter of reading distinctly, audibly, and with expression. Expression results naturally if we can let the eyes travel ahead of the voice and in this way grasp the meaning of the words before we speak them. Of course, the problem of meaning is solved if we are familiar with the poem.

Because of the rhythm of poetry some people have a tendency to read it in a singsong, or monotonously rhythmical manner. This fault of reading all poetry with accented regularity can be avoided by bearing in mind that much poetry is irregular, as explained on pages 466 to 467.

Furthermore, regardless of verse form, words are pronounced as they would be in ordinary speech. The result is that the accented syllables are not all equally stressed and the unaccented syllables, also, differ slightly.

I like to watch the cars go by.

Of the accented syllables, *cars* is naturally stressed more than *by* and of the unaccented syllables *go* more than *the*. Pauses come where the sense of the words and the punctuation require them. In poetry with rhyme there should be no unnatural stress on rhyming words.

Some poems have qualities which make them suitable for group reading or speaking. These qualities are:

1. A well-marked rhythm in either measured verse or free verse
2. Subject matter which has general interest
3. Contrast, to permit the use of different types of voices and different numbers of speakers

Many of the poems in this book have these qualities, and are, therefore, suitable for group reading. A few of these which have not been commonly used are:

"The Secret of the Machines," page 6
"On Hearing Jazz," page 34
"The Gargoyle in the Snow," page 140
"Mountain Hamlet," page 210
"Cobbler," page 221
"Spanish Waters," page 318
"Reveille," page 326
"He Who Loves the Ocean," page 329
"I Hear America Singing," page 343

"Lone Dog," page 401
"Echo," page 437

Understanding a Poem

Sometimes a reader is a bit puzzled by the meaning of a oem. This feeling of uncertainty is described as follows by hristopher Morley in his poem, "Thin Air."

> Most people read poetry
> As our wire-haired terrier snaps a soap-bubble:
> An empty gulp,
> A frail vapory sparkle on her nose—
> Not even wondering where it went.

A reader who finds himself in this predicament may well sk what he can do. First, of course, he had better reread e poem, trying to understand it. If he failed the first time, erhaps it was because some of the words, expressions, or eferences are unusual and difficult. To find the meaning of ese, he should consult the notes, which are frequently rovided, such as those at the back of this book. If these fail o give the desired information, or if there are no notes, he hould consult a dictionary, an encyclopedia, or someone ho can help him.

Occasionally, poems written years ago contain words not eadily understood by people living today. Such words are uzzling because their meanings have changed with time. hese older meanings are given only in the larger diction-ries. For example, in a poem by Shakespeare, "To His ove," page 265, occurs this line:

> Nor lose possession of that fair thou owest

An unabridged dictionary will make clear to the puzzle reader that *fair* formerly meant beauty. *Owest* is, of cours from *owe* which formerly meant possess.

At other times the reader's difficulty may be due to th figurative use of words that in themselves are perfect familiar. The poet may be comparing one thing to anoth because he sees it in a new light. He may be using person fication or apostrophe to express his feeling more strikingl Under such circumstances the reader must try to tune in o the poet's imagination.

However, it is possible to understand all the words bot literal and figurative, as well as the references, and sti not understand the poem. Perhaps the word order is ur usual, or words—especially verbs—are left out, because th poet is trying to express his ideas more vividly by the unusua order or by economy of words. For example, the ide expressed by "Something there is that doesn't love a wall" is more emphatic than it would be if expressed in the usua word order "There is something that doesn't love a wall" ("Mending Wall," page 86); and "Noise of hammer once I heard" is more effective than "Once I heard a nois of hammers" ("The Hammers," page 192). "Tempest with out" is as clear and more forceful than the longer expressio "There is a tempest without" ("Hands," page 181). Th following stanza from "Across Illinois," page 15, contains no verb, yet it presents a perfectly definite picture.

The light of a locomotive adown the level track,
A straight white line of brightness cutting the blanket o
black.

If the reader feels that the order of words or the omissior of words makes the poem difficult, a more careful examinaon of the troublesome passages will usually enable him to iscover the ideas that the poet was trying to express.

Finally, somebody may ask the reader what he thinks f a poem. Of course, if he is to take part in a discussion, e must have definite ideas and opinions. The following uestions may help to bring these out:

1. What experience probably led to the writing of the poem?
2. What experience, in any way similar, have I had, heard of, or read of?
3. What thoughts, pictures, or sensations does the poem suggest?
4. What features of the poem do I particularly like or dislike? (Features to consider are: ideas and opinions, word pictures, sound of words, rhythm, and style.)

THE MECHANICS OF POETRY

JUST as many people like to understand how a machine i put together, so some readers of poetry like to under stand the structure of a poem. It must be remembered, o course, that mere knowledge of the mechanics of verse wil not produce poetry or enable us to understand it, althoug such knowledge may help us to appreciate better its artis try and power.

The mechanics of poetry is called versification or prosody and applies to measured verse only. It includes an under standing of meter, rhyme, and stanza structure.

Metrical Structure

The first step in studying the mechanics of a poem is tc determine the rhythm. This is done by noting the accented and the unaccented syllables according to natural pronunciation of the words. In the following illustration an *accent* (′) marks an accented syllable, and a *short*, or *breve* (˘) marks an unaccented syllable.

> Ĭ heár thĕm gríndĭng, gríndĭng thróugh thĕ níght,
> Thĕ gáunt măchínes wĭth ártĕríes ŏf fíre.

If the accents occur with fair regularity, as in the lines marked, we conclude that the rhythm is measured, or metrical, rather than free.

The next step is to determine the meter. The unit of measure in verse is the *foot*. A foot ordinarily contains one accented syllable and one or more unaccented syllables. The feet may be separated by vertical lines.

> I hear|them grind|ing, grind|ing through|the night,
> The gaunt|ma chines|with ar|ter ies|of fire.

Each of these divisions is a foot. Thus, we have two lines each containing five feet.

There are different meters depending upon the number and arrangement of syllables in the foot and the number of feet in each line. Following are definitions and illustrations of the commonest kinds of feet in English verse. Their names came originally from Greek.

The common two-syllable feet are:

Iamb, *iambus*, or *iambic:* one unaccented syllable and one accented syllable (⏑ʹ). The word *be lieve* is iambic. Two iambic lines are marked in the preceding illustration.

Trochee: one accented syllable and one unaccented syllable (ʹ⏑). The name is from a word that means *running*, and the word *run ning* is trochaic.

> Up, lad,|up, 'tis|late for|ly ing.

The common three-syllable feet are:

Dactyl: one accented syllable and two unaccented syllables (ʹ⏑⏑). The name comes from a word meaning *finger*. The dactyl resembles a finger in that the accented or long syllable corresponds to the long first joint and the unaccented or short syllables correspond to the two shorter joints. The word *sud den ly* is dactylic.

> Hark to the|song in him!

Anapaest: two unaccented syllables and one accented syllable (˘˘′). The name means a dactyl reversed. The phrase *of the best* is anapaestic.

In the des|ert he sings|of a rose.

Two other kinds of two-syllable feet are sometimes used to give variety to the rhythm of lines:

Spondee: two accented syllables (′′). The name is derived from that of a slow-moving Greek ceremonial melody. The words *high tide* are spondaic.

Pyrrhic: two unaccented syllables (˘˘). The name comes from a lively Greek dance. Two adjoining unimportant words like *and the* may be pyrrhic.

Since verse is based on the recurrence of accented and unaccented syllables, it is evident that no line of any length can be composed entirely of spondees and certainly not of pyrrhics. These feet are generally mixed with the more usual types. "Sea Fever" by John Masefield, page 331, contains an unusually large number of spondees and pyrrhics.

And the|wheel's kick|and the|wind's song|and the|white
sail's|shak ing.

Of the various types of feet named, the iambic is so common that it may be considered the standard, the others being used for special effects. In a general way, the trochee is rapid, the dactyl soothing, and the anapaest buoyant. The spondee and the pyrrhic, as their names indicate, are slow and fast respectively.

By his choice of the kind and combination of feet, the poet can suggest a mood: cheer, melancholy, reverence, ıspiration, humor. Of course, much depends also on the ıeaning and sound of the words, the length of the lines, and ıch special sound effects as rhyme, assonance, and allitera- on, explained later on pages 469–472.

A metrical line may contain any number of feet up to ight, from two to six being commonest. The different kinds f metrical lines have names. Each of these, as will be een from the following examples, ends in *meter*, meaning ıeasure, and begins with a prefix which signifies the num- er of feet. The feet used in these examples are iambic, for urposes of comparison; but trochaic, dactyllic, or ana- aestic feet could also be used to illustrate most of the differ- nt patterns.

Monometer: a line of one foot.

Mă chínes.

Dimeter: a line of two feet.

Thĕ tráck|lĕss fóam.

Trimeter: a line of three feet.

Thĕ éa|glĕ sóars|ĭn aír.

Tetrameter: a line of four feet.

Ă lít|tlĕ ár|gŭ mént|ĭs góod.

Pentameter: a line of five feet.

Thĕre ís|nŏ ún|ĭm prés|sĭve spót|ŏn eárth.

Hexameter: a line of six feet.

Ăs íf|ă gí|ănt wóke,|ănd túrned| . . . ănd slépt|ă gaín.

A line of iambic hexameter, like the foregoing, is usuall called an "Alexandrine." The term "hexameter" mor often refers to dactylic hexameter, as used by Longfellow i "Evangeline":

This is the|for est pri|me val. The|mur mur ing|pines an
the|hem locks.

Heptameter, also called "septenary": a line of seven feet.

King Fran|cis was|a heart|y king|and loved|a roy|al spor

A line of iambic heptameter is sometimes written as tw lines: a line of iambic tetrameter followed by a line c iambic trimeter. In the ballad stanza on page 472 the firs and third lines are tetrameter while the second and fourt lines are trimeter.

Octameter: a line of eight feet.

I bridge|the void|'twixt soul|and soul;|I bring|the long|in
lov|ers near.

In reading all but very short lines there is a slight natura break or pause in the rhythm, usually near the middle This break, called a *caesura*, is usually quite evident becaus it is determined by the grouping of the words. It may o may not be marked by punctuation. In the preceding octa meter line, there is a semicolon at the pause.

By means of variations in the normal pattern of verse poets produce unusual and pleasing rhythms; in fact, per fectly regular meter is rare.

One of these variations consists of using, here and there, a foot of a different type. A favorite way of achieving emphais and variety is by using a trochaic foot at the beginning of an iambic line.

> Au tumn,|for sake|these hills|and dwell|with towns.

Another variation consists of using lines with different numbers of feet.

> Oh, you|may sing|your gyp|sy songs
> Of wind|ing trails|and free.

Often both kinds of variation occur in the same poem.

> New ton,|him self,|be neath|his tree,
> Would pon|der this|and frown.

Sometimes a line contains a syllable, accented or unaccented, which does not seem to belong to any foot. A syllable of this kind may be considered a one-syllable foot. However, in determining the number of feet in a line, it is not counted unless accented, because a foot ordinarily has an accented syllable.

An extra unaccented syllable often occurs after an accented syllable at the end of a line.

> Who dares|be lieve|his lau|rel is|im mor|tal?

This line is iambic pentameter because most of the feet are iambic, and there are five accents. True, it could be divided equally well into trochaic feet with the unaccented syllable at the beginning, but such a division is not customary, and the poem (“¿Quién Sabe?,” page 120) is mainly iambic.

A single accented syllable instead of a complete trochaic foot often ends a trochaic line.

Noise of|ham mers|once I|heard.

This line is trochaic tetrameter because most of the feet a trochaic and there are four accents. It could also be divide into iambic feet with the single accented syllable at th beginning, but again, this division is not customary, an the poen ("The Hammers," page 192) is mainly trochaic.

Rarely, a one-syllable foot occurs within a line. In th following line the single syllable is unaccented, but it cann be counted with the next foot to form an anapaest becau of the pause (caesura) demanded by the parallel ideas.

Be yond|the East|the sun|rise;|be yond|the West|the sea

A single syllable such as those illustrated may be though of as an incomplete foot, the missing part being a paus like a rest in music. These slight pauses do not interrup the rhythm of verse, any more than rests interrupt th rhythm of music.

Scanning a poem consists of first reading it intelligently an naturally, then indicating the accented and unaccente syllables, and finally dividing the lines into feet as in th preceding illustrations.

Indicating the accented and unaccented syllables shoul be easy, but dividing the lines into feet may be difficult if th poem is irregular. It is a good plan to look first for the pre vailing type of foot. Indicating these regular feet wi establish the general pattern; then identifying the irregula ones should be less difficult.

Usually lines show a rather definite pattern; that is, the are composed principally of two-syllable feet or three syllable feet. A line may contain nothing but two-syllabl feet, as

The path|lies blue|a cross|the bay.

A pure three-syllable-foot line is rare.

These are the|best of him.

Sometimes a line has two-syllable feet and three-syllable feet about evenly mixed as

This is the|song of the|wa ters|churn ing.

The two-syllable foot pattern is the one most frequently used in poetry. In this pattern the iambic foot is commoner than the trochaic.

After enough lines have been scanned, the poem may be found to have a general pattern, as iambic pentameter (⏑′5), trochaic tetrameter (′⏑4), or any of the other meters. These patterns seldom exist without variation; in fact, some poems are so irregular that it is difficult or impossible to classify them metrically.

Rhyme, Assonance, and Alliteration

Many of the special "sound" effects in poetry are gained by the use of rhyme, assonance, and alliteration. Each of these three is effective because the ear takes pleasure in listening for the repetition of a sound or sounds already uttered.

I went a-riding, a-riding,
Over a great long plain.
And the great plain went a-sliding, a-sliding
Away from my bridle rein.

Rhyme is the correspondence of sounds at the end of words, as *plain-rein, riding-sliding*. Since only the sound of words determines the rhyme, the spelling is not considered. Rhyme is a feature of much poetry, but is by no means essential.

Rhyming words usually occur at the end of lines. Such rhymes are called *end rhymes*.

> Machines in haughty and presumptuous pr*ide*
> Are mankind magnif*ied*.

If, however, at least one of the rhyming words occurs within the line, the rhyme is called an *internal rhyme*.

Valor and l*ove*, and a king ab*ove*, and the royal beasts below.

Though most people have an instinctive sense of rhyme, there are definite rules governing it. The corresponding sounds must begin with an accented vowel and continue to the end of the words as pl*ay*—ob*ey*, cl*aim*—g*ame*, h*ammer*—cl*amor*.

Of course, *sing* and *playing* do not rhyme because the *ing* in *playing* is not accented. However, the last syllable of some words, although not having the primary accent, may have enough secondary stress to be accented in verse as magni*fied* which can be rhymed with *pride*.

The sounds preceding the corresponding sounds must be different, as *o*bey—*pl*ay, with two exceptions: (1) One of the words may have no sound preceding the rhyming sound, as aim—*cl*aim. (2) The consonant sounds immediately preceding the rhyming vowels may be the same provided that the syllables of which they are a part begin with sounds that are different, as b*l*ame—*cl*aim; d*r*eam—st*r*eam; *c*orn—*sc*orn.

The rhyming sound may extend through one or more following words which are unaccented in the line as *in it* to rhyme with *minute*, *before us* with *chorus*, and such combinaons as *cheer it—steer it, about you—doubt you, best of him—jest* *him.*

Most rhyming words are words of one syllable or words ccented on the last syllable as *wheel—steel, design—mine, pairs—affairs.* Such rhymes are called single or masculine hymes. When the accented syllable is followed by one naccented syllable as *churning—turning,* the rhyme is called double or feminine rhyme. When it is followed by two naccented syllables as *lyrical—satirical,* the rhyme is called riple rhyme. Triple rhymes are rare, and rhymes with till more syllables are scarcely ever found.

Verse without rhyme is known as *blank verse.* Though any nrhymed measured verse is blank verse, the term is aplied principally to unrhymed iambic pentameter. This is he form of measured verse most closely resembling the atural rhythm of speech. For this reason it is much used for onger poems and plays. Shakespeare's plays are, for the nost part, in blank verse.

Blank verse, which is composed of metrical lines, should ot be confused with free verse, discussed on pages 455, 456, 478, and 479. However, if blank verse contains enough rregularities, it comes close to being free verse.

Assonance is a repetition of the same vowel sounds, usually in the accented syllables. Unlike rhyme, however, he consonant sounds are different, as *came—lane, coming—unning.* Notice the repetition of the short *o* sounds in the ines:

> The fog comes
> on little cat feet

The term "assonance" is also used to include other resemblances in sound. In some cases the vowel sounds of the accented syllables are not quite the same, but any sound following the vowels correspond, as *throw—now*, *come—loom*. In rare instances, neither the vowel sounds of the accented syllables nor the following sounds are quite the same there is only a suggested resemblance, as *moss—was*. These sound resemblances, which are sometimes called "false rhymes," are common in ballads and other folk poetry.

> Half ower, half ower to Aberdour
> It's fifty faddom *deep;*
> And there lies guid Sir Patrick Spens
> Wi' the Scots lords at his *feet.*

Alliteration is the repetition of a sound at the beginning of words. Most people have not only an instinctive sense of rhyme, but also an instinctive sense of alliteration, which shows itself in such familiar expressions as "mice and men," "time and tide."

The effect is obtained by repeating the same sound (usually a single consonant) in the accented syllable (usually the first syllable) of different words. These words should be close enough for the ear to detect the similarity.

> *S*inuous *s*outhward and *s*inuous northward the shimmering *b*and
> Of the *s*and *b*each *f*astens the *f*ringe of the marsh to the *f*olds of the land.

Both assonance and alliteration are used in rhymed and unrhymed metrical verse and in free verse.

Stanza Structure

A *stanza* is a group of lines forming a division of a poem. *Stanza* and *verse* are often used interchangeably, but *verse* roperly means a single line, or rhythmical lines in general, ather than a group of lines. The word *strophe* is sometimes sed in place of stanza, especially for the irregular, unhymed divisions of free verse.

In the strict sense, a stanza is a pattern of lines repeated ver and over in a poem, each stanza having the same tructure. Rhyme is generally used in the pattern to produce a closer relationship between the lines and thus make he stanza a unit. Rhyme schemes are numerous; the poet nay rhyme successive lines, alternate lines, or any combinaion of lines that suits his fancy, using both end rhymes and nternal rhymes.

A convenient method of representing rhyme schemes is to ise letters. The letters which are repeated stand for rhyming vords, those which are not repeated for non-rhyming words. 'or example:

The snow is lying very deep, *a*
My house is sheltered from the blast. *b*
I hear each muffled step outside, *c*
I hear each voice go past. *b*

In the preceding stanza, *a b c b* means that the second and ourth lines rhyme, but the first and third do not.

With rue my heart is laden *a*
For golden friends I had, *b*
For many a rose-lipped maiden *a*
And many a lightfoot lad. *b*

In this instance, *a b a b* indicates a rhyme scheme in which the first and third lines rhyme, as do the second and fourth.

A *couplet* is two successive lines which rhyme: *a a.*

A *tercet* (or *triplet*) is a stanza of three lines, usually rhyming *a a a*.

A *quatrain* is a stanza of four lines usually having one of the following rhyme patterns: *a b a b*, *a b c b*, *a b b a*, *a a b a*, *a b b b*. The first two are the commonest.

Other frequently used stanzas consist of five, six, seven, eight, or nine lines.

A few stanzas and certain entire poems which have definite patterns of meter and rhyme are given special names. Most of them will not be discussed here, for they would be of interest only to the advanced student. Two, however, are used so often that their names are well known. They are the ballad and the sonnet.

A *ballad* is a poem that tells a story in short, similar stanzas. The old ballads which originated as songs among the common people are known as traditional or folk ballads. Such a ballad is "Sir Patrick Spens," page 379. Sir Walter Scott made a collection of these old ballads, and he and other poets down to the present time have imitated them. Longfellow's "The Wreck of the Hesperus" and Kipling's "The Ballad of East and West" are familiar examples.

Variations of some of the best-known folk ballads are still sung in the Southern mountains and in some other sections of our country. "The Two Sisters," page 381, is one of these familiar ballads. It is also an example of a ballad having a refrain, that is, a line or lines repeated in, or at the end of, succeeding stanzas. When read or sung each stanza has the same pattern as the first.

Ballads are usually simple in form. They may be written in various meters, but one particular form is known as *ballad meter*. It consists of a four-line stanza, rhyming *a b c b*, in which the first and third lines have four accents (tetrameter) and the second and fourth three accents (trimeter).

The king sits in Dumferling town
Drinking the bluid-red wine:
"Oh, whar will I get a guid sailor
To sail this ship of mine?"

The meter is roughly iambic. However, irregularities often occur in the structure of ballads, especially in the old ones, which probably developed from the songs of the people over a period of years.

Sometimes the first and second lines of a ballad are written as one, and the third and fourth as one, making couplets in heptameter. Such an arrangement is used in "The Glove and the Lions," page 370.

Ballad meter is the same as the *common meter* of hymns, except that common meter is more strictly iambic, and the first and third lines often rhyme, as well as the second and fourth.

A *sonnet* consists of fourteen lines of iambic pentameter having a definite rhyme scheme. Because of its form and brevity, it is much used for expressing a single idea of rare value. Though many variations in form are possible, there are two main types of sonnets, the Italian and the English.

The *Italian* sonnet is also called "Petrarchan," because Petrarch, Italian poet of the fourteenth century, was one of the first to use this form extensively. The lines are arranged in two groups, one of eight lines called the *octave* (*a b b a a b b a*) and one of six lines called the *sestet* (*c d e c d e*, *d c d c d c*, or some other arrangement of two or three rhyming sounds). The octave is sometimes thought of as divided into a pair of quatrains and the sestet as divided into a pair of tercets. This division is cleverly brought out in a sonnet written by Lope De Vega, Spanish poet and dramatist (1562–1635) and translated by James Y. Gibson. It is known as "A Sonnet on the Sonnet."

To write a sonnet doth Juana press me; *a*
I've never found me in such stress and pain; *b*
A sonnet numbers fourteen lines 'tis plain, *b*
And three are gone ere I can say, God bless me! *a*

I thought that spinning rhymes might sore oppress me, *a*
Yet here I'm midway in the last quatrain *b*
And if the foremost tercet I can gain, *b*
The quatrains need not any more distress me. *a*

To the first tercet I have got at last *c*
And travel through it with such right good will, *d*
That with this line I've finished it I ween. *e*

I'm in the second now and see how fast *c*
The thirteenth line comes tripping from my quill; *d*
Hurrah, 'tis done. Count if there be fourteen. *e*

In a strict Italian sonnet the octave makes a general statement and the sestet an application of that statement. An illustration of this type of sonnet is "A Modern Columbus," page 254.

The *Miltonic* sonnet is a special kind of Italian sonnet. In structure it is the same, but the thought, instead of following the division into octave and sestet, passes without break from the one into the other. This type of sonnet is illustrated by "The World Is Too Much with Us," page 76.

The *English* sonnet is also known as the "Shakespearean" sonnet because it is the form Shakespeare used. It consists of three quatrains (*a b a b*, *c d c d*, *e f e f*) and a concluding couplet (*g g*). The thought falls somewhat into an octave-sestet division as in the Italian form, but more markedly into a quatrain division progressing naturally to the end of the poem where it is emphasized by the couplet. "Aladdin Throws Away His Lamp," page 8, is written in this form.

In the words of William Sharp, Scottish poet and writer of the late nineteenth century, "the Shakespearean sonnet is like a red-hot bar being molded upon a forge, till—in the closing couplet—it receives the final clinching blow from the heavy hammer."

Making a similar comparison, we may say that the Italian sonnet is like a girder being made from crude ore. First—in the octave—the steel, a general substance, is produced; then—in the sestet—it is formed into the girder, a definite object.

Continuing the comparison, we might say that the Miltonic sonnet is like a building being constructed, a continuous process, not one that can readily be separated into two distinct steps.

A Miltonic sonnet should preferably be written or printed as a single stanza, but Italian and English sonnets may have their natural divisions indicated by separate stanzas. Such division into stanzas, like the indentation of lines to suggest the rhyme scheme, is purely a matter of choice.

Modern poets are inclined to disregard some of the restrictions of the sonnet, as well as distinctions between the different types. Any poem of fourteen lines written in iambic pentameter with a more or less systematic rhyme scheme is usually considered a sonnet. "Autumn, Forsake These Hills," page 68, is an illustration.

Free verse is so named because it is free from the restrictions placed upon metrical verse. Although verse rhythms and occasional metrical feet are sometimes used in free verse, the poet usually seeks to use new combinations which will break up any set metrical pattern. Free verse is also unrhymed. It may be divided into groups of lines resembling stanzas, but these divisions are not considered stanzas in the strictest sense because they lack regularity and rhyme. Instead they are sometimes referred to as strophes.

In America Walt Whitman was one of the first to write truly impressive poems that were free from conventional rhythms. Recent poets, like Amy Lowell and Carl Sandburg, have done much to popularize free verse, but free verse is not a new thing. In fact, it is older than the metrical form—so old that it goes back to ancient times. A similar form occurs in the Old Testament of the Bible.

> I will lift up mine eyes unto the hills,
> From whence cometh my help.
> My help cometh from the Lord,
> Which made heaven and earth.

This same rhythm of thought expressed by recurring words, similar phrases, or similar lines is also the basis of modern free verse.

> Smoke of the fields in spring is one,
> Smoke of the leaves in autumn another.
> Smoke of a steel-mill roof or a battleship funnel,

They all go up in a line with the smokestack,
Or they twist . . . in the slow twist . . . of the wind.

Free verse is rugged and unrestrained, like the roll of the surf or the sound of the wind. Instead of trying to fit what he has to say into a more or less rigid form, the poet prefers to let the accents fall according to the free rhythm of speech and to emphasize the rhythm of ideas.

NOTES

NOTES

PAGE

4. A Song of Power

Aladdin's story, the story of "Aladdin and the Wonderful Lamp" in the *Arabian Nights*. Aladdin was a poor Chinese boy who became the possessor of a magic lamp. Whenever this lamp was rubbed, a supernatural being called a "genie" ("jinn" or "jinni") would appear and grant any wish. Thus Aladdin grew rich, married the Sultan's daughter, and eventually became Sultan.

6. The Secret of the Machines

Mauretania, for years the fastest and one of the largest of the transatlantic liners. She was scrapped in 1935. Another vessel of the same name began service in 1939.

8. Aladdin Throws Away His Lamp. See note for page 4, on *Aladdin's story*.

10. *From* Smoke and Steel

11. *runner of fire*, tongue of flame; the application of heat in the making and shaping of steel.

Pittsburgh, Youngstown, Gary, steel-manufacturing cities in Pennsylvania, Ohio, and Indiana respectively.

Homestead, Braddock, Birmingham, the first two, boroughs near Pittsburgh; the last a city in Alabama—all sites of important steel plants.

12. *clamshells*, buckets which open and close like clams. Suspended by cables, they are used for moving loose material.

runners, chutes used to convey ore, limestone, or coal from bins to the holds of boats.

handlers, buckets used to unload ore, stone, or coal from boats.

pour is timed. Steel made in a furnace is tapped or drawn off into a container or ladle. In the bottom of the ladle there is a small opening one and a half inches in diameter. When the ladle is lifted, the steel flows through the hole into the molds. This process is called "pouring." Since the temperature of the steel and the speed of filling the molds into which the steel is poured are accurately controlled, the poet speaks of the pour being "timed."

billets, short bars of metal.

14. THE IRON HORSE

wanderlust, a strong desire to wander or travel.

16. CHANT OF THE BOX CARS

gride, move with a harsh, grinding sound.

17. INDUCED CURRENT. This poem appeared in *Blackwood's Edinburgh Magazine*, March, 1847. A note preceding it states: "Faraday was the first to elicit the electric spark from the magnet; he found that it is visible at the instants of breaking and of renewing the contact of the conducting wires; and *only then*."

Faraday, Michael, English chemist and physicist of the nineteenth century.

Volta, Alessandro, Italian physicist of the eighteenth and nineteenth centuries who first produced an electric current by chemical action.

18. GREAT TOWERS OF STEEL

blowzy, rough.

19. FIRST FLIGHT

unroll The parchment of new heaven and new earth. "And the heaven departed as a scroll when it is rolled together; and every mountain and island were moved out of their places."—Revelation 6: 14.

eagle in the dream That Dante dreamt. In the *Divine Comedy*, "Purgatory," Book 9, lines 19 to 33, Dante, Italian poet of the thirteenth and fourteenth centuries, tells of his dream in which an eagle "having wheeled a little . . . descended, terrible as a flash of lightning, and snatched me up."

20. *Fire, water, air, and earth*, suggests the old belief that all things were composed of these four elements.

angel lovelier Than those Ezekiel saw in awe and wonder. The account of the vision is in Ezekiel, Chapters 1 and 10.

whispering gallery, a room with rounded walls and ceiling which reflect and concentrate sound, so that a person at a particular spot can hear a whisper spoken from another spot a considerable distance away. There are whispering galleries in the Capitol at Washington; St. Paul's Cathedral, London; and Gloucester Cathedral, England. The radio has made every house such a gallery.

21. *More slaves than Pharaoh dreamt of*. Pharaoh was the title given to the rulers of ancient Egypt. The early Pharaohs used multitudes of slaves in building the pyramids. Herodotus, Greek historian of the first century B.C., estimated that building the Great Pyramid of Cheops took relays of 100,000 subjects working for twenty years.

New Jerusalem. "And I saw a new heaven and a new earth: for the first heaven and the first earth were passed away. . . . And I John saw the holy city, new Jerusalem, coming down from God out of heaven."—Revelation 21: 1–2.

Strapped in a ventricle of the human brain, strapped in a cavity of the human brain, since the cabin of an airplane is the product of man's brain.

wheels beneath it old as the pyramids. The wheel was used before the building of the pyramids. These were begun, it is estimated, about 5,000 B.C.

22. *Apocalypse*, the vision of St. John the Divine: "And the city had no need of the sun, neither of the moon, to shine in it: for the glory of God did lighten it."—Revelation 21: 23.

in under, below.

23. *Antietam*, a creek in Maryland, the scene of a battle of the Civil War.

windrows, rows; usually refers to hay or sheaves of grain raked into rows to dry before being piled; may also mean deep furrows.

Their fathers seed of Abraham and Noah. The allusion is to the following Biblical verses: "And God blessed Noah and his sons, and said unto them, Be fruitful and multiply, and replenish the earth."—Genesis 9: 1. " . . . thy name shall be Abraham. . . . And I will give thee, and to thy seed after thee, the land wherein thou art a stranger."—Genesis 17: 5, 8.

The thought of this line and those immediately following is th the airplane, symbolic of modern civilization, has given ma power to do things which his ancestors, even those of the la generation, would have believed impossible.

26. . . . *his feet*

Moved with the unpredictable and strange
Loveliness, like God, upon the mountains.

The reference is to the following Biblical verse: "How beaut ful upon the mountains are the feet of him that bringeth goo tidings, that publisheth peace; that bringeth good tidings of goo that bringeth salvation; that saith unto Zion, Thy God reigneth! —Isaiah 52: 7.

27. *ridges of the Shenandoah*, mountains bordering the Shenandoah Rive valley in northwest Virginia.

Milky Way, the irregular, faintly luminous band which stretche across the sky. It is composed of countless numbers of stars a vast distances from the earth. The Milky Way is seen to bes advantage on moonless nights when the air is free from haze, an in places away from city lights.

28. *aeons*, ages.

symmetry, harmony.

Mayfly, a slender, delicate insect which lives but a few hours or days

sons of God, the stars and other heavenly bodies.

eternal morning, continual light.

Whose lips are full of ancient praise of God. The allusion is to the follow- ing Biblical verse: "The heavens declare the glory of God; and the firmament showeth his handiwork."—Psalms 19: 1.

29. *leviathans*, huge water animals, possibly whales, mentioned in the Old Testament of the Bible.

31. *From* CENTRAL

older Fates, sister goddesses, the Three Fates, of Greek and Roman mythology: Clotho, who spun the thread of life; Lachesis, who measured it; Atropos, who severed it.

32. MANDARIN ON THE AIR

pellucid, clear.

Mandarin, a Chinese public officer.
unapprehended, unperceived, unnoticed.
autonomous, independent.
inspissated, thickened.
thridded his lumbars, (*thridded*, form of "threaded") passed through his loins, that part of the body between the lowest ribs and the hip bones.
entrails were embryo with palaver, internal organs were in a state of undeveloped talk.
Electric with spores of speech, alive with seeds of speech.
circumambient, surrounding.

33. *kilocycles*, here, vibrations of radio waves.
amplitudes, sizes of vibrations.

33. THE SURGEON
obedient to a star. The reference is probably to the belief that the stars control the destinies of human beings.

38. HOUSE DEMOLISHED
nuzzles, digs up with the nose.
maw, stomach.

41. POWER
scrip, small bag or wallet.

42. TEXAS

43. *basilisk*, a fabled creature resembling a serpent, lizard, or dragon, whose look and breath were supposed to be fatal. A basilisk is also a variety of lizard.
dogie steers (dō′gĭ), motherless calves in a range or trail herd; sometimes any cattle.
Hold up, slow up or stop.
paint horse, a horse of different colors, usually spotted bay (reddish brown) and white, probably so called because it looks "painted."

45. ODE TO MACHINES. An ode is a poem which deals progressively with a subject in a dignified way.

Raised by groans of workers under new
And greedier Pharaoh's lids,
Are age-old pyramids.

See note for page 21, on *More slaves than Pharaoh dreamt of.*

46. *Millenium*, the thousand years mentioned in the Bible (Revelatic 20), during which good is to be triumphant in the world; hen a period of happiness and good government.

55. COMPOSED UPON WESTMINSTER BRIDGE, SEPTEMBER 3, 180 Westminster Bridge crosses the Thames River in London, ne the Houses of Parliament.

56. MANHATTAN. The title of the poem is the Indian name for tl Island on which New York City has been built. The city no includes much surrounding territory, and the term *Manhattan* used to designate specifically that part, or borough, of the ci which occupies Manhattan Island.

pagan, irreligious.

Bowling Green, a park at the southern tip of Manhattan.

East Side, a densely populated section of Manhattan.

Milano (mē-lä′nō), Milan, an Italian city famous as a center c music.

Bleecker Street, a crowded commercial street in the Italian section c Manhattan.

60. ELLIS PARK. A park located in Chicago.

62. THE LIGHTS OF NEW YORK

broidery, old form of "embroidery."

Babylon, a luxurious ancient city, now in ruins, located on the Eu phrates River in what is now Iraq, southwestern Asia.

flambeaux, torches.

Saturnalia, festivities to honor Saturn, an ancient Roman deity associated with seed sowing and agriculture.

But you have found a good and filched from him
A fire that neither rain nor wind can dim.

According to mythology, Prometheus, a Titan, stole fire from the gods and gave it to man.

63. City Birds

Times Square, an open area in the theater district of New York, formed by the intersection of Broadway, Seventh Avenue, and Forty-Second Street. In the center is the *New York Times* building.

66. To the Greatest City in the World

Prepare, prepare To see your towers falling! These lines are quoted from "Twentieth Century Slave-Gang," a poem by Genevieve Taggard, which prophesies the fall of modern cities and links this event with the fall of Babylon.

71. He Climbs a Hill and Turns His Face

Vega, a bluish-white star, the sixth brightest in the sky. It is in the constellation Lyra.

Orion, a large, brilliant constellation which is identified by three bright stars in a line. It is most conspicuous during the fall and winter.

76. The World Is Too Much With Us

pagan, irreligious person; here, one who worships the old Greek and Roman deities.

Proteus, in mythology, a minor sea god, a wise old man of the sea. Proteus had charge of Neptune's seals, and would rise with them from the water at midday to rest in an island cave.

Triton, a minor deity, the son of Neptune, god of the sea. He was his father's trumpeter, and by blowing his conch-shell trumpet raised or calmed the waves.

78. *From* Senlin: A Biography, a long poem which is a study of man. The titles of its divisions are "His Dark Origins," "His Futile Preoccupations" (from which this selection is taken), and "His Cloudy Destiny."

Senlin, a fictitious character representing man. The author explains that he merely invented the name, on the Latin basis *senex*, *senilis*—meaning "old man," or "old,"—with the diminutive ending added; hence, "little old man."

chinaberry tree, a handsome shade tree which grows in warm regions.

82. THE LITTLE GODS. The title suggests the Lares and Penates, household gods of the ancient Romans; hence, one's household goods or personal belongings.

84. CONTRARY JOE

mazehead, one in a state of bewilderment.

86. MENDING WALL

frozen-ground-swell, a heaving of the ground caused by expansion in freezing, like the lift of broad ocean waves.

87. *Old Stone savage*, a savage of the early Stone Age, when men used unpolished stone implements.

88. THE POET

Romany, gypsy.

90. HOUSEHOLD GODS. See note for page 82, on "The Little Gods."

92. A MAN'S A MAN FOR A' THAT. A poem like this one, written in Scottish dialect, at first looks difficult to read. A more careful examination shows that most of the words which look strange are easily recognizable as English words with slightly different spellings: *ane*, one; *frae*, from; *maun*, must; *sae*, so; *wad*, would. The dropping of final consonants is especially common: *a'*, all; *awa'*, away; *fu'*, full; *o'*, of; *wi'*, with. Even though a Scottish word does not seem to be like an English word, its meaning may often be determined from the way it is used. For instance, *bonnie* may have a variety of meanings: pretty, handsome, fine, gay, strong. It may be applied to a lassie, a flower, a bird, a river, a person's brow—in fact to almost anything worthy of praise.

a' (aw), all.

guinea, a former English gold coin worth twenty-one shillings. It was first made of gold from Guinea, a region of the west coast of Africa.

gowd (goud), gold.

hodden gray, coarse, gray woolen cloth.

birkie (bûr′kĭ), haughty fellow.

coof (ko͞of), blockhead.

93. *fa'*, attempt.

gree, prize.

95. THE DISCOVERY

caravels, sailing vessels.

97. THE CONGO. The title refers to the Congo River in central Africa. A note by the author states: "This poem, particularly the third section, was suggested by an allusion in a sermon by my pastor, F. W. Burnham, to the heroic life and death of Ray Eldred (1872–1913). Eldred was a missionary of the Disciples of Christ who perished while swimming in a treacherous branch of the Congo."

Barrel-house, low drinking-place.

blood-lust, bloodthirsty.

98. *witch doctors*, medicine men who are supposed to detect witches and counteract their influence by magic.

voodoo, referring to voodooism, a religion which originated in Africa. In practice it makes use of charms and witchcraft.

Mountains of the Moon, the snow-capped Ruwenzori Mountains in Africa, at the source of the Nile. (See also note for page 324, on *Mountains of the Moon*.)

Mumbo Jumbo, a god worshiped with superstitious fear.

hoodoo, bring bad luck to.

juba, a characteristic lively, shuffling dance accompanied by the onlookers who sing, stamp their feet, and pat their knees.

guyed, made fun of.

99. *cakewalk*, a form of entertainment in which a cake is awarded as a prize for the most elaborate steps in walking, usually to a musical accompaniment.

PAGE

100. *camp meeting*, a religious gathering in the open air or in a tent.

jubilee revival shout, a triumphant shouting, as during a time reawakened interest in religion.

Jacob, and the golden stairs. The reference is to Jacob's vision, as told i the Bible. "And he dreamed, and behold a ladder set up on th earth, and the top of it reached to heaven: and behold the ange of God ascending and descending on it."—Genesis 28: 12.

102. The Man with the Hoe. This poem had for its inspiration th painting of a French peasant by Jean François Millet who lived i the nineteenth century. Markham used this bowed and toil-wor figure as a symbol of all those who must endure drudgery. Whe the poem was first published in the *San Francisco Examiner*, i attracted immediate attention. It appeared in all parts of th country and was translated into many languages, the numbe now having reached thirty-eight. It has been called "the battl cry of the next thousand years."

103. *Plato*, a great philosopher of ancient Greece.

Pleiades, a cluster of stars, about seven of which are visible to the unaided eye. This group is easily recognized because the stars are so close together.

immemorial infamies, disgraces so old that they extend beyond the reach of memory.

Perfidious, treacherous.

immedicable, incurable.

105. Factory Windows Are Always Broken

Yahoo, in Swift's *Gulliver's Travels*, one of a race of filthy animals under the control of the Houyhnhnms, a superior race of horses having the ability to reason. The Yahoos resembled man in body and possessed his follies and vices. They were particularly malicious.

Something is rotten—I think, in Denmark. This statement implies that something is fundamentally wrong. In Shakespeare's *Hamlet*, Marcellus, his suspicions aroused by the appearance of the ghost of Hamlet's father, remarks: "Something is rotten in the state of Denmark."—Act I, scene 4.

6. Caliban in the Coal Mines

Caliban, in Shakespeare's *The Tempest,* the deformed slave, son of the witch Sycorax. In spite of his natural savagery, Caliban shows a longing for better things, for he says to his master Prospero:

. . . When thou camest first
Thou strok'dst me and mad'st much of me, wouldst give me
Water with berries in 't, and teach me how
To name the bigger light, and how the less,
That burn by day and night; and then I loved thee.

—Act I, scene 2

Caliban has come to be the symbol of primitive man in search of religion or the higher things of life. In this poem, the miner speaks as a Caliban of our civilization.

08. Report on the Planet, Earth

Solar System, the sun, and the planets, satellites, asteroids, meteors, and comets associated with it.

10. *peacock feathers,* display. The peacock is commonly used as the symbol of vanity.

11. *cosmic,* of the universe.

13. Recessional. A hymn sung near the close of a church service is called a "Recessional." Kipling composed this poem after witnessing a naval review off the south coast of England in 1897, during Queen Victoria's Diamond Jubilee. He undoubtedly felt that the poem was a fitting recessional to the ceremonies on that occasion.

Lest we forget. "Then beware lest thou forget the Lord, which brought thee forth out of the land of Egypt, from the house of bondage."—Deuteronomy 6: 12. "The wicked shall be turned into hell, and all the nations that forget God."—Psalms 9: 17.

Still stands Thine ancient sacrifice,
An humble and a contrite heart.

"The sacrifices of God are a broken spirit: a broken and a contrite heart, O God, thou wilt not despise."—Psalms 51: 17.

Nineveh, capital of the ancient empire of Assyria in southwest Asia.

PAGE

Tyre, capital of the ancient country of Phoenicia at the eastern e of the Mediterranean Sea.

Such boastings as the Gentiles use,
Or lesser breeds without the Law.

In the Bible, boastfulness was considered one of the sins of t Gentiles. The term Gentiles was used to designate nations whi were not of the Biblical faith, that is, had not received the La of God, and so were "without the Law," or heathens. He Kipling used the phrase to indicate nations which are not Go fearing.

117. The Great Lover
inenarrable, indescribable.

118. *faëry*, pertaining to the world of fairies; hence, miniature, delicat

120. ¿Quién Sabe? (keyańe sah′bay), Spanish for "who knows?" I Spanish it is customary to put a question mark before, as we as after, questions.
Córdoba (côr′do-vä), a city in southern Spain.
Plaza, a public square.
peon (pē′ŏn), laborer.
tortillas (tôr-tē′yäs), thin cakes.
Yo no sé (yō nō sā), I don't know.
laurel, used by the ancient Greeks in wreaths to crown the victor in the Pythian Games held in honor of Apollo at Delphi; henc laurel came to be the symbol of fame.

124. To an Athlete Dying Young
chaired, carried in triumph on a chair or seat (English usage).
cut, broken.

129. Invictus. The title is the Latin word meaning "unconquered."
fell, cruel.
strait, narrow.

130. With Rue My Heart Is Laden
rue, sorrow.

GE

3. On His Blindness. At the age of forty-four Milton became totally blind. (See also the poem "Milton," page 243, and the note for that poem.)

34. To a Mouse. For reading Scottish dialect, see note for page 92, on "A Man's a Man for A' That."

bickerin', hasty.

brattle, scamper.

pattle, a plowstaff, used to remove mud that clings to the plowshare.

whyles, sometimes.

daimen icker in a thrave, occasional ear in a quantity of grain.

lave, rest.

silly, weak.

foggage (fŏg′ĭj), coarse grass.

snell, sharp.

35. *colter*, a cutter on a plow to cut a grassy surface.

But house or hald (hawd), without house or shelter.

thole, endure.

cranreuch (krȧn′ruch), hoarfrost.

agley (ȧ-glē′), crooked, wrong.

137. Young and Old

every dog his day. The allusion is probably to the following lines from Shakespeare's *Hamlet:*

Let Hercules himself do what he may,
The cat will mew and dog will have his day.
—Act V, scene 1

138. Ode on a Grecian Urn. An ode is a poem which deals progressively with a subject in a dignified way.

Grecian urn, a terra cotta vase about three feet tall, surrounded by bands of pictures one above the other, each band telling its own story.

foster child, a child receiving care and support, though not related by blood.

Tempe (tĕm′pē̆), a valley in Greece renowned for its beauty.

PAGE

Arcady (är'kȧ-dĭ), a mountainous region in Greece inhabited duri ancient times by shepherds and hunters.

139. *Attic*, pertaining to Attica, an ancient division of Greece whi included Athens; hence, having qualities characteristic of t Athenians, especially purity and simplicity in art.

brede, ornamentation.

Pastoral, a representation of rural life and scenes.

140. THE GARGOYLE IN THE SNOW

gargoyle, in Gothic architecture a stone waterspout, usually grotesquely carved person or animal, projecting from the uppe part of a building. The reference here is to one of the gargoyle on the Cathedral of Notre Dame, Paris, France.

Seine, the river which flows through Paris.

141. RECIPE FOR A HAPPY LIFE. This poem has been attributed t Margaret, Queen of Navarre, who lived from 1492 to 1549 The Kingdom of Navarre was located in southwestern Franc and the adjoining northwestern part of Spain. Margaret was th author of many poems. Whether she actually wrote this one may be doubted, since it is supposed to have been written in the yea 1500 when she was only eight years old. However, she is know to have been a precocious child, and it is not impossible that she could have written this "Recipe."

drachms, (drămz), drams. A dram, in apothecaries' weight, is an eighth of an ounce or sixty grains.

Orisons, prayers.

142. MIRACLES

Manhattan. See note for page 56, on "Manhattan."

144. THE PARABOLA

Sir Isaac Newton, English mathematician of the late seventeenth and early eighteenth centuries.

46. Faith

asphodel, a plant of the narcissus family. In Greek mythology, it is associated with the dead and the lower world; hence, with life after death.

49. The Happiest Heart

Who drives the horses of the sun Shall lord it but a day. In Greek mythology, Apollo, the god of the sun, swore to grant his son Phaëthon any request. Phaëthon asked for the privilege of driving for one day the horses which drew the golden chariot of the sun. The journey was disastrous. Phaëthon lost control of the horses and the chariot came too close to the world, setting it on fire. Finally Zeus was obliged to destroy the overambitious driver with a thunderbolt.

50. Dream the Great Dream

Arcturus, one of the brightest stars, thirty-three light years or some 200,000,000,000,000 miles distant.

151. Vitaï Lampada (wē′tī läm′pä-dä), Latin for *The Torch of Life.* One form of the torch race of the ancient Greeks was a relay race in which a lighted torch was passed from one runner to the other. Lucretius, Roman poet of the first century B.C., used this idea in the following comparison: "Some races wax while others wane, and in brief space the tribes of men are changed and like runners hand on the torch of life."—*On the Nature of Things*, Book 2, line 79.

Close, an enclosed space; here, a school playing field.

Ten to make and the match to win—
A bumping pitch and a blinding light,
An hour to play and the last man in.

The reference is to cricket, a game as popular in England as baseball is in the United States. It is played with a ball, bats, and wickets by opposing teams of eleven men each. The *pitch* is the space between wickets. Over this the ball is bowled (thrown overhead with the arm stiff) so that it bounces before reaching

PAGE

the batter. A *bumping* pitch is an uneven pitch which causes t ball to bounce deceptively. The batter in the poem, therefor faces a deceptively bouncing ball against the "blinding ligh of the setting sun. The fate of his team depends on him for wi ten runs to make, an hour to play, and the last man of his sic at bat he must keep batting and running in spite of his opponent efforts to put him out.

square, a hollow, square, defensive infantry formation. The fror rank kneels, the next two stoop, and the rest (usually two) stan The stanza refers to the fighting of the British Expeditionar Force in the Sudan, Africa, 1883–1885.

Gatling, a type of machine gun used in the latter part of the nine teenth century and named after its inventor, Richard Jorda Gatling, an American. It consisted of a cluster of barrels (usuall ten) resembling somewhat a bundle of stout sticks. This wa revolved about the long axis by turning a crank, each barre being loaded and fired once during a revolution. It could fir about six hundred shots a minute.

154. A Dreamer

warp and woof. In weaving, the warp means the threads running lengthwise of the loom; the woof, the threads that cross the warp.

161. Cat's Eye

Galaxies, the million or more groups of stars like the Milky Way of which our sun is a part. Some of the most distant galaxies so far discovered are estimated to be sextillions of miles away.

162. Philosopher's Garden

Philosopher (Greek for lover of wisdom), one who thinks deeply about the meaning of life.

166. Derricks and Rainbows

The hostage given man by God, the pledge given man by God. "And God said, This is the token of the covenant which I make between me and you and every living creature that is with you, for perpetual generations: I do set my bow in the cloud, and it shall be for a token of a covenant between me and the earth. And it shall come to pass, when I bring a cloud over the earth, that the bow shall be seen in the cloud: And I will remember my covenant, which is between me and you and every living creature of all flesh; and the waters shall no more become a flood to destroy all flesh."—Genesis 9: 12–15.

67. SIGHT

stall, a stand, or booth, for the display of goods.

Krakatoa, island volcano in the strait of Sunda between the islands of Sumatra and Java of the Dutch East Indies; the scene of a disastrous eruption in 1883.

Tyre, capital of the ancient country of Phoenicia at the Eastern end of the Mediterranean Sea.

Paradise, the Garden of Eden.

176. MATHEMATICS

Mars . . . Venus . . . Saturn, planets of the solar system.

Celestial, heavenly.

Where the comet wanes and comes Are essential axioms. The path of a comet may be an ellipse, a parabola, or a hyperbola—all mathematical figures.

177. STEAM SHOVEL

dinosaurs, large extinct reptiles. (See also note for page 443, on "The Dinosaur.")

177. THERE IS NO FRIGATE LIKE A BOOK

traverse, journey.

frugal, economical.

178. YOU, ANDREW MARVELL. The significance of the title is that Andrew Marvell, English poet of the seventeenth century, is the author of lines expressing the idea on which this poem is based. In Marvell's poem "To His Coy Mistress," a lover states that he would not care how much time he spent in wooing,

PAGE

But at my back I always hear
Time's winged chariot hurrying near:
And yonder all before us lie
Deserts of vast eternity.

The always rising of the night. In this line the poet suggests the passing of time. Since each of the places in his poem is farther west than the one preceding, the sun is later in setting. As he explains "The movement of the poem is not the movement of the revolving earth from west to east but the movement (or what seems to be the movement) of the night from east to west—the night moving upon the face of the earth."

Ecbatan, ancient name of modern Hamadan, a city in northwest Persia.

Persia, Iran, kingdom in southwest Asia.

Kermanshah (kĕr-män-shä′), city in northwest Persia.

Bagdad, capital of Iraq.

Arabia, country in southwest Asia.

Palmyra (păl-mī′rȧ), ruins of a city in Syria.

Lebanon, self-governing territory in western Syria.

Crete, mountainous island belonging to Greece, southeast of the Grecian peninsula.

overblown, with the wind blowing over, exposed to the wind.

179. *Sicily,* island in the Mediterranean Sea, belonging to Italy.

Nor now the long light on the sea. The extra space between the lines has the force of punctuation. Like a dash, it suggests a pause, a change of thought, a summarization.

180. THE TICKET AGENT

Aden, seaport of southwest Arabia in Asia Minor.

Bombay, city on the west coast of India.

Nome, city on the west coast of Alaska.

183. BLIND

Cumberland Market, London, a picturesque square, formerly the site of a hay market.

185. FLAMES

maze, here amazement.

integral, whole, unimpaired.

187. LIQUIDS

humors, liquids.

187. RADIUM

But giving, giving, eager with the gift,
Exhaustless as the soul.

Radium gives forth energy at a steady rate throughout its existence of thousands of years.

188. ALLENBY ENTERS JERUSALEM! During the World War (1914–1918), Sir Edmund Allenby, British general, was placed in charge of the campaign against the Turkish forces in Palestine. After defeating the enemy at Beersheba, he drove them north toward Jerusalem. Almost at its gates they offered stubborn resistance but could not check the British advance. The city surrendered December 9, 1917, and Allenby entered it officially December 11. The Holy City, so bitterly fought for during the Crusades, had been in the hands of the Mohammedans almost continuously for twelve centuries.

Richard, Coeur de Lion. French for Richard the Lion Heart, a name given to Richard I, King of England at the end of the twelfth century and leader of the Third Crusade.

Ascalon (ăs′kȧ-lŏn), village on the coast of Palestine, the scene of a battle in 1099 during the First Crusade.

Zion, a hill in Jerusalem.

Red Cross. The cross was the emblem of the Crusaders.

Crusaders, members of a number of military expeditions sent out by Christian powers between 1096 and 1270 to regain the Holy Land from the Mohammedans.

Sepulcher, the tomb of Christ, marked by the Church of the Holy Sepulcher in Jerusalem.

Gethsemane, an enclosed space or garden outside Jerusalem, the scene of the spiritual suffering and the betrayal of Christ.

Calvary, the place outside Jerusalem where Christ was crucified.

Godfrey de Bouillon (gôd-frwä′ dĕ bo͞o-yôn′), a Frenchman who wa[s] one of the leaders of the First Crusade, toward the end of th[e] eleventh century. After the Christian forces had capture[d] Jerusalem in 1099, he became Baron of that city, and dreamed o[f] a splendid future for it. To strengthen his position, he engaged in further military operations but died of fever before he could carry them out. He is buried in the Church of the Holy Sepulcher.

Crescent, the emblem of the Turkish empire and, therefore, of Mohammedan power.

Saladin, sultan of Egypt and Syria, at the end of the twelfth century, who waged war against the Crusaders.

Dead Sea, an inland salt lake about fifteen miles southeast of Jerusalem.

St. George, patron saint of England who lived during the latter part of the third century.

189. Return

St. Francis, St. Francis of Assisi, Italian friar and founder of the Order of Franciscans, who lived in the late twelfth and early thirteenth centuries. He had a deep love for nature and according to legend was the friend and protector of all forms of animal life. One story tells of his preaching a sermon to the birds, in which he urged them to be thankful to their Creator for food, protective covering, and the liberty to fly about.

191. Hawaiian Hilltop

Babylonian, of Babylon, ancient city, now in ruins, on the Euphrates River in what is now Iraq, southwestern Asia.

192. David and Goliath

David, a shepherd boy who became king of Israel about 1000 B.C.

Goliath, the Philistine giant slain by David with a sling shot. The story is told in 1 Samuel, chapter 17.

193. Hands

jasmine-petaled hands, like the petals of jasmine, a white flower.

extreme unction, a sacrament of the Roman Catholic Church, administered by a priest who anoints with holy oil a person believed to be near death, and offers prayers for his spiritual and physical well-being.

95. THOSE WHO SOAR

Progenitors, ancestors.

forbears, ancestors.

201. THE ROUNDHOUSE

Rembrandt, famous Dutch painter of the seventeenth century.

Hydra, in mythology, a many-headed serpent. In the *Aeneid*, Vergil gives a description of the frightful monsters which guard the entrance to Hades and speaks of "Hydras hissing."

Tartarus, in mythology, the region of the lower world for the punishment of the wicked; Hades.

gryphons (also griffins), in mythology, monsters having the bodies and legs of lions, and the heads and wings of eagles. Since they built their nests of gold, they were obliged to keep watchful guard over them.

203. SILVER

shoon, old form of "shoes."

204. THE WINDMILLS. One of a group entitled "Arizona Poems."

manzanita (măn-zȧ-nē′tȧ), a variety of shrub found in the southwestern United States.

206. APPLES IN NEW HAMPSHIRE

207. *The apple crop is heavy this year in New Hampshire;*

Next year the trees will rest and apples will be few. According to C. F. Kinman, senior pomologist, United States Department of Agriculture: "If weather conditions and the vigor of the tree are favorable, an extra heavy crop of fruit may be set, and to bring this crop to maturity may so deplete the resources of the tree that comparatively few, if any, fruit buds are formed for the

PAGE

following year. Bearing little or no fruit the following year, the tree can build up its resources for a very heavy crop for the next year. In this way some apple varieties become what are called alternate bearers."

208. LONDON SNOW

manna, the food with which God fed the children of Israel in the wilderness. "And when the dew fell upon the camp in the night, the manna fell upon it."—Numbers 11: 9. " . . . and it was like coriander seed, white; and the taste of it was like wafers made with honey."—Exodus 16: 31.

209. *Paul's*, St. Paul's Cathedral.

210. MOUNTAIN HAMLET

211. *Gunflint Pass*, a Rocky Mountain pass in western Montana.

214. SMELLS

gramarye, magic.

217. THE STATISTICIAN

Chartres (shär'tr), the Cathedral of Chartres, in northern France, one of the most beautiful cathedrals in Europe.

Titian (tĭsh'ăn), Tiziano Vecellio, Venetian painter of the early sixteenth century.

219. PORTRAIT

sycophants, servile flatterers.

220. THE FIDDLER OF DOONEY. All the places mentioned are, of course, in Ireland (now Eire).

Dooney, perhaps Doony, a town in County Cork.

Kilvarnet, a parish in County Sligo.

Mocharabuiee, perhaps Magheraboy, one of a number of places by that name.

Sligo, a town on Sligo Bay on the northwest coast.

222. OLD GRAY SQUIRREL

Golden Gate, the entrance to San Francisco Bay.

penny dreadfuls, sensational stories, the equivalent of dime novels.

Norroway, old Scottish form of Norway.

Sunderland, seaport in northeast England.

223. *capstan*, a cylindrical drum rotating on a vertical axis, used for moving or raising heavy weights. If operated by machinery, it is turned by means of a cable passing around the drum. If operated by hand, it is turned by means of bars thrust into holes at the top of the drum.

totting, adding.

228. PORTRAIT OF A BOY

Cross, the Southern Cross, a constellation.

Mars, one of the planets, distinguished by its redness.

Centaur, brilliant southern constellation.

wattled, having loose red flesh under the throat, as a rooster has.

syenite, a crystalline gray rock.

Doubloons, former Spanish and Spanish-American gold coins.

232. THE SCHOOLBOY READS HIS ILIAD

Iliad, a Greek poem attributed to Homer, which tells the story of the last year of the siege of Ilium (Troy), a city in northwest Asia Minor.

Helen, in Greek legend Helen of Troy, the wife of Menelaus, a son of the king of Sparta. She was carried away by Paris, a son of the king of Troy, to his native city. This incident caused the Greek warriors to sail to Troy and lay siege to it. Helen's beauty, the cause of that expedition, inspired the famous lines from Christopher Marlowe's *The Tragical History of Doctor Faustus:*

> Was this the face that launched a thousand ships
> And burnt the topless towers of Ilium?

visited with gods. The gods and goddesses, according to the legend, took an active interest in the Trojan War.

234. GUNGA DIN (gōōn′gȧ dēn′). The foreign expressions used in this poem are Hindustani, the dialect of most of India, or the British soldier's idea of it.

penny-fights, fights that do not amount to anything.

Aldershot it, spent time at Aldershot, a famous military trainin camp, located in southern England.

'Er Majesty the Queen, Queen Victoria, who ruled in the nineteent century.

bhisti (beast'i), a native water carrier attached to a British regimen in India.

Slippy hitherao (hither-ä'o), come here and be quick about it (*slipp* be quick; *hitherao*, come here).

Panee lao (pä'nē lä'ō), bring water.

squidgy-nosed, short-nosed.

Harry By, *Harry*, a slang term; *By* (bhai), brother.

wopped, beat.

235. *juldee* (jŭl'dee), "quickly."

marrow, hit.

dot an' carry one, from arithmetic, meaning put down and carry a number over; hence, keep going. Here it means limp along on bare, tired feet.

mussick (mŭs' sick), water skin, the goatskin water bag previously referred to.

236. *dooli* (dōō'lĭ), a litter of canvas, suspended from a wooden frame, used for carrying the wounded.

Lazarushian-leather, a combination of *Lazarus* and *leather*. *Lazarus* suggests the Bible story (Luke 16: 19–31) of the beggar by that name who desired to be fed with the crumbs which fell from the rich man's table. Later, the rich man, in hell, cried: "Father Abraham, have mercy on me, and send Lazarus that he may dip the tip of his finger in water, and cool my tongue, for I am tormented in this flame." *Leather* probably refers to the *mussick*, the goatskin water bag, which Gunga Din carried.

belted, struck.

flayed, reproved harshly.

242. MARY SHAKESPEARE

Saint George, patron saint of England, who lived during the latter part of the third century. April 23 is celebrated as Saint George's Day.

limn, depict.

243. MILTON. John Milton, English poet and writer of the seventeenth century, author of the epic poem *Paradise Lost*. Milton was a patriotic, liberty-loving idealist. Living during a period of unrest, when the Puritans were rebelling against the Church of England, and Parliament was rebelling against the king, he felt that it was his duty to enter into public affairs. Since his sympathy was with the Puritan party and the people, he wrote pamphlets fearlessly attacking both church and state. His article in defense of unlicensed printing did much to establish the principle of the freedom of the press. (See also the poem "On His Blindness," page 133.) This poem was written in 1802, in the reign of George III, a time of political and economic unrest caused by the Napoleonic Wars and the Industrial Revolution.

244. HOW COULD YOU KNOW?

in many an aery wheel, quoted from *Paradise Lost*, Book III, line 741.

Uriel, one of the archangels. In *Paradise Lost*, Milton makes him "Regent of the Sun" and "the sharpest-sighted Spirit of all Heaven."

a shooting star, quoted from *Paradise Lost*, Book IV, line 556.

sail-broad vans, quoted from *Paradise Lost*, Book II, line 927. Here the word *vans* means wings.

a pyramid of fire, quoted from *Paradise Lost*, Book II, line 1013.

246. BEETHOVEN

spheric music. According to the theory of Pythagoras, Greek philosopher of the sixth century B.C., the harmonious motions of the heavenly bodies (as he understood them) must produce a harmony of sound. This idea gave rise to the expression "the music of the spheres."

247. CARLYLE AND EMERSON. Thomas *Carlyle*, Scottish essayist, historian, and philosopher of the nineteenth century. The style of much of his writing is impulsive and fiery. Ralph Waldo *Emerson*, American essayist, poet, and philosopher of the nineteenth century.

The style of his writing is studied and calm. When Emerson wa traveling in Scotland, he visited Carlyle. This meeting resulte in a lifelong friendship between the two, based on the dee respect each had for the other's moral courage and frankness.

balefire, signal fire, usually on a hill.

248. CRAWFORD LONG AND WILLIAM MORTON

249. *inlay*, a filling cemented into a tooth.

Massachusetts General, hospital in Boston, where, on October 16, 1846, Dr. Morton administered the anaesthetic for a public surgical operation.

250. LINCOLN, THE MAN OF THE PEOPLE

Norn Mother, in early Norse mythology, Urd, the goddess of fate. The Anglo-Saxon form is Wyrd, from which comes the word *weird*. As time passed, two more Norns were added; Urd is, therefore, regarded as the Norn Mother. In later mythology the Norns were three sisters: Urd (the past), Verdandi (the present), and Skuld (the future), similar to the Three Fates of the Greeks and Romans. (See also note for page 31, on *older Fates*.)

Heaven of Heroes. In Norse mythology, Asgard, the abode of the gods, contained Valhalla, the Hall of the Slain, the dwelling place of heroes killed in battle.

251. *Matterhorn*, high, rugged mountain of the Alps on the Italian-Swiss border.

254. A MODERN COLUMBUS

Genoese, a native or inhabitant of Genoa, Italy.

258. SONG

jasmine, any of various shrubs having fragrant, usually white, flowers.

lea, meadow.

265. TO HIS LOVE

every fair from fair sometime declines. In Shakespeare's time, "fair" meant "beauty"; therefore, he probably meant that everything beautiful will, in time, lose its beauty.

untrimmed, dismantled, its beauty taken away.

267. THAT TIME OF YEAR
choirs, places where choirs sing; here, the branches of trees.

268. JEAN. Burns's note concerning this poem reads: "The air is by Marshall, the song I composed out of compliment to Mrs. Burns. N.B.—It was during the honeymoon."

For reading Scottish dialect, see note for page 92, on "A Man's a Man for A' That."

airts (ârts), directions.
shaw, small wood or grove.

269. JOHN ANDERSON MY JO. For reading Scottish dialect, see note for page 92, on "A Man's a Man for A' That."

jo, sweetheart.
brent, smooth.
beld, bald.
pow, poll, head.
canty, happy.

274. DUNCAN GRAY. For reading Scottish dialect, see note for page 92, on "A Man's a Man for A' That."

fou, full, drunk.
coost, cast.
Looked asklent an' unco skeigh, looked aslant and very disdainfully.
Gart poor Duncan stand abeigh, made poor Duncan stand aloof.
fleeched, coaxed.
Ailsa Craig, a large rock off the coast of Ayr county, Scotland.
Grat his e'en baith bleart an' blin, wept his eyes both bleared and blind.
Spak o' lowpin' ower a linn, spoke of leaping over a waterfall.
hizzie, hussy, worthless girl.

275. *smoored*, smothered.
crouse an' canty baith, both lively and happy.

278. THE BANKS O' DOON. For reading Scottish dialect, see note for page 92, on "A Man's a Man for A' That."

PAGE

Doon, a river in Ayr county, Scotland.
braes, hillsides.
ilka, every.

281. *From* SPRING
unhoods The falcon. In falconry, a method of hunting birds, a hood is kept over the head of the falcon (a trained hawk) to keep it quiet until released.

282. *eft*, the red eft, an animal two or three inches long resembling a lizard, but having a smooth, moist skin.

284. A BALLADE OF SPRING'S UNREST. A ballade (bȧ-lȧd′) is a verse form, originally French. There are three stanzas of eight lines, each having the same rhyming sounds in the order *a b a b b c b c* (see page 473), and a concluding quatrain (called the "envoy") which rhymes *b c b c*. The final line of the first stanza, known as the refrain, recurs as the final line of all the succeeding stanzas including the envoy. The ballade should not be confused with the ballad. The latter is discussed on page 474.

286. UP! UP! MY FRIEND, AND QUIT YOUR BOOKS
throstle, thrush.

288. HILLS
pleachèd, bordered or overarched by trees or bushes having their branches interwoven.

292. STREAMS
banyan, an East Indian tree from whose branches roots grow down to the ground and form additional trunks.

293. THE MARSHES OF GLYNN. Glynn is a county in southeast Georgia bordering on the Atlantic Ocean.

294. *mete*, boundary.

298. WHEN THE FROST IS ON THE PUNKIN
shock, sheaves of grain set up in a field.

guineys, guinea fowl, birds resembling chickens. The feathers are dark gray speckled with white. The species originally came from Guinea, a region on the west coast of Africa.

furries, furrows; here, plowed land or fields.

299. *souse*, something pickled in brine, such as pigs' feet.

305. ODE TO THE WEST WIND. Shelley's note: "This poem was conceived and chiefly written in a wood that skirts the Arno [River], near Florence [Italy] and on a day when that tempestuous wind whose temperature is at once mild and animating, was collecting the vapors which pour down the autumnal rains. They began, as I foresaw, at sunset, with a violent tempest of hail and rain, attended by that magnificent thunder and lightning peculiar to the Cisalpine regions [regions on the Italian side of the Alps].

"The phenomenon alluded to at the conclusion of the third stanza is well known to naturalists. The vegetation at the bottom of the sea, of rivers, and of lakes sympathizes with that of the land in the change of seasons, and is consequently influenced by the winds which announce it."

ode, a poem which deals progressively with a subject in a dignified way.

Maenad (mē′nad), in mythology, a nymph attendant on Dionysus (Bacchus), the god of wine.

306. *coil*, tumult.

Baiae (Bī′ē), modern Baia, a village situated on a small bay west of Naples, Italy. Because of its mild climate, beautiful scenery, and warm mineral springs it was a favorite resort of the ancient Romans, who built magnificent villas and baths there. The ruins of these are still to be seen.

318. SPANISH WATERS. The title refers to the Caribbean Sea off the "Spanish Main," or the northern coast of South America. During the seventeenth and eighteenth centuries, the Caribbean was a favorite hunting ground for pirates, who plundered the Spanish ships carrying wealth from Mexico and South America.

Los Muertos (lōs mo͞o-ĕr′tōs), Spanish words meaning "the dead," the name of an island off the south coast of Puerto Rico, formerl a refuge of pirates.

Cay, low, small island.

lazareet (lăz-ȧ-rēt′), a storeroom of a ship, usually near the stern.

319. *Lima Town*, a city near the coast of Peru. For two hundred year following the middle of the sixteenth century, Lima was th center of Spanish trade and a place of great wealth.

doubloons, former Spanish and Spanish-American gold coins.

moidores (moi′dōrs), former Portuguese and Brazilian coins.

louis d'ors (lo͞o-i dôr′), French gold coins.

portagues (pōr′tȧ-gūz), former Portuguese coins.

bezoar stones (bē′zōr), stones from the digestive organs of certain ruminant animals, such as the Peruvian llama, once used as an antidote for poison.

Guayaquil (gwī-ä-kēl′), a city on the coast of Ecuador.

Arica (ä-rē′kä), a seaport in the extreme northern part of Chile.

Incas, Indians who inhabited the region nów known as Peru.

Dons, Spaniards.

Mulatas Cays (mo͞o-lah′tahs cās), a group of small islands off the northeast coast of Panama.

320. THE VAGABOND

lave, rest.

322. THE UNCONQUERED AIR

Rhea, great nature goddess, mother of Zeus.

Neptune, god of the sea.

Olympian, godlike, since Mount Olympus in Greece was the abode of the gods.

Titans, in mythology, giants with power greater than that of men but not equal to that of the Olympian gods, against whom they waged an unsuccessful war. They were the children of Uranus (Heaven) and Gaea (Earth).

Icarian, of Icarus, a youth who, according to mythology, escaped from the island of Crete by means of artificial wings. However, he flew too near the sun, so that the heat melted the wax by which his wings were attached. As a result he fell into the sea and was drowned.

Apollo's steeds, the four horses which pulled the golden chariot of the sun through the heavens. Only Apollo, the sun god, could drive them. (See also note for page 149, on "The Happiest Heart.")

wield the thunderbolt. The thunderbolt was the weapon of Zeus, chief of the gods.

323. THE GYPSY HEART

furze, spiny evergreen shrub.

patteran, handfuls of material such as grass or leaves thrown down at intervals by gypsies to indicate the way they have gone.

324. ELDORADO (Spanish meaning "the gilded"), originally the chief of a South American tribe. According to one story, each ruler at the time of his inauguration had himself covered with gold dust which he then washed off in a sacred lake. Later, the name came to be applied to an imaginary country rich in gold and precious stones. The Spaniards of the sixteenth century supposed this to be in the northern part of South America. Eldorado was eagerly sought by adventurers of the time.

bedight, dressed.

Mountains Of the Moon, the snow-capped Ruwenzori Mountains in Africa at the source of the Nile. Although mentioned by Ptolemy, Greek astronomer, geographer, and mathematician of the second century, their actual existence was not proved until 1888 when they were found by Sir Henry Morton Stanley, English explorer. In the time of Poe they were believed to be imaginary.

Valley of the Shadow. "Yea, though I walk through the valley of the shadow of death, I will fear no evil . . . "—Psalms 23: 4.

326. REVEILLE

Forelands, headlands, promontories.

thews, muscles, sinews.

cumber, burden.

PAGE

329. He Who Loves the Ocean

330. *skysails*, the highest sails of a square-rigged ship.

royals, the sails next below the skysails.

caravel, sailing vessel.

curvet, leap like a horse.

332. Sea Longing

sea mews, sea gulls.

334. Three Tarry Men

Port Sudan, a city of Anglo-Egyptian Sudan in northeast Africa, on the Red Sea.

Port-au-Prince, the chief seaport, as well as the capital, of Haiti, in the West Indies.

Seychelles (sā-shĕl′), islands about a thousand miles east of Africa.

Hebrides (hĕb′ rĭ-dēz), islands off the west coast of Scotland.

336. A Wet Sheet and a Flowing Sea

sheet, a rope or chain attached to the lower corner of a sail for spreading it out.

339. No Gull's Wings. "No creature under heaven knows the sea so well as the gull—mute bird of the Loneliness."—O. E. Rölvaag.

O. E. Rölvaag, American novelist (1876–1931). Rölvaag was born in a little fishing hamlet on the island of Dönna, off the coast of Norway and just south of the Arctic Circle. During his early life the sea made a deep impression on him. When he was twenty, he came to the United States where, after further education, he became a professor at St. Olaf College (Northfield, Minnesota), as well as an author. Two of his best-known books are *Giants in the Earth* and *Peder Victorious*. Although his stories are about the Norwegian settlers of the prairies, they frequently reveal his love for the sea and for his home in Norway.

Here he can sleep, far inland from the sea. Rölvaag is buried in Oaklawn Cemetery, Northfield, Minnesota.

homesick birds that fly into the west. Nearly twelve years after his arrival in America, Rölvaag wrote to the Reverend O. E.

Farseth: "Would that I might be in Rölvaag a few days now and help them get ready for the Lofoten sailing. . . . It seems to me that I can feel the eager but trembling forward movement of the boat as it rides the wave and the spray beats against my face." Rölvaag chose as his surname the name of the cove near which he was born.

cormorant, large dark-colored sea bird.

345. THE HARBOR

sea wrack, marine vegetation or other floating material cast up on the shore.

Wexford, the county at the southeast corner of Ireland.

Arklow, a town.

Cahore, Cahore Point, about twenty miles south of Arklow.

colloguing, talking.

Angelus, a church bell rung in the belfry of Catholic churches three times a day: morning, noon, and evening. It is a call to recite the prayer having the Latin title "Angelus," since "Angelus" is its first word.

346. THE ANCESTRAL DWELLINGS

fanlight, a semi-circular window with sash bars radiating like the ribs of a fan.

gambrel roof, a roof having its slope broken by an obtuse angle. It is so called because the angle is suggestive of a gambrel, the joint above the foot in the hind leg of an animal, especially a horse. Oliver Wendell Holmes described such a roof in the following lines:

"Gambrel?—Gambrel?" Let me beg
You'll look at a horse's hinder leg—
First great angle above the hoof—
That's the *gambrel;* hence gambrel roof.

—*The Autocrat of the Breakfast Table*, Number 12.

347. *Quaker*, of the religious sect, the Society of Friends.

gabled, built with the upper part of the wall forming a triangle between the slopes of a double-sloping roof.

stoops, steps.

Puritans, the Pilgrim settlers of New England, who belonged to the religious sect known as the Puritans.

348. *dormer windows,* vertical windows extending out from sloping roofs, usually opening into sleeping rooms—hence the name, related to the word "dormitory,"

Charleston, seaport city in South Carolina.

349. WHERE A ROMAN VILLA STOOD, ABOVE FREIBURG

Freiburg, a city in southwest Germany.

354. THE VOICES

Kentish, of Kent, the county in the southeast corner of England.

356. ATTACK

barrage, artillery fire coming from behind troops and falling in front of them so as to produce a barrier.

357. THE SPIRES OF OXFORD. The university at Oxford in southern England.

quad, quadrangle, a four-sided piece of ground more or less surrounded by buildings. Most of the colleges of Oxford are built according to this plan.

359. IN FLANDERS FIELDS

Flanders, two provinces, East Flanders and West Flanders, in Belgium. In the World War (1914–1918), the former was occupied by the German troops, the latter defended by the Belgians and the British.

poppies blow Between the crosses, row on row. Crosses marked the graves of the soldiers who had fallen in the World War. The poppies, which grow wild in that region, produced under the white crosses a faint flush of red.

360. GRASS

Austerlitz (ôs′tĕr-lĭts), a town located in Czecho-Slovakia. It was the scene of a battle in 1805, where Napoleon Bonaparte defeated the Austrians and Russians.

PAGE

Waterloo, a village near Brussels, Belgium. Here in 1815 the English and their allies under Wellington defeated the armies of Napoleon Bonaparte.

Gettysburg, a borough in southern Pennsylvania where Meade defeated Lee in 1863.

Ypres (ē′pr), a town in Belgium, the scene of battles during the World War (1914–1918).

Verdun (vĕr-dŭn′), a town in northeast France, the scene of battles during the World War (1914–1918).

363. HE FELL AMONG THIEVES

Yassin river . . . Laspur hills, in extreme northwestern India.

Afghan snows, the snows on the distant mountains in Afghanistan, the country adjoining India.

Norman arch, an arch of the Gothic type of architecture introduced into England by the Normans.

364. *Close*, an enclosed space; grounds.

Dons, members of the university faculty.

366. ACHILLES DEATHERIDGE

367. *Johnnie*, name sometimes given to a Southern soldier in the War between the States.

368. THE CHRYSANTHEMUM LEGEND

Kyoto, the former capital of Japan.

369. *isolate*, isolated, solitary.

370. THE GLOVE AND THE LIONS

King Francis, King Francis I of France who lived in the early part of the sixteenth century.

374. THE HIGHWAYMAN

galleon, a large sailing vessel.

stable wicket, a small door in a larger stable door.

379. SIR PATRICK SPENS. The extent to which the incidents in this ballad are historical is not known.

For reading Scottish dialect, see note for page 92, on "A Man's a Man for A' That."

Dumferling, Dunfermline, a town on the southeast coast of Scotland.

braid, broad, that is "open" rather than "closed," rolled into a scroll.

To send me out this time o' the year To sail upon the sea. A note to this ballad in *Reliques of Ancient English Poetry*, collected by Thomas Percy, contains a statement to the effect that in the winter season ships sailing the North Sea were very likely to be wrecked. As a consequence, a law was passed during the reign of James the Third, King of Scotland in the fifteenth century, that no ship was to leave the kingdom from the end of October to the beginning of February.

380. *yestreen*, last evening.

new moon Wi' the auld moon in her arm, the crescent moon with the dark part made visible by sunlight reflected from the earth. The faintly illuminated part is particularly noticeable when the air is very clear, a condition which sometimes indicates storm.

shoon, old form of "shoes."

Their hats they swam aboon, "they" refers to hats; "aboon" means above.

Half ower, half way over.

Aberdour, a village on the northeast coast of Scotland, about 150 miles by water from Dunfermline.

381. The Two Sisters. This is a version of one of the traditional English and Scottish ballads. It is still sung in the mountain regions of the South. For singing or group reading, the indented lines are repeated in the other stanzas.

balance, in dancing, to move toward and then back away from another person.

fair, pretty girl.

382. The Gol-Darned Wheel

tarnel, eternal, that can last long enough to put up a good fight.

longhorn, a breed of cattle having very long horns, sometimes seven feet from tip to tip. This breed is now practically extinct.

Brazos, a river that flows through the central part of Texas from northwest to southeast.

tenderfoot, an inexperienced person.

handy cutter, one skillful at driving or "cutting" from a herd a particular animal to be branded, or treated for screw worms.

383. *hotter than a mink*. A mink, when cornered, is a savage fighter.

chink, money, so called because of the sharp, metallic sound, or chink, which coins make.

whipcrackers, crackings of whips. Hair was long and whiplike inasmuch as there were no barbers on the plains.

canthy, long and stringy.

punchers, cowboys. "Punching" cattle is driving or herding cattle, since "punching" means prodding, as with a stick.

muzzle, the projecting nose and mouth of an animal.

a-galliflutin', with a noisy "hither and yon" movement.

384. *hollowed*, shouted.

meachin', suspicion.

385. CERELLE

chaparral, a low-growing thicket characteristic of Mexico and the southwestern United States. The term comes from the Spanish word "chaparro," meaning "dwarf evergreen oak," but is applied to any thicket of shrubs, cacti, or dwarf trees.

387. WASHINGTON'S LAST BIRTHDAY. On February 22, 1799, Eleanor (Nelly) Parke Custis, Washington's stepgrandchild, was married to Lawrence Lewis, his nephew. Eleanor Custis was the daughter of John Parke Custis, who was the son of Daniel Parke Custis and Martha Custis. Martha Custis, after the death of her first husband, became the wife of George Washington. Lawrence Lewis was the son of Elizabeth (Betty) Lewis, the sister of George Washington.

389. FIVE PEAS ON A BARRELHEAD

loco, insane.

stark, harsh.

rotgut gin, bad quality, usually adulterated, liquor.

berserker, violently mad. In Norse mythology a "berserk" was a fighter who was supposed to assume the form of a bear or wolf and become frenzied. At such times he was invulnerable to fire and iron.

390. *run amuck*, rush about in a state of frenzy attacking everyone.

393. *voyageur*, in the Northwest and Canada, a boatman and trapper.
Lac la Croix, a lake on the Minnesota-Ontario border.
M'sieu, Monsieur, French for "Mister."

394. *Sacré*, a weak oath having the force of "confound it!"

396. *lantern jaw*, long, thin jaw.

402. THE TOMCAT
Malevolent, wishing evil.
brindled, gray or dull yellowish brown with dark streaks or spots.
bard, in ancient times a poet and singer; a poet.
leers, casts a sidelong glance, usually suggestive of evil intent.

403. IN HONOR OF TAFFY TOPAZ
Freudian wish, suppressed desires.

406. THE DONKEY
errant, wandering.
parody, ludicrous imitation.
There was a shout about my ears,
And palms before my feet.

When Jesus rode into Jerusalem seated on an ass's colt, the people "Took branches of palm trees, and went forth to meet him, and cried, Hosanna: Blessed is the King of Israel that cometh in the name of the Lord."—John, 12: 13.

410. CLIPPED WINGS
stool, a pole to which a bird is fastened to attract other birds.
wildling, wild one.

413. AN AUGUST MIDNIGHT
blind, window shade.

dumbledore, beetle which flies with a buzzing noise.

414. THE MOLLUSK. Refers to a shellfish, such as a clam or an oyster.
Sèvres (sâ′vr), fine chinaware from Sèvres, a city in the north of France.

419. THE UNTUTORED GIRAFFE
Mus Ridiculus, *Felis*, *Caniculus*, burlesques of the scientific names of animals: mouse being *Mus musculus*; cat, *Felis domestica;* and dog, *Canis familiaris*.

422. LINES TO DR. DITMARS. Dr. Ditmars, an authority on animals, is curator of mammals and reptiles at the New York Zoological Gardens.
Orinoco (ō-ri-nō′kō) large river in Venezuela, South America.
Sargasso (sär-găs′ō), the Sargasso Sea, a region of the south Atlantic, so named from the prevalence of seaweed. *Sargazo* is Spanish for "seaweed."
Bocas (bō′cäs), Spanish for "mouths." The Bocas del Dragon (Dragon's Mouths) is the northerly group of straits separating Trinidad, a British island, from Venezuela.
Port of Spain, the capital of Trinidad.
loveless Virgins, the Virgin Islands, a small group in the West Indies named in honor of St. Ursula and her attendant virgins. According to legend, St. Ursula was a princess of Cornwall, England, about the fourth century. While on a pilgrimage, she and her companions were slain by the Huns at the city of Cologne.
boa constrictors, large, nonpoisonous snakes of tropical America, which crush their prey in their coils.
fer-de-lances, large poisonous snakes of tropical America. They are allied to rattlesnakes but have no rattles.
coral snakes, small, poisonous, brilliant red-and-black snakes of tropical America.

423. *vampire bats*, large blood-sucking bats of Central America and South America.
bushmaster, the largest poisonous snake in the Western Hemisphere. It inhabits Central America and South America.

430. The Street of Doctors

Pekin, Peiping (Peking), city in eastern China, formerly the capital.

prophylact, doctor.

"*Feasts of Lanterns.*" The Feast of Lanterns is a Chinese festival next in importance to that of the New Year. It seems to have originated as an ancient ceremony welcoming the increasing light and warmth of the sun. Beginning on the thirteenth day of the first moon of the year, it continues for six days. On the fifteenth, the great day of celebration, paper lanterns are carried by the people and hung along the streets in great abundance.

Hoyle, Edmund, eighteenth century English authority on the rules of games.

Dyspepsia, indigestion.

431. *osteopath*, a physician who believes that health is dependent on the structural integrity of the body, and treats disease by the correction of disturbances in structure.

hydropath, a physician who treats disease by administering water.

Nux vomica, a substance used in medicine, the poisonous seed of an Asiatic tree.

432. To a Poet

paens, songs of praise.

433. *Omar*, Omar Khayyam, Persian poet of the twelfth century, noted for his poem called *Rubáiyát*.

Parnassian, of Parnassus, a mountain in Greece sacred to Apollo and the Muses; hence, associated with poetry.

438. A Scot's Farewell to His Golf Ball. For reading Scottish dialect, see note for page 92, on "A Man's a Man for A' That."

brawly, heartily.

441. A Pure Mathematician

nought to him's a Primrose on The river's border. The suggestion for these lines comes from Wordsworth's "Peter Bell":

> A primrose by the river's brim
> A yellow primrose was to him
> And it was nothing more.

AGE

Parallelepipedon, a six-sided prism whose sides are parallelograms, the opposite pairs being equal and parallel.

Zealots, individuals filled with zeal or enthusiasm for some cause.

142. THE MUSIC OF THE FUTURE

fugues, musical compositions in which a number of parts combine in developing a single theme.

sonatas, musical compositions of three or four distinct divisions, each having a unity of its own, but so related as to form a whole.

143. THE DINOSAUR. An extinct reptile somewhat resembling an alligator or lizard, as revealed by the fossil remains. Some of the dinosaurs reached great size, having a length of nearly a hundred feet and a weight estimated at as much as thirty-five tons. No larger land animal is known to have existed.

a priori, Latin expression meaning "from the former," used to designate reasoning from the general to the particular, or from causes to effects—deductive reasoning.

a posteriori, Latin expression meaning "from the latter," used to designate reasoning from the particular to the general, or from effects to causes—inductive reasoning.

ACKNOWLEDGMENTS

ACKNOWLEDGMENTS

The compilers of this collection wish to thank those who have so generously co-operated directly or indirectly in its production: Dr. Albert L. Colston, Principal of the Brooklyn Technical High School, for sponsoring the idea; authors, publishers, and others who have granted the use of poems; authors who have read the manuscript of notes, made suggestions, and supplied information; members of the English Department and the Library Staff of the Brooklyn Technical High School; the staffs of various branches of the New York and Brooklyn Public Libraries, particularly the Reference Department of the New York Public Library; those who have read the manuscript and contributed ideas for it; the authors of the various works of reference which have supplied much useful information; and all those too numerous to mention who have made contributions toward the book.

For permission to use copyrighted material, grateful acknowledgment is made to:

Conrad Aiken for: The selection from "Senlin: a Biography" from *Selected Poems* published by Charles Scribner's Sons, copyright 1925 by Horace Liveright, Inc., reproduced by permission of the Author. "Music I Heard with You" from *Selected Poems* published by Charles Scribner's Sons, copyright 1918, 1921, 1929 by Conrad Aiken, reproduced by permission of the Author.

George Allen & Unwin, Ltd., for "Beethoven" from *The Story of Eros and Psyche* by Edward Carpenter.

American Poetry Magazine and the authors for: "On Hearing Jazz" by Alice Phelps-Rider. "Distribution" by Elsie B. Purcell.

D. Appleton-Century Company for: "¿Quien Sabe?" from *Narratives in Verse* by Ruth Comfort Mitchell. "Report on the Planet Earth" from *War and Laughter* by James Oppenheim, copyright, used by permission of D. Appleton-Century Company, Publishers, New York, N.Y.

J. J. Augustin, Inc., Publisher, for "The Two Sisters" from *Folk Song from the Southern Highlands*, collected and edited by Mellinger E Henry.

The Bell Syndicate, Inc. and James Montague for "The Mollusk" and "A Scot's Farewell to His Golf Ball."

Rosemary and Stephen Vincent Benét for "Crawford Long and William Morton" and "Wilbur Wright and Orville Wright" from *A Book of Americans* published by Farrar and Rinehart, Inc., copyright 1933 by Rosemary and Stephen Vincent Benét, reprinted by permission of the Authors.

Stephen Vincent Benét for "Portrait of a Boy" from *Ballads and Poems* published by Farrar and Rinehart, Inc.; copyright 1918, 1920, 1923, 1925, 1929, 1930, 1931 by Stephen Vincent Benét; reprinted by permission of the Author.

Basil Blackwell & Mott, Ltd., for "Adventure" from *Contacts* by T. W. Earp.

Blackwood's Magazine for: "Induced Current" by Herbert Mayo. "The Voices" (anonymous).

The Bobbs-Merrill Company for: "A Parting Guest" from *Morning* by James Whitcomb Riley, copyright 1907, 1935, and "When the Frost Is on the Punkin" from *Neighborly Poems* by James Whitcomb Riley, copyright 1891, 1919; Used by special permission of the publishers, The Bobbs-Merrill Company.

Berton Braley for "The Thinker" from *Songs from the Workaday World*, and "A Song of Power" first published in the *Public Utilities Fortnightly*.

June Breining for "Inexperience."

Richard E. Byrd for the selection from *Alone*.

Alice B. Campbell for "Sally and Manda."

Mrs. Stephen Chalmers and Joseph Lawren, Publisher, for "Allenby Enters Jerusalem" from *The Hermit Thrush* by Stephen Chalmers.

Chicago Tribune for "A Ballade of Spring's Unrest" and "The Dinosaur" by Bert Leston Taylor.

City Teachers Club Bulletin (Santa Barbara, Calif.) for "A Timely Warning." (Attempts to find the author have been unsuccessful.)

The Clarendon Press for "London Snow" from *The Shorter Poems of Robert Bridges*, Clarendon Press, Oxford, 1931, by permission of the publishers.

Country Life (London) and Isabel Butchart for "Dawn."

Covici Friede, Inc., for "Fences" and "Horizons" from *The Cheerful Cherub* by Rebecca McCann.

Dodd, Mead & Company, Inc., for: "The Great Lover" and "The Soldier" from *The Collected Poems of Rupert Brooke*. "A Vagabond Song" from *Bliss Carman's Poems*. "Cerelle" from *Lanterns in the Dusk* by Margaret Bell Houston. "At the Crossroads" from *Last Songs from Vagabondia*, and "Love in the Winds" and a selection from "Spring" from *Along the Trail* by Richard Hovey. "The Courtship of Miles Standish" from *Norsk Nightingale* by William F. Kirk. "I Meant to Do My Work Today" from *The Lonely Dancer and Other Poems* by Richard Le Gallienne. "The Fisher's Widow" from *Poems by Arthur Symons*. "A Mongrel Pup" from *A Riband on My Rein* by Nancy Byrd Turner. "To a Poet—By Spring" from *Baubles* by Carolyn Wells. All used by permission of the publishers, Dodd, Mead & Company, Inc.

Doubleday, Doran & Company, Inc., for: "The Rich Man" from *Tobogganing on Parnassus* by Franklin P. Adams, copyright 1911 by Doubleday, Doran & Co., Inc. "Distance" from *Banners* by Babette Deutsch, copyright 1919 by Doubleday, Doran & Co., Inc. "Cat's

Eye" from *American Song* by Paul Engle, copyright 1933, 1934, b Doubleday, Doran & Co., Inc. "Krazy: Reflection No. 5" from *Ot Cat* by Baron Ireland, copyright 1931, 1934, reprinted with permis sion from Doubleday, Doran & Co., Inc. "Trees" from *Trees an Other Poems* by Joyce Kilmer, copyright 1914 by Doubleday, Dora & Co., Inc. "Gunga Din" from *Barrack Room Ballads* by Rudyar Kipling, copyright 1892, 1920; "If" from *Rewards and Fairies* b Rudyard Kipling, copyright 1910; "Recessional" from *The Fiv Nations* by Rudyard Kipling, copyright 1903, 1931; and "Th Secret of the Machines" from *A History of England* by Rudyard Kip ling, copyright 1911; all reprinted with permission from Mrs Kipling and Doubleday, Doran & Co., Inc. "The Tomcat" from *Poems and Portraits* by Don Marquis, copyright 1922 by Doubleday, Doran & Co., Inc. "The Discovery" from *Poems, First Series* by John Collings Squire, copyright 1919, reprinted with permission from Doubleday, Doran & Co., Inc., and from the author. "I Hear America Singing," "Miracles," selections from "Song of Myself" and "Song of the Open Road," "This Moment Yearning and Thoughtful," "When I Heard the Learned Astronomer," and "When I Peruse the Conquered Fame" from *Leaves of Grass* by Walt Whitman, all reprinted by permission from Doubleday, Doran & Co., Inc. "Sportsmen in Paradise" from *A Waste Paper Philosophy* by T. P. Cameron Wilson, copyright 1920 by Doubleday, Doran & Co., Inc.

E. P. Dutton & Co., Inc., for: "The Donkey" taken from *The Wild Knight and Other Poems* by G. K. Chesterton, published by E. P. Dutton & Co., Inc., New York. "Incorrigible" taken from *Youngsters* by Burges Johnson, published and copyrighted by E. P. Dutton & Co., Inc., New York. "The Spires of Oxford" taken from *The Spires of Oxford and Other Poems* by Winifred Letts, published and copyrighted by E. P. Dutton & Co., Inc., New York. "The Harbor" taken from *Songs of Leinster* by Winifred M. Letts, published by E. P. Dutton & Co., Inc., New York. "There Is Shrill Music," Sonnet #293 taken from *Man with a Bull-Tongue Plow* by Jesse Stuart, published and copyrighted by E. P. Dutton & Co., Inc., New York. "Pretense" taken from *Singing Drums* by Helen Welshimer, published by E. P. Dutton & Co., Inc., New York.

nma Beer Ehrlich, literary executor of Morris Abel Beer, for his "Achievement" from *Street Lamps.*

ul Elder & Company for "Recipe for a Happy Life" by Margaret of Navarre from a volume of that title.

arrar & Rinehart, Inc., for: "Steam Shovel" from *Upper Pasture: Poems*, copyright, 1930, by Charles Malam, and reprinted by permission of Farrar & Rinehart, Inc. "No Words Are Lost" from *Hill Garden* by Margaret Widdemer, copyright 1936 and reprinted by permission of Farrar & Rinehart, Inc.

ohn Gould Fletcher for "The Skaters" from *Some Imagist Poems*, and "The Windmills" from *Breakers and Granite.*

ollett Publishing Company for "Motor Cars" from *Around a Toadstool Table* by Rowena Bastin Bennett, Follett Publishing Company, Chicago.

The Forum and the authors for: "Sonnet on Turning a Radio Dial" by Anderson M. Scruggs. "The Statistician" by Charles Wharton Stork.

W. J. Funk and The Oglethorpe University Press for "The Surgeon" published in *Bozart and Contemporary Verse.*

Hamlin Garland for "Do You Fear the Force of the Wind?" and "The Mountains Are a Lonely Folk."

Good Housekeeping and the authors for: "Envy" by Edgar Daniel Kramer. "Road Song" by Margaret E. Sangster. "Hummingbird" by Violet Alleyn Storey.

Hooper Reynolds Goodwin and the *Manchester Union-Leader* for "The Parabola."

Edwin O. Grover for: "Days like These" by Ella Elizabeth Egbert. "Sea Urge" (anonymous) from *Nature Lover's Knapsack.* (Attempts to find the authors have been unsuccessful.)

Harcourt, Brace and Company, Inc., for: "Cobbler" from *Animosities* Peggy Bacon, copyright 1931, by Harcourt, Brace and Compar Inc. "Between Two Loves" and "Een Napoli" from *Selected Poems T. A. Daly*, reprinted by permission of Harcourt, Brace and Cor pany, Inc., holders of the copyright. "Enigma in Altman's" fro *One More Manhattan* by Phillis McGinley, copyright, 1937, by Ha court, Brace and Company, Inc. "Liquids" from *The Noise Th Time Makes* by Merrill Moore. A selection from *Smoke and Steel* l Carl Sandburg, copyright, 1920, by Harcourt, Brace and Compan Inc. "Caliban in the Coal Mines" and "Prayer" from *Select Poems and Parodies of Louis Untermeyer*, reprinted by permission Harcourt, Brace and Company, Inc., holders of the copyrigh "The Factories" from *Factories and Other Poems* by Margaret Wic demer, reprinted by permission of Harcourt, Brace and Company Inc. Persis Greely Anderson's "The Question Mark," Marie Gi christ's "Apples in New Hampshire," Kenneth Allan Robinson' "Lines to Dr. Ditmars," and Mildred Weston's "Argument" an "Echo," all from *The New Yorker Book of Verse*, copyright, 1935, b the F-R Publishing Corporation; reprinted by permission of Har court, Brace and Company, Inc.

Harper & Brothers for: "Song" from *Poems* by Dana Burnet. "Al Goats" from *Atlas and Beyond* by Elizabeth Coatsworth. "Power" from *This Golden Summit* by Grace Noll Crowell. "For a Pessimist" from *Color* by Countee Cullen. "The Ambiguous Dog" and "A Pure Mathematician" from *The Laughing Muse*. "A Dreamer" and "Thunderstorm" from *Ballads of Old New York*. "Hills" from *The Mirthful Lyre* by Arthur Guiterman.

Harper's Magazine and the authors for: "The Ticket Agent" by Edmund Leamy. "Street Beggar" by Anderson M. Scruggs. "Expatriate" by Mary Brown Onstott. (Attempts to get in touch with the author have been unsuccessful.)

The Harpoon and Oliver Jenkins for "Captain's Walk: Salem."

The Hogarth Press for "The Woman with the Baby to the Philosopher" from *Different Days* by Frances Cornford.

enry Holt and Company, Inc., for: "Silver" from *Collected Poems, 1901–1918* by Walter de la Mare. "Mending Wall" and "An Old Man's Winter Night" from *Collected Poems* by Robert Frost. "Machines" and "Say That He Loved Old Ships" from *Bright Harbor* by Daniel Whitehead Hicky. "Fog" and "Skyscraper" from *Chicago Poems,* and "Grass" and "Prayers of Steel" from *Cornhuskers* by Carl Sandburg. "Angus McGregor," "Clipped Wings," "Five Peas on a Barrelhead," and "Mountain Hamlet" from *Wings against the Moon;* "Four Little Foxes" from *Slow Smoke;* and "The Wolf Cry" from *Many, Many Moons* by Lew Sarett.

oughton Mifflin Company for: "Memory" from *The Complete Poems of Thomas Bailey Aldrich.* "The White Man's Road" from *Out Where the West Begins and Other Western Verses* by Arthur Chapman. "The Happiest Heart" from *Poems* by John Vance Cheney. "Dream the Great Dream," "Song," and "The Unconquered Air" from *Poems* by Florence Earle Coates. "Challenge" from *Poems, 1908–1919* by John Drinkwater. "Faith" from *Clouds and Cobblestones* by Hortense Flexner. "Jim Bludso of the *Prairie Belle*" from *The Complete Poetical Works of John Hay,* and "Nature" from *Collected Poems* by Henry Wadsworth Longfellow, used by permission of, and by arrangement with, Houghton Mifflin Company, the authorized publishers. "Texas" from *What's O'clock* by Amy Lowell. "You, Andrew Marvell" from *Poems, 1924–1933* by Archibald MacLeish. "My Wage" from *The Door of Dreams* by Jessie B. Rittenhouse. "Opportunity" from *Poems* by Edward Rowland Sill.

Rolfe Humphries for "Heresy for a Classroom" and "To the Greatest City in the World" from *Europa, and Other Poems and Sonnets.*

Spud Johnson for "City Birds."

Johnson Publishing Company for "I Scarcely Grieve, O Nature," Sonnet from the Memorial Edition of *Poems of Henry Timrod,* used by permission of the Johnson Publishing Co., Richmond, Va.

The Kaleidograph Press for "Summer Evening" by Sara Henderson Hay from *Field of Honor.*

Harry Kemp for "Blind" from *Chanteys and Ballads.*

Mitchell Kennerley and the author for "At the Aquarium" from *Ch of the Amazons and Other Poems* by Max Eastman.

Theda Kenyon for "City Bird" in the *New York Times.*

Richard Kirk for "A Conversational Neighbor" from *A Tallow Dip* pub lished by the Order of Bookfellows.

Alfred A. Knopf, Inc., for: "The Wayfarer" reprinted from *War Is Kin* by Stephen Crane. "As to Being Alone" and "The Slave" reprinte from *Songs for the New Age* by James Oppenheim. "The Lazy Writer" reprinted from *A Penny Whistle* by Bert Leston Taylor. "Sanctuary" reprinted from *Collected Poems of Elinor Wylie.* All by permission c and special arrangement with Alfred A. Knopf, Inc., authorize publishers.

Alfred Kreymborg for "Idealists" from *Mushrooms.*

L'Alouette: A Magazine of Verse and Irene Shirley Moran for "Lilacs for Remembrance."

The Lantern and Lulu E. Thompson for "In Hardin County, 1809."

Margaret Lathrop Law for "Hands" and "Those Who Soar" from *Horizon Smoke.*

Agnes Lee for "Convention" from *Faces and Open Doors* published by Ralph Fletcher Seymour, and "Radium" from *The Sharing.*

Mary Sinton Leitch for "The Poet" from *The Wagon and the Star* published by B. J. Brimmer Company.

Elias Lieberman for "Aladdin Throws Away His Lamp" published in the New York *Sun*, and "Brothers" from *Paved Streets* published by Cornhill Publishing Company. Copyright by the author.

B. Lippincott Company for "In Honor of Taffy Topaz" from *Chimney-smoke*, "Mandarin on the Air" from *Streamlines* (also to *The Saturday Review of Literature* for original publication), and "Smells" and "To a Very Young Gentleman" from *The Rocking Horse* by Christopher Morley.

Little, Brown & Company for "There Is No Frigate like a Book" from *The Poems of Emily Dickinson, Centenary Edition*, edited by Martha Dickinson Bianchi and Alfred Leete Hampson. Reprinted by permission of Little, Brown & Company.

Dr. Francis Litz for "David and Goliath," "Influence," and "Leaf and Soul" from *The Poetry of Father Tabb* by John Banister Tabb, published by Dodd Mead & Company, Inc.

Liveright Publishing Corporation for: "Express Trains" from *Machinery* by MacKnight Black. "Ode to Machines" and "Waterfalls of Stone" from *The Everlasting Minute and Other Lyrics* by Louis Ginsberg. "Observation" from *Year In, You're Out* by Samuel Hoffenstein. "The Gargoyle in the Snow" from *The Beggar at the Gate*, and "1929" from *The Hermit Thrush* by Kathleen Millay. All published by Liveright Publishing Corporation.

John A. Lomax for "The Gol-darned Wheel" from *Cowboy Songs and Other Frontier Ballads*.

Longmans, Green & Co., for: "The Dromedary" from *Poems* by Archibald Y. Campbell. "Autumn, Forsake These Hills" and "This Is the City Children Made" from *Stone Dust* by Frank Ernest Hill.

The Macmillan Company, publishers, for: "Derricks and Rainbows" from *More than Bread* by Joseph Auslander. "Laughter and Death" from *Poetical Works* by Wilfrid Scawen Blunt. "The Rabbits' Song Outside the Tavern" from *Away Goes Sally* by Elizabeth Coatsworth (also to *The Saturday Review of Literature* for original publication). "First Flight" from *Strange Holiness* by Robert P. Tristram Coffin. "Indifference" from *Garden Grace* by Louise Driscoll. "Hands" and "Sight" from *Collected Poems* by Wilfrid Wilson Gibson. "An

August Midnight" from *Collected Poems* by Thomas Hardy. "Th Hammers" from *The Last Blackbird and Other Lines* by Ralph Hodg son. "Failure" from *Wild Plum* by Orrick Johns. "Young and Old from *The Water Babies* by Charles Kingsley. "The Congo" in pa and "Factory Windows Are Always Broken" from *Collected Poems* b Vachel Lindsay. "Sea Fever" and "Spanish Waters" from *Poem* by John Masefield. "Let Me Live Out My Years" from *Collecte Poems* by John G. Neihardt. "The Last Antelope" from *Barbe Wire and Wayfarers* by Edwin Ford Piper. "Uphill" from *Poetica Works* by Christina Rosetti. "The Lights of New York" from *River to the Sea*, and "Sunset: St. Louis" from *Flame and Shadow* by Sar Teasdale. "The Eagle" from *Works of Tennyson.* "The Fiddler o Dooney" from *Collected Poems* by W. B. Yeats. All by permission o The Macmillan Company, publishers.

Edwin Markham for "Lincoln, the Man of the People" from *Lincoln and Other Poems*, and "The Joy of the Hills" and "The Man with the Hoe" from *The Man with the Hoe and Other Poems*. Copyrighted by the author and used by his permission.

Edgar Lee Masters for "Achilles Deatheridge" from *Collected Poems*, and "Silence" from *Songs and Satires*.

Florence Ripley Mastin for "Old Hound" from *Cables of Cobweb* published by Henry Harrison (also to *The Saturday Review of Literature* for original publication).

Methuen and Co., Ltd., for "Mary Shakespeare" from *The Widow* by Ada Jackson. Used with permission of author and publisher.

Edna St. Vincent Millay for "City Trees" from *Second April and Other Poems* published by Harper and Brothers, copyright 1921 by Edna St. Vincent Millay, reprinted by permission of the Author.

Kathleen Millay for "Relativity."

John Richard Moreland for "Captive" from *A Blue Wave Breaking* published by the Kaleidograph Press.

ıomas B. Mosher, Publisher, for: "Sometimes" from *The Rose-Jar* by Thomas S. Jones, Jr. "The Dust" and "A Little Song of Life" from *A Wayside Lute* by Lizette Woodworth Reese.

awrence Emerson Nelson for "My Pompous Friend" from *Gypsy Scarlet* (also to *Horizons* for original publication).

he New Republic and Max Endicoff for "The Excavation."

he New York Herald Tribune and the authors for: "The Chrysanthemum Legend" by Arthur Davison Ficke. "Interlude" by Holger Lundbergh. "Washington's Last Birthday" by Alfred Noyes. "Gentle Storm" by Martha Banning Thomas.

The New York Times and the authors for: "The Little Gods" by Abigail Cresson. "Futility" and "Return" by Mary S. Hawling. "Machines —or Men?" by Elizabeth Newport Hepburn. "Night Shower" by Brock Milton. "The Iron Horse" by Israel Newman.

Captain Francis Newbolt for "He Fell among Thieves" and "Vitaï Lampada," reprinted by permission from *Poems New and Old* by Henry Newbolt, published by John Murray; and "Where a Roman Villa Stood, above Freiburg" reprinted by permission from *Poems by Mary E. Coleridge*, published by Elkin Mathews.

John Oxenham for "Philosopher's Garden" and "The Ways." By permission from *Bees in Amber*.

Packard and Company for "Filling Station" from *Dawn Is Forever* by E. Merrill Root.

L. C. Page & Company for "On a Flyleaf of Burns's Songs" from *On Life's Stairway* by Frederic Lawrence Knowles.

Esther Pinch and the Tyndall Press for "City Nature" and "Friction" from *One a Penny*.

Poetry, a Magazine of Verse for "Ellis Park" by Helen Hoyt.

Harry Noyes Pratt and the Order of Bookfellows for "The Gypsy Hea published in *The Step Ladder*.

Princeton University Press for John Stoltze's "Across Illinois" from *Book of Princeton Verse II.*

G. P. Putnam's Sons, and Mary Sinton Leitch for "He Who Loves tl Ocean" from *Spider Architect;* to Putnam's and John McCrae Kilgo for "In Flanders Fields" from *In Flanders Fields and Other Poems* b John McCrae; to Putnam's and David Morton for "Mariners" an "The Schoolboy Reads His Iliad" from *Ships in Harbor*.

Fleming H. Revell Company for "Town Child" from *The Keys of Heave* by Barbara Young.

Jessie B. Rittenhouse, literary executor of Clinton Scollard, and Th Macmillan Company for "Streams" from *The Singing Heart*.

A. M. Robertson, Publishers, for "The Black Vulture" from *The House of Orchids*, and "Then and Now" from *Beyond the Breakers* by George Sterling.

E. Merrill Root for "Flames" from *Lost Eden* published by The Unicorn Press.

Siegfried Sassoon for "Attack" from *Counter-Attack and Other Poems*.

The Saturday Review (London) and Mrs. W. Hodgson Burnet for "Autumn Leaves" by W. Hodgson Burnet.

The Saturday Review of Literature and the authors for: "How Could You Know?" by Ben Ray Redman. "Thin Air" from "The Bowling Green" by Christopher Morley.

Henri DeWitt Saylor for "Steel" from *Mauve and Magenta*.

Montgomery Schuyler and Robert L. Schuyler for "Carlyle and Emerson" by their father, Montgomery Schuyler.

Charles Scribner's Sons for: "Seein' Things" from *The Poems of Eugene Field.* "Invictus" from *Poems* by William Ernest Henley. "The Music of the Future" and "The Untutored Giraffe" from *The Bashful Earthquake* by Oliver Herford. "Wanted" from *The Complete Poetical Writings of J. G. Holland.* "The Marshes of Glynn" from *The Poems of Sidney Lanier.* "Subway Builders" from *The Tomb of Thomas Jefferson* by Lawrence Lee. "Richard Cory" from *The Children of the Night* by Edwin Arlington Robinson. "I Have a Rendezvous with Death" from *Poems* by Alan Seeger. "The Vagabond" from *Poems and Ballads* by Robert Louis Stevenson. "The Ancestral Dwellings" and "Work" from *The Poems of Henry van Dyke.*

Anderson M. Scruggs for "City Trees" and "Pines" from *Glory of Earth.*

Thomas Seltzer, Inc., for "The Discoverer" from *Lava Lane* by Nathalia Crane.

Eleanor Foote Soderbeck and the *Au Sable News*, published by the Consumers Power Company, for "Great Towers of Steel."

Southern Agriculturist and Katharine Atherton Grimes for "The Farm Boy."

The Spectator (London) and the authors for: "Household Gods" by J. H. Macnair. "Contrary Joe" by L. A. G. Strong.

Spirit and Dorothy Brown Thompson for "Parlor Car."

The (New York) *Sun* and the authors for: "The Flesh Is Weak" by Stanton A. Coblentz. "Cockpit in the Clouds" by Dick Dorrance. "Chant of the Box Cars" by Harry Kemp. "Three Tarry Men" by Edmund Leamy. "House Demolished" by Charles Malam. "Apartment House," "Lineman," and "New Dynamo" by Gerald Raftery. "Portrait" by Sydney King Russell. "Pastorale" by Mildred Weston. "Trees That Shade a House" by Katharine Worth.

Frederick A. Stokes Company for: "The Highwayman," reprinted by permission from *Collected Poems*, Volume I, by Alfred Noyes, copyright, 1906, by Alfred Noyes. "Old Gray Squirrel," reprinted by permission from *Collected Poems*, Volume III, by Alfred Noyes, Copyright, 1915, by Alfred Noyes.

Genevieve Taggard for "Hawaiian Hilltop" from the volume of that name, published by Gelber, Lilienthal, Inc.

John Curtis Underwood for stanzas from "Central" taken from *Americans*.

The Viking Press, Inc., for: "In Two Months Now" from *Boy in the Wind* by George Dillon, copyright 1927 by The Viking Press, Inc., New York. "Lone Dog" from *Songs to Save a Soul* by Irene Rutherford McLeod. "Thought for a Sunshiny Morning" from *Not So Deep As a Well* by Dorothy Parker, copyright 1926, 1928, 1931 and 1936. "He Climbs a Hill and Turns His Face" and "Mathematics" from *Landscape with Figures* by Lionel Wiggam, copyright 1936. All published by The Viking Press, Inc., New York.

Lorna Gill Walsh, literary executor of Thomas Walsh, for "The Street of Doctors" from *Selected Poems of Thomas Walsh*.

Sir Henry Webb, Bt., for "A Prayer" by Thomas Harry Basil Webb.

Will-o'-the-Wisp and Margaret Elward Lawless for "Manhattan."

Eleanor Robbins Wilson and *Education*, published by The Palmer Company, for "A Modern Columbus."

Woman's Home Companion and Charles Hanson Towne for "Thanksgiving."

The World Tomorrow and Hazel I. Dannecker for "Balloon Man."

Yale University Press for: "The Roundhouse" and "To My Wife" from *Merchants from Cathay*, and "Wings" from *The Falconer of God and Other Poems* by William Rose Benét. "No Gull's Wings" from *This Worn Earth* by Paul Engle. "Sea Longing" from *White April* by Harold Vinal. "Epitaph" and "Winter Breath" from *The Deer Come Down* by Edward Weismiller.

INDEX

INDEX

(Titles of selections appear in italics; names of authors, in capitals; and first lines, in ordinary type.)

A

B

C

D

E

F

G

H

I

J

K

L

M

N

O

P

Q

R

S

T

U

V

W

Y